Red
Shelley

PAUL FOOT

BOOKMARKS

RED SHELLEY
by Paul Foot

Published by Bookmarks July 1984
Reprinted April 1988
Bookmarks, 265 Seven Sisters Road, London N4 2DE, England
Bookmarks, PO Box 16085, Chicago, IL 60616, USA
Bookmarks, GPO Box 1473N, Melbourne 3001, Australia
First published by Sidgwick and Jackson, London, 1980

ISBN 0 906224 13 6

Printed by Cox and Wyman Limited, Reading, England
Cover design by Tim Saunders

Bookmarks is linked to an international grouping of
socialist organisations:

AUSTRALIA: **International Socialists**, GPO Box 1473N,
 Melbourne 3001.
BELGIUM: **Socialisme International**, 9 rue Marexhe,
 4400 Herstal, Liege.
BRITAIN: **Socialist Workers Party**, PO Box 82, London
 E3.
CANADA: **International Socialists**, PO Box 339, Station
 E, Toronto, Ontario M6H 4E3.
DENMARK: **Internationale Socialister**, Morten
 Borupsgade 18, kld, 8000 Arhus C.
FRANCE: **Socialisme International** (correspondence to
 Yves Coleman, BP 407, Paris Cedex 05).
IRELAND: **Socialist Workers Movement**, PO Box 1648,
 Dublin 8.
NORWAY: **Internasjonale Sosialister**, Postboks 5370,
 Majorstua, 0304 Oslo 3.
UNITED STATES: **International Socialist Organization**,
 PO Box 16085, Chicago, Illinois 60616.
WEST GERMANY: **Sozialistische Arbeiter Gruppe**,
 Wolfgangstrasse 81, D–6000 Frankfurt 1.

Contents

Paul Foot is a journalist and a member of the Socialist Workers Party. He writes a weekly column for the **Daily Mirror**. His other books include **The Politics of Harold Wilson** (1968), **Why you should be a socialist** (1977) and **The Helen Smith Story** (1983).

This book is published with the aid of the **Bookmarks Publishing Co-operative**. Many socialists have a few savings put aside, probably in a bank or savings bank. While it is there, this money is being loaned out by the bank to some business or other to further the capitalist search for profit. We believe it is better loaned to a socialist venture to further the struggle for socialism. That's how the co-operative works: in return for a loan, repayable at a month's notice, members receive free copies of books published by Bookmarks, plus other advantages. The co-operative has more than 250 members at the time this book is published, from as far apart as London and Australia, Canada and Malaysia.

Like to know more? Write to the **Bookmarks Publishing Co-operative**, 265 Seven Sisters Road, Finsbury Park, London N4 2DE, England.

Introduction

I share with Shelley a rotten education at University College, Oxford.

On many journeys to the college's football changing rooms, I passed, with only a moment's hesitation, a huge gilded cage, under a dome. Inside, on a marble slab borne up by angels and sea lions, as though from the deep, was, and still is, the statue of a beautiful young man, emphatically naked. A typewritten note stuck rather shamefacedly on the wall told me that this was Percy Bysshe Shelley, who had been an 'alumnus' of University College, Oxford, from 1810 to 1811. I remember asking the dean of the college why Shelley had spent so little time at the university. 'Oh,' muttered the dean, embarrassed, 'he was drowned.' And so, of course, he was – eleven years after he had been expelled from University College for writing the first atheist pamphlet ever published in English.

The naked Shelley was the subject of much sport each summer I was at Oxford. As a climax to what is known as Eights Week, the future leaders of the nation would mourn yet another disaster for the University College First Eight by squeezing between the bars of Shelley's cage, and wreaking havoc on his statue. 'We've got Shelley's balls!' was the plummy cry of triumph which would echo through the quadrangles at three or four in the morning.

The authorities shrugged their shoulders and sought out

a mason, who replaced the missing parts.

The castration of Shelley at British places of learning has not been confined to rowing oafs. Ladies and gentlemen of letters have been at it far longer, and with far greater effect. I still have a slim navy blue volume, entitled *Shelley*,[1] which I was forced to buy at school. Its editor is one A. M. D. Hughes. In his 'selected works', there is no *Queen Mab*, no *Revolt of Islam*, no *Mask of Anarchy*, no *Peter Bell*, no *Swellfoot the Tyrant* – no *ideas* of any description. In the Penguin edition of Shelley, published in my last year at school (1956), the editor, a celebrated lady of letters called Isobel Quigly, writes: 'No poet better repays cutting; no great poet was ever less worth reading in his entirety.'[2] She sets to her scissors with a will, extracting with devoted thoroughness every trace of political or social thought from Shelley's work.

In the beautiful Nonesuch edition of *Shelley: Selected Poetry, Prose and Letters*, published in 1951, the editor, a well-read gentleman called A. S. B. Glover, rejoices as he leaves out two of Shelley's greatest longer poems, both political from start to finish. '*Peter Bell* and *Oedipus* [*Swellfoot the Tyrant*],' writes Mr Glover, 'are mainly of interest as proof that a great lyric poet may fail lamentably outside his own proper field. . .'

Similarly, Kathleen Raine in her selection of Shelley in the Penguin 'Poet to Poet' series,[3] writes: 'Without regret, I have omitted *Laon and Cythna* (later revised and renamed *The Revolt of Islam*), and a great deal of occasional political verse by Shelley the student activist in which the inspirers had no hand.'

These are just a few examples from my own literary upbringing and education. They are repeated over and over again in perhaps a hundred castrated editions of Shelley over the last 150 years.

The castration is horrible. The treatment of Shelley's 'Philosophical View of Reform', for instance, is almost incredible. It was written at the height of Shelley's literary powers. It ranks in style and in content with the most famous radical pamphlets of our history – with Tom Paine's *Rights of Man*, with Mary Wollstonecraft's *Vindication of the Rights of Women*, with the pamphlets of Bentham or Robert Owen or Marx and Engels. It was available and known to all the people who had access to Shelley's notebooks after his death. Yet it stayed there, not even transcribed, for *one hundred years* after it was written. And even then – in 1920 – it was published only as a collector's item for members of the Shelley Society.

Shelley's most explicit work on sex and love, *A Discourse on the Manners of the Ancient Greeks, Relative to the Subject of Love*, was held back even longer. It first appeared in an edition edited by Roger Ingpen in 1931, 113 years after it was written, and even then it was privately printed.

By this process of censorship and omission, Shelley has been sheltered from young people at school and university even more carefully than have most other radical or revolutionary writers. He is regarded as 'too complicated' for study by 'O' level classes. And, to judge from the questions asked about him at 'A' level, he is very complicated indeed! The questions are almost exclusively about Shelley's 'linguistic' or 'lyrical' qualities. In 1967, for instance, students for the 'A' level English literature paper set by the Joint Matriculation Board (Liverpool, Sheffield, Leeds, Manchester and Birmingham Universities) were asked to study *Prometheus Unbound*. The question put to them after all their study was: 'What are the oustanding poetic qualities of the songs and lyrics in *Prometheus Unbound*?'

In all the English literature papers set by the three main examination boards – the Joint Matriculation Board, Oxford, and Cambridge – from 1961 to 1977, there is only one question, from Oxford in 1974 – 'How does Shelley handle the theme of liberty?' – which concedes that Shelley had any political ideas at all.

The most time-honoured rule for teaching anything at our schools and universities is that people should stick to what Mr A. S. B. Glover calls 'their proper field'. Science is science, law is law, literature is literature and politics is

politics. Each must be isolated. The separation is enforced
with special fervour for poetry and politics. For poetry can
inspire people. And it is extremely important for the 'fabric
of society' that inspirations should be kept away from politics, and especially from anything which smells of subver-
sion. So poetry is judged 'as poetry', by standards set down
by 'experts' on poetry. Politics, students are reminded
sharply, has nothing to do with it.

It is all humbug. George Orwell, who could sniff out
humbug quicker than most, wrote shortly before he died:

The more I see the more I doubt whether people ever really make
aesthetic judgements at all. Everything is judged on political
grounds which are then given an aesthetic disguise. When, for
instance, Eliot can't see anything good in Shelley or anything bad
in Kipling, the real underlying reason must be that one is a radical
and the other a conservative, of sorts. Yet evidently one does
have aesthetic reactions, especially as a lot of art and even literature
is politically neutral, and also certain unmistakable standards do
exist, e.g. Homer is better than Edgar Wallace. Perhaps the way
we should put it is: the more one is aware of political bias the
more one can be independent of it, & the more one claims to be
impartial the more one is biassed.'[4]

To remove from writers their political ideas is even more
insulting than to judge them solely on their politics. What
people think usually, if not always, determines what they
write. When writers think about their fellow human beings
and the political relationships between them, those thoughts
become essential to their writing, and to the understanding
and enjoyment of it.

In Shelley's case, censorship of his ideas is more than
insulting. It is totally destructive. For Shelley thought about
politics intensely, all his life. His revolutionary ideas were
the main inspiration for the great bulk of his poems and
essays.

For people who agree even with some of those ideas, the
discovery of the real Shelley is an astonishing experience.
'At last,' wrote the philosopher Bertrand Russell, 'at the age

of 17 I came across Shelley, whom no one had ever told me about. He remained for many years the man I loved most among the great men of the past.'[5]

At last! At the age of seventeen! It took me twice as long, but it was no less exciting. I read the unadulterated Shelley with a mixture of fury and excitement: fury at what had been hidden by my education; excitement at what was opening out in front of me. The feeble fop on that marble slab vanished altogether. In his place appeared a restless agitator, who spent his short life challenging every received opinion and every arbitrary authority. Behind the other-worldly lyrics I had learned at school, I found poems which had inspired generations of workers to political action. I came face to face with Shelley's gigantic intellect, and was re-educated. He became for me like a great tree of knowledge and I like a squirrel, scampering down each undiscovered branch.

The 'Romantic poets' (Byron, Keats, Wordsworth, Southey) became not Romantic at all but every one of them creatures of the social convulsions which shook Europe in the wake of the French Revolution. Shelley introduced me, perhaps most crucially and most disturbingly, to feminism, to its literature and its struggles. He led me back to Condorcet, Diderot and Mary Wollstonecraft, and on to the nineteenth-century feminists, to the suffragettes and to the Women's Liberation movement, which is still fighting for the ideas expressed so eloquently by Cythna in *The Revolt of Islam*. All these things were hidden both from my patrician education and from the curiously masculine Marxism to which I graduated.

The purpose of this book, then, is to restore to Shelley the political ideas without which his poetry loses its magic, its music and its meaning. I want to pass on Shelley's political enthusiasms to today's socialists, radicals and feminists, in the hope that their commitment will be strengthened and enriched by Shelley, as mine has been. I have tried, too, to take Shelley out of the academic prison in which he has been firmly trapped for half a century. I am comforted in this attempt by the fact that most of the people who have read and enjoyed Shelley over the last 150 years never went near a university.

I owe a special debt to two mighty books. The first is Edward Thompson's *The Making of the English Working Class*,[6] which covers, almost exactly, the period of Shelley's life.

It is a marvellous history book. Kings and queens, politicians and generals have walk-on parts. The main characters are the working people, the main dramas their struggles for survival against a new exploitation. Edward Thompson brings these people to life. Above all, his history is connected with what is going on today. It is part of his commitment to the cause of the working people, then and now. For anyone who wants to understand Shelley, and must therefore want to understand the working people of his time, *The Making of The English Working Class* is indispensable.

The other book uncovered the real Shelley for me. It is Richard Holmes's towering biography, *Shelley the Pursuit*.[7] It was the first book I read about Shelley, and it led me to perhaps fifty others, none of which come within a million miles of Richard Holmes's.

Other people have helped me more directly. Janet Montefiore, an English lecturer at Liverpool University, researched a host of G.C.E. examination papers on my account. David Palmer, a lecturer at High Melton teachers' training college near Doncaster (now scheduled for closure), was watching Lord Clark's television series 'Civilisation', when he heard Clark sneer, 'Where is Shelley now?' This stung him to write a thesis on the posthumous reputation of Shelley, which I was lucky to read and, with his permission, to plunder. If, as I suspect will happen, interest in Shelley does increase, then someone should take David Palmer's work off the shelves at Sheffield University and publish it.

Nicholas Walter put me right on blasphemy prosecutions in the 1840s. Rose Foot ploughed through two generations of communist and socialist newspapers looking, without much success, for references to Shelley. She also found the references to Shelley in the Clarion and in Blatchford in the final chapter. Jill Craigie delved deep into her voluminous feminist library to search out the influence of Shelley among women's rights campaigners through the ages. Almost all the section on the suffraggists comes from her.

After this book was finished I attended a conference at Gregynog, in the middle of Wales. It was reported to be the first Shelley conference this century, and it attracted many idols, whose books on Shelley I had read: Geoffrey Matthews, of Reading University, author of the British Council's little book on Shelley; Desmond King-Hele, who spoke on Erasmus Darwin's influence on Shelley;[8] Judith Chernaik, whose lovely book, *The Lyrics of Shelley*,[9] had always been a special favourite of mine. I learned so much in these three days that I plucked my manuscript back from the publisher and rewrote several sections. Geoffrey Matthews read the manuscript and painstakingly corrected at least some of the mistakes. Judith Chernaik forced me to rethink my earlier antipathy to Mary Shelley. Thanks to her for that (though I still don't accept *her* antipathy to Claire Clairmont), and for patiently insisting that I rewrite the whole section.

Paul Dawson, of Sidney Sussex, Cambridge, one of the many young dons who are reviving Shelley in the universities, sent me Shelley's fragment on birth control, and let me read his thesis on Shelley's politics, quite absurdly entitled 'The Gradual Path'.

Thanks too to Judith Condon of *Women's Voice*, who is a fan of F. R. Leavis, and who forced me not to dismiss him without an argument; and to the drama teacher at Hampstead School who approached me after my first attempt to speak about Shelley with the shocking question: 'Can you tell me why Shelley was such a shit to his women?' I could not answer her then. I have tried to in this book.

This book reached Sidgwick and Jackson in the summer of 1979 without a single note of reference. Geoffrey Matthews, who read the draft, wrote to me, 'I do not think you err on the side of pedantry.' There are now over 500 notes of reference, and the quotations make some pretence at accuracy and scholarship. This has nothing whatever to do with me, but everything to do with the book's editor Jane Heller, her assistant Jane Birdsell, and copy-editor Caroline Hartnell. Thanks to them (a ridiculous understatement).

No thanks at all to Lord de Lisle and Dudley, V.C., K.G. In May 1977, I saw an advertisement in *The Times* for an exhibition of Shelley manuscripts at Penshurst Place, near Tonbridge, Kent. The public were 'welcome'. On arrival that afternoon with my wife and son, I was told by an embarrassed man at the gate that the 'Shelley people' had arrived for a sherry party that morning. They couldn't find anyone to stand guard over the manuscripts, and had therefore locked up the exhibiton room and gone home.

Surely, I remonstrated, someone had a key and could let us look at the exhibition for half an hour? What about the man who lived here?

'Oh, you mean Lord de Lisle,' said the man at the gate. 'You might find him up at the house.'

Lord de Lisle! The occupant of Penshurst Place was none other than the chairman of the National Association of Freedom, an extremist right-wing organization whose chief concern was to protect the 'freedom' of employers not to recognize trade unions, and therefore to make more money for themselves. My curiosity got the better of me. For a large sum of money we were allowed into the grounds, as far as the artificial lake, and into part of the stately home. There, from pamphlets which cost still more money, I discovered that Lord de Lisle has an ancestral connection with the (Philip) Sidneys, and was vaguely related to the Shelley family. He was, therefore, president of the Keats–Shelley Memorial Association.

Of the Shelley exhibition we saw nothing. We were told politely and firmly that the door was locked, that 'his Lordship had the key', that 'his Lordship was taking tea', and that 'his Lordship was on no account to be disturbed'.

That evening I wrote a letter to Lord de Lisle expounding in uncharacteristically immoderate language on the theme of the 'freedom' to advertise exhibitions to the public and then to bar the public from them. He replied with an 'apology': 'It was an error on the part of the person to whom you spoke not to inform me, and for this I apologise. It is, of course, possible that you employed as vehement a manner in addressing the member of my staff as you used in your letter to me, and he was deterred thereby. Not everyone is able to estimate the value of such a very idiosyncratic style.'

I keep his letter as a pointer to what Shelley meant by Ozymandias's 'sneer of cold command'.

For the paperback edition I have corrected a few mistakes and added the short section on the controversy in *Plebs* in 1921 (page 249 and following). My thanks to Martin Adams for directing me to this, and to the Marx Memorial Library for digging it out and letting me read it.

Paul Foot
London, April 1984

1

The Ghastly Masquerade: England 1810–22

I met Murder on the way—
He had a mask like Castlereagh—
Very smooth he looked, yet grim;
Seven blood-hounds followed him.

All were fat; and well they might
Be in admirable plight,
For one by one, and two by two,
He tossed them human hearts to chew
Which from his wide cloak he drew.

Next came Fraud, and he had on,
Like Eldon, an ermined gown;
His big tears, for he wept well,
Turned to millstones as they fell;

And the little children, who
Round his feet played to and fro,
Thinking every tear a gem,
Had their brains knocked out by them.

Clothed with the Bible, as with light,
And the shadows of the night,
Like Sidmouth next, Hypocrisy
On a crocodile rode by.

And many more Destructions played
In this ghastly masquerade,
All disguised, even to the eyes,
Like Bishops, lawyers, peers, or spies.

The Mask of Anarchy, 1819[1]

In the twelve years of Shelley's adult life (1810–22), Britain had its worst government ever. That government devoted all its energies to two monstrous wars. The first was against Napoleon and the French armies. The second was against the mass of the British people.

This was a period of uninterrupted tyranny, which appeared all the more horrible against the period of enlightenment which preceded it. For ten years before the French Revolution of 1789, Britain's Tory government under William Pitt had listened eagerly to Parliamentary opposition. Even the King, George III, stunned by his ignominious failure to hold the American colonies, held back from too arbitrary expression of the monarch's power. The French Revolution of 1789 was hailed by liberals and working people everywhere as the dawn of the new era. From now on, it was believed, the people would have some say in their government. Government by monarchs, riches, force or superstition was finished. The Tory government in Britain was prepared for a few short months to tolerate such idealistic talk and thought. Liberal politicians in the House of Commons were allowed openly to side with the revolutionaries. The Duke of Norfolk toasted a dinner in London to the 'Majesty of the People' instead of the Majesty of the King. He kept his head and his dukedom.

Little-read young poets like Wordsworth, Coleridge and Southey were allowed to enthuse at will on the great developments in France. When Wordsworth wrote:

Bliss was it in that dawn to be alive
And to be young was very heaven.

he was writing about the time when people of decent birth

were allowed to be enthusiastic about the French Revolution.

But such enthusiasm was intolerable when it spread to the working people. They were outside politics. They tilled the fields and worked in the newly dug mines. They wove and spun the cloth. But they weren't expected to *think*, still less to transfer thoughts into action.

Tom Paine, who had been trained as a stay-maker in Norfolk, was an early exception to that rule. He travelled to America in 1774, and the pamphlets he wrote there inspired the American people in their fight for independence from the British Crown. Paine hated kings and courtiers. He argued in his pamphlets that the only government worth obeying was a government which took its power from the people. When he returned to Britain after the American victory, Paine was fêted by wealthy liberals. He stayed a week with the Duke of Portland and another with Edmund Burke, the orator. But Paine's political beliefs did not change.

Two years after the French Revolution, Edmund Burke wrote a book, *Reflections on the Revolution in France*, which defended property rights, kings, queens and noblemen against the 'swinish multitude'. It was a bestseller in the fashionable areas where people bought books. Paine replied at once with *The Rights of Man*. This was not just an attack on Burke's snobbery and pretentiousness. It was a call to the British people to establish for themselves an elected government under which everyone, whatever their wealth or breeding, had a right to vote.

This was treason to the government and its paymasters, who were already looking nervously across the water to where kings, queens and noblemen were losing their heads as fast as corrupt and absentee landlords were losing their land. They resolved to hit out twice: first in open warfare against Napoleon; secondly in a less open but just as murderous war against the kind of people who were likely to read Thomas Paine's book and act upon it. The sceptical journalist William Hazlitt wrote at the time that *The Rights of Man* was so popular that 'the government was obliged to suspend the constitution and go to war to counteract the effect of its popularity'.² That is exactly what happened. The war against Napoleon went on until the Battle of Waterloo in 1815. The war against the British working people is still going on today.

Three men in particular won the praise of the king, the official newspapers and the Church for their energetic and ruthless conduct of both these wars.

The first was John Scott, an ambitious lawyer who had been born the third son of a Tory coal barge owner in Newcastle. This was bad breeding for a successful career, but Scott soon improved his outlook by eloping with the daughter of a rich Newcastle banker. He now had money, though he was still short of ability. So, with the help of his wife's fortune, he bought himself a seat in the House of Commons for the 'constituency' of Weobley in Herefordshire, whose Parliamentary candidature was 'owned' by the Duke of Weymouth. While the Tory government was prepared to listen to opposition and even to institute reforms, young Scott was just another useless backbencher. But when Pitt took to repression he looked around for law officers without ability or scruple.

John Scott fitted the bill admirably. He was appointed Attorney-General, and ushered in the Habeas Corpus Suspension Act of 1794 which restricted the right to be freed from prison or be brought at once to trial, and under which hundreds of people were imprisoned without trial. In the same year he acted as chief prosecutor against the organizers of the London Corresponding Society, the first ever working class political organization in Britain, which had been formed to propound radical ideas and which had about 3,000 members. Scott's case was so weak and his rhetoric so verbose that the jury found the accused not guilty of sedition. So Scott rushed through Parliament the Treasonable Practices and Seditious Meetings Act of 1795 banning protest meetings, under which most of the London Corresponding Society organizers and leading members were eventually jailed. Scott also spawned the Newspaper Proprietors Registration Act, which made it very difficult for anyone who wasn't rich to produce a newspaper. He developed the legal concept of 'constructive treason', whereby people could be found guilty of plotting against the monarch if they complained about the price of corn. He hated Catholics and strongly supported slavery. He got on very well with the King, who called him 'Old Bags'.

He was boring and sententious. When he sentenced people to transportation and to death, he had a habit of weeping and wiping away his tears with his gown. These qualities marked him out for promotion, and in 1799 he became Lord Chief Justice of England and Lord Eldon of Durham. In 1807 he became Lord Chancellor, and helped to run the Tory government almost without interruption for nearly twenty years.

Hazlitt wrote of Eldon:

He seems to be on his guard against everything liberal and humane as his weak side. Others relax in their obsequiousness either from satiety or disgust, or a hankering after popularity, or a wish to be thought above narrow prejudices. The Lord Chancellor alone is fixed and immovable. . . . He signs a warrant in council devoting ten thousand men to an untimely death with steady nerves. Is it that he is cruel or unfeeling? No; but he thinks neither of their suffering nor of their cries. He sees only the gracious smile, the ready hand stretched out to thank him for his compliance with the dictates of rooted hate. He dooms a continent to slavery. Is it that he is a tyrant or an enemy to the human race? No. But he cannot find it in his heart to resist the commands or give pain to a kind and generous benefactor.[3]

So kind and generous were Lord Eldon's benefactors that when he finally died, aged eighty-seven, in 1838 he left £700,000 – the revenue from the gifts, sinecures and corruptions which studded the Lord Chancellor's life.

At the apex of the triangle was Robert Stewart, the son of an Irish Protestant, placeman and politician who had won an undeserved reputation as a reformer. The young Stewart showed some aptitude as a public speaker at Cambridge, and his family spent their entire fortune – about £60,000 – in buying him a seat in the British Parliament for the safe Protestant area of Down. The young genius went into the army and rose quickly to the rank of lieutenant-colonel, where he was safe from the enemy. More importantly, he married the daughter of the Earl of Buckinghamshire and was duly enobled with the name by which he is best known (though he was born and died with a different one): Viscount Castlereagh. In his twenties Castlereagh continued in his father's footsteps as a sham reformer, and even wrote a tract supporting the vote for propertied Catholics. In 1797 he became Keeper of the Irish Privy Seal and in 1799, Chief Secretary for Ireland.

Castlereagh understood in advance of his class that the weak link in the British empire was Ireland. He saw what Napoleon in his new-found imperialist role did not see: that if the French had concentrated their armies on Ireland rather than on Austria, Russia and Spain, they would have struck Britain's Achilles heel. The unspeakable exploitation of Ireland by British landlords and businessmen had resulted in universal hostility among the Irish masses to the British government, and a French invasion, properly timed – particularly in 1797 when the British navy was paralysed by a series of mutinies – could have wrested Ireland from the British, united the Protestant and Catholic poor and so transformed the future of Ireland. But Napoleon was by now deaf to the pleas of freedom-fighters from places like Ireland. He was set on routine imperialist advance. What was a small island when the great Russian empire invited conquest? The pleas of the Irish were fobbed off with a small expeditionary force, which was delayed and eventually turned back by the weather.

While the French dithered, Castlereagh recruited an army of spies to provoke an Irish uprising and to isolate it among the Catholic peasantry of the South. This rising, though more ferocious than even Castlereagh can have imagined, was, inevitably, crushed. The reprisals exceeded in brutality anything in even the long and bloody history of British rule in Ireland. Castlereagh's regime in Ireland was marked throughout by bloodshed and torture.

In 1797, in order to flush out the United Irishmen, a riding school in Marlborough Street, Dublin, was converted into a flogging arena where anyone remotely suspected of connection with the rebels was flayed with the cat o'nine tails until either the bones showed beneath the flesh or some friend or comrade was exposed. Castlereagh thoroughly approved this development and claimed to have patented it. Throughout Castlereagh's time as Keeper of the Irish Privy Seal and Chief Secretary, the Royal Exchange in Dublin was converted into a torture chamber for the extraction of information. R. R. Madden, the historian of the United Irishmen, wrote: 'The Exchange immediately adjoins the Castle and from it the cries of the sufferers might have been heard in Lord Castlereagh's office, where his personal interposition, or the mere expression of his will, might have prevented the continuance of torture.'[4]

With the rebellion crushed, Castlereagh set himself to dissolving the Irish Parliament into the British Parliament, by means of the Act of Union. His problem was how to persuade the Irish Parliament to dissolve itself when few Irish M.P.s could see any advantage in doing so. His solution was simple. He bought them. When the dissolution Bill was flung out in 1799 – by two votes – he was forced to buy on a massive scale. Never in all history have more Irish peers been created. Hundreds of thousands of pounds were doled out in sinecures and pensions to secure the Castlereagh plan. In addition, Castlereagh promised the emancipation of the Catholic middle class as soon as the union was achieved, thus effectively silencing Catholic opposition to the union. This promise was duly broken – King George III 'would not stand' for *any* votes for Irish Catholics – and Castlereagh resigned for a short period. But he was soon back again; indeed he was the driving force of the British Cabinet from 1805 to 1822. Then, in the very summer that Shelley was drowned in Italy, he went mad and cut his throat.

The psycopathic introspection which led to his suicide was not far below the surface all his life. Lord Cornwallis, who led the British army against the Irish insurrection, said of Castlereagh: 'He is so cold that nothing can warm him.'[5] This quality showed itself in a relentless prosecution of the war against Napoleon while Secretary of State for War; a stubborn defence of the East India Company's desecration of Bengal in order to sell opium to China; and, above all, a deep hatred for the common people whenever they dared to ask for rights or food. He was rightly identified as the chief architect of war and repression. In 1820 he could not move through the streets in public without being booed. When he died and his pall was carried to Westminster Abbey by the Duke of Wellington, a huge crowd collected to cheer and celebrate. William Cobbett, one of Castlereagh's most confirmed enemies, wrote in his *Weekly Political Register*: 'PEOPLE OF ENGLAND REJOICE! CASTLEREAGH IS DEAD!'

The third member of the troika was, if possible, even more reactionary and repressive than Castlereagh and Eldon. Henry Addington was born into a prosperous South London family. Like Eldon, he was a third-rate lawyer: like both Eldon and Castlereagh, he bought himself into Parliament. There he acted as Speaker during the 1790s, and became a close favourite of the King. The King was suspicious of Pitt because Pitt sometimes spoke his mind in the royal presence. Henry Addington had no mind to speak, and if he had had one would never have dared to speak it in front of the King. When Pitt and Castlereagh resigned over Irish Catholic emancipation in 1801, the King appointed Addington as Prime Minister; later he made him Chancellor of the Exchequer. He was known as 'the King's Chancellor'. Money could always be found from taxes on the working people to help out the royal family, and especially to defray the Prince Regent's endless gambling debts. In 1805, the King gave him the huge White Lodge estate in Richmond Park, and made him Viscount Sidmouth. In that same year, Sidmouth gave his son the 'clerkship of the pells', a sinecure which entailed no work but brought with it £20,000 a year.

Sidmouth was Home Secretary from 1812 to 1822. He was responsible for the war against the British people. He set up an army of spies, whose work led to the capture and execution of countless reformers. He introduced a stream of laws to put down free speech, free newspapers, free meetings. He was especially popular with the landed gentry and the Church. He was a devoted churchman, who never failed to attend service on the Sabbath. In 1807, his main measure to deal with poverty was a Bill to build another 117 churches. He argued that this Bill would 'create work' and 'when the work was done, would provide a solace for the workless'. He was a man without talent of any kind, save only a relentless dedication to protect the property of his king, his Church and his class.

These three 'self-made men' – self-made, that is, not through initiative or dynamism but through inheritance and corruption – exemplified not just the government of the twelve years from 1810 to 1822 but the political atmosphere of the time.

The first of the two wars which the troika waged so furiously – the war against Napoleon and the French – dominated the first half of the period, and certainly dominated Shelley's early political ideas. School history books still write of the Napoleonic Wars as though they were fought chiefly in Europe and were distinguished by a long string of British victories. The truth is different. The Napoleonic Wars took the British army and navy all over the world. In the first period of the war, about 60,000 British lives were sacrificed to Pitt's aspirations of military grandeur in the West Indies. At Rosetta, Egypt, in 1807, a British force of 5,000 was wiped out almost to a man. Nor were the British expeditions into Europe the bloodless successes they are often made out to be. The Peninsular Wars, for instance, in which the British masqueraded as the champions of the 'oppressed Spanish peoples' against the French invasion, cost thousands' of soldiers' lives.

In 1809 Wellington's forces – about 20,000 men – were

driven out of Spain after the indecisive battle of Talavera (hailed by the government at home as a triumph). Following the siege of Badajos in 1811, in which 20,000 Spanish troops were killed or taken prisoner by the French, General Blake's army was routed on 9 June at Barza, and later at Puch. About 2,000 soldiers were killed in these two battles. In 1812, Blake was again routed at Valencia, and even at the battle of Salamanca, which Wellington won, some 5,000 British soldiers were killed or taken prisoner.[6]

The dispatch of the armies to the Peninsula in 1809 was seen by Castlereagh as part of a 'two-pronged' attack, of which the other part was an expedition to Walcheren in Holland. This was a disaster. Twenty thousand British soldiers and sailors died of famine and fever without fighting a major battle. The British generals continually postponed a life-saving return to Britain for fear of losing prestige.

The manpower required for these holocausts was prodigious. In 1801 the Census showed 470,598 under arms out of a population of 10.4 million. By 1811 the armed forces had grown by a staggering 35 per cent: to 640,000, out of a population only 14 per cent larger at just under 12 million.[7]

This army, of course, was not a volunteer force. Large numbers of soldiers and sailors were 'pressed' into service by military gangs who roamed the streets at night with powers to recruit at will. Conditions in the army were atrocious. The men's food was almost always inferior to the food for the officers' horses. The structure of command was enforced with the most savage brutality. Flogging for the most trivial disobedience was widespread. The attitude of officers towards their men was sensitively summed up by the Duke of Wellington when he described 'other ranks' as 'the scum of the earth enlisted for drink'.[8]

The scum had to be kept alive, however, and armed for battle, and that cost money. The government had also to find hundreds of thousands of pounds for 'subsidies' for their quavering partners in the Grand Coalition of Despotisms. They found it from the working people. Taxes rose out of all proportion to anything which had been known before. A low income tax, introduced to howls of rage from the Tories, produced, by 1815, £25 million a year. Indirect taxes – that is, mainly, on food and on other necessities like clothes and fuel – produced, in the same year, £67 million. A labourer earning 10s. a week found that half of it went in 'indirect' taxes.[9] To supplement its income, the government borrowed from wealthy individuals and other governments all over the world. At the beginning of the war the interest on the national debt was £9.4 million a year. At the end of the war it was £30.4 million – and that had to be paid back out of still higher taxes when the war ended.

At the same time the wages of farm workers were held down by the notorious Speenhamland system of dole, which obliged parish councils to supplement farm workers' wages on a starvation rate, based on the price of bread. This allowed the large farmers to pay ridiculously low wages, at the same time as they were enclosing common lands and forcing small peasant farmers off their land. Throughout these twelve years the south of England was stricken by high unemployment and low wages. In the manufacturing areas of the north, new machinery was throwing thousands of skilled workers out of their jobs. Of 1,400 shearers in Leeds in 1811, 450 were out of work in 1812. The unemployment cut into every one of the old skills: stockingers, weavers, croppers. At the same time, prices of basic foods rose unbelievably and intolerably. In the crisis year of 1812, the price of wheat rose 30 per cent from its all-time high in 1811, and still the government insisted on restricting the import of corn.[10] The year 1815 began with a series of demonstrations against Corn Law import controls, which resulted in another sharp increase in food prices in 1816.

The coming of peace in 1816 brought none of the prosperity which had been promised. The collapse of the war economy brought a collapse of markets, especially for heavy industry and mining. At the same time taxes had to be kept high to pay off the interest on the national debt. The resulting poverty was worse than anything yet experienced in Britain. The great iron works at Stafford were closed down

– with such appalling results that even a minister of the Church could be provoked to write (in a letter which appears in that year's Annual Register, 24 July 1816): 'Multitudes went through the country offering to work at anything merely for a little food, not even expecting wages. But still their wives and children were at home in the greatest possible distress. Some who have fared the best when our manufactories were flourishing around us have said: "We would rather die, Sir, than be dependent on the parish." ' Then, as now, many of those entitled to the dole preferred to starve rather than 'scrounge'. The letter concluded: 'I have myself repeatedly saved a man, his wife and six children from absolute starvation, who were reduced to eat the cabbage stalks and the refuse of their little cottage garden as the only food they could obtain.'

Thousands *did* die of starvation. The Yorkshire correspondent of the *Leeds Mercury* wrote to his paper from Deanhouse, Stainland, on 15 November 1816:

When Joseph Tweed, head of the family, was found, he was laid upon his bed in a miserable chamber with an infant child two years old, who, like himself, was a lifeless corpse, clasped in his arms. His wife lay dead in the lower room upon the hearth having divested herself of every article of clothing, with one of her grandchildren who was still alive stretched upon her body. The daughter of these wretched parents, who was 12 years of age, roused probably from the stupor into which want and sickness had plunged her by the dying groans of her mother, appears to have attempted to make her way downstairs; but her enfeebled limbs refusing to perform their office, she had fallen, and when found her corpse was laid stretched upon the stairs with her head downwards and one of her feet locked against the stairs and the wall.

Small wonder that in April 1819 the trade union newspaper, *The Gorgon*, could report on a meeting of 3,000 working people at Leeds who pleaded to be transported to Australia since they could not survive at home.

Throughout the twelve years of Shelley's adult life, the degradation into which the people who actually produced the wealth were plunged had no noticeable effect whatever on the behaviour of the wealthy few who produced no wealth at all. George, the Prince Regent, later George IV, was one of the great wasters of history. When the royal physicians finally confirmed that George III was mad, his son George took over. This called for celebration. A 'party to end all parties' was arranged. The *Morning Chronicle* reported:

His Royal Highness, the Prince Regent, entered the State departments about a quarter past nine o'clock, dressed in a scarlet coat, most richly and elegantly ornamented in a very modern style with gold lace, with a brilliant star of the Order of the Garter . . . the conservatory presented the fine effect of a lofty aisle in an ancient cathedral. The grand table extended the whole length of the conservatory and across Carlton House to the length of 200 feet. Along the centre of the table, about six inches above the surface, a canal of pure water continued flowing from a silver fountain, beautifully constructed at the head of the table. Its faintly waving artificial banks were covered with green moss and aquatic. Gold and silver fish, gudgeons etc. were seen to swim and sport through the bubbling current . . .

The feast went on until the early hours of the morning.

This inauguration set the tone for high society. Fêtes and parties of the most astonishing extravagance took place at the least possible excuse. To celebrate the first anniversary of the appointment of Lord Greville as Chancellor of Oxford University, for instance, a 'grand fête' went on for *four days*. The end of the war provided a suitable occasion for a series of fêtes and dinners to entertain the victorious brigands of Europe. The visit of the Emperor of Russia in June 1814 was celebrated with a series of dinners whose exorbitance disgusted even the court reporters. August 1814, a month of terrible deprivation for the unemployed stockingers of the Midlands, saw, according to the *Chronicle*, 'an almost constant succession of spectacles of grandeur and festivity'. When the old, mad George III finally died, his son took the opportunity to hold yet another party, the like of which had never been seen before (and few since). The 'solemnization festivity' authorities proudly published the statistics to a starving nation. One evening's royal entertainment disposed of 7,442 pounds of beef, 7,033 pounds of veal, 20,474 pounds of mutton, 1,850 chickens and 8,400 eggs. To wash this down 350 dozen bottles of sherry and port, 20 dozen burgundy, 50 dozen hock and 100 dozen of champagne were drunk.[11]

So the period known in British history as 'the Regency', the period which almost exactly covers Shelley's adult life, ended as it had begun. Even the conventional historians could not forbear from commenting. G. M. Trevelyan, in his *History of England*, wrote of the war period: 'The upper class throve on enhanced rents – and paid too small a proportion in wages.' And again: 'Never was a country house life more thriving or jovial, with its fox-hunting, shooting and leisure in spacious and well-stocked libraries. Never was sporting life more attractive.'[12]

The wealth of the wealthy had to be supplemented from the public purse. Huge sums were paid to anyone even remotely connected with the royal family. The support of the royal 'establishment' at Windsor cost £100,000 a year. In 1819, £50,000 was allotted for the personal expenditure of the King, who was so mad that he could not leave his room. And a grant of £10,000 was made to the Duke of York for being personally responsible for looking after the King! Five other dukes – Clarence, Kent, Cumberland, Sussex and Cambridge – all received between £18,000 and £25,000 a year tax-free as 'a basic emolument', plus another £20,000 a year from the Admiralty for their command of regiments. Their clothes and those of their entourages were also paid for by the public. They also had ready access to 'loans'.[13] In 1813, for instance, the Duke of Clarence was lent £20,000, to be paid back at the rate of £500 a quarter. By October 1818, twenty-one quarters later, he had repaid £3,000, six quarters' worth – and there the payment seems to have stopped.[14] Non-royalty often had to rely on the innumerable sinecures which were in the appointment of the government. In May 1812, for instance, a backbencher called attention to two 'tellerships of the Exchequer' granted to the Marquis of Buckingham and Lord Camden. Lord Camden was a member of the Cabinet and President of the Council. The 'tellerships', which had no duties attached to them, were worth £23,000 a year each in 1808. According to one report, Spencer Perceval, Chancellor of the Exchequer and Prime Minister, who was assassinated the following week by someone whom he had annoyed, summed up ministerial thinking on these matters as follows:

The tellerships of the exchequer were ancient offices, and legally within the gift of the crown. The right of those noblemen to them was a vested right which could not be touched, and he conceived the emoluments to be also vested interests which must be protected. There would be much more danger and mischief from breaking down the barriers of private property in this instance, than in allowing the receipt of the 40 or 50 thousand a year which were now the emoluments of those offices.[15]

These 'rights' had to be defended from people who did not believe in them – that is, the vast majority of the people of Britain. For this purpose the wealthy organized a carnival of repression. Eldon's 'Two Acts' of 1794, which suspended habeas corpus until 1801 and restricted the press, proved inadequate to deal with the rising fury of the masses after the Napoleonic Wars. In 1817, habeas corpus was suspended again and imprisonment without trial was legalized. In the same year, Sidmouth introduced two more 'gagging Acts' to prevent meetings of more than fifty people for any purpose whatever. In 1819, following the massacre of Peterloo, the government introduced six more Acts which gave unprecedented powers to magistrates to convict anyone suspected of conspiring or meeting to discuss any political question. It gave them powers to enter homes without warrants and to hound and bully any of their suspects. At the same time the Combination Acts, passed by Pitt's government in 1800 and 1801, were widely used to break up the growing trade union organizations in factories and mines.

The Acts were enforced almost entirely by the magistrates, and the cases have not been recorded. What is known is that the magistrates met at least twice a week, and in the northern towns they dealt at almost every meeting with a case of a breach of the Combination Acts. Ringleaders of trade union organizations were hounded with ridiculous fines and stiff prison sentences if they did not pay.

All these laws, taken together with a common law which had been drawn up over centuries with the single purpose of defending the property of those who had it, were enforced by a brutal system of punishment. Stealing of almost any kind was punishable by death. For the 'muggers' of the day, known as footpads or highwaymen, the death sentence was compounded by the 'gibbet', from which the starved bodies of hanged men and women would be chained to a stake in places of public resort (such as Hounslow Heath). In Manchester in 1819, after food riots, two women were hanged for stealing two potatoes from a cart which had been overturned in the street. And the *Taunton Courier* of 28 August 1818 reported: 'William Hopwood was found guilty of stealing a sack of oats from Mr. George Butler, and sentenced by Judge Park to 18 months imprisonment and hard labour. On sentence being pronounced, he thought it proper to ask who was to pay the wages for this labour; for which offence the learned judge altered his sentence to transportation for seven years.'

These laws were jealously guarded. Sir Samuel Romilly, a rich liberal lawyer, spent much of his life arguing in Parliament for small reforms of the penal code. In February 1811, for instance, he moved in the House of Commons to abolish the death penalty for stealing 40s. or more from a dwelling house, and for stealing from navigable rivers and canals. He argued that these punishments did not work as deterrents; that stealing rose and fell not with the severity of punishment but with economic deprivation. He even managed to convince the gerrymandered House of Commons of his case. His Bill's Second and Third Readings were passed by small majorities. But the Bill was broken in the

Lords. Lord Eldon accurately summed up the feelings of his profession: 'The universal opinion of those who are engaged in the administration of justice,' he said, 'is against the Bill.'[16]

For those who dared to speak or write against the government there was a whole host of newly introduced interpretations of the laws on libel. At no other period has the criminal libel law been used with such abandon.

Peter Finnerty, an Irish journalist, travelled at his own expense to report the British expedition to the Walcheren in 1809. Hardly had he arrived than he was sought out by the commanding officers and sent back to Britain. Finnerty wrote a letter to the *Morning Chronicle* protesting that Castlereagh, who hated Finnerty for former attacks on his bloody rule in Ireland, had ordered him to be sent home before he could do any damange to the expedition. The letter also attacked Castlereagh's administration in Ireland in forthright terms. Finnerty was found guilty of 'seditious libel' and sent to prison for eighteen months. The Lord Chief Justice, Ellenborough, refused him permission to introduce evidence about the Castlereagh regime in Ireland as justification for what he had written. A notorious saying was revived and celebrated: 'The greater the truth the greater the libel.'

That was in January 1811. The following month, John and Leigh Hunt, two liberal journalists who ran the *Examiner* newspaper, were charged with seditious libel for attacking flogging in the army. Lord Chief Justice Ellenborough impartially told the jury that the Hunts' article was libel, but they returned a verdict of not guilty. The publishers of the *Stamford News*, however, who had originally published the anti-flogging article, were found guilty of libel and went down for eighteen months.

Later the same year the government charged Henry White, editor of the *Independent Whig*, with libel. White was in prison for another offence and could not even have seen an article in his paper which attacked conditions in the British army, compared them unfavourably with those in the French army, and complained that the only people who received medals for bravery in the field were senior officers.

Lord Ellenborough, the judge, in the words of a contemporary report, 'dwelt with the animation of a pleader upon the injustice done to the national spirit and government by charging members of the administration with imbecility and corruption'. 'Publications directly defaming the government,' he said, '*are* libels.'[17] The jury disagreed. They found White not guilty – though largely because he was not immediately responsible for the publication.

Usually the prosecutions were successful. In March 1812, Daniel Eaton was sentenced to eighteen months for publishing the works of Tom Paine. Lord Ellenborough explained: 'In this country the Christian religion is fenced about by the laws of libel.'[18] In November of the same year, Daniel Lovell, proprieter of the *Statesman*, went down for eighteen months for criticizing the prison service. In December, the Hunt brothers came up again, this time for publishing a spirited attack on the Prince Regent ('a libertine, a companion of gamblers and demireps'). Once again Ellenborough refused the Hunts' lawyers permission to prove that the Prince was indeed what the Hunts had called him, and a lot worse besides. After a hysterical direction from the judge, the jury found the Hunts guilty and they went to prison for two years.

The prosecutions abated somewhat as the economic crisis of 1812 eased, but with the new agitation following the 'peace crisis of 1816 and 1817' they started up again. In 1817 the government lost a seditious libel case against the *Black Dwarf* and its publisher, Thomas Wooler. It lost three cases against the satirist William Hone when he was charged with libel for parodies on the Litany. Lord Ellenborough delivered his solemn opinion, 'as he was required by Act of Parliament to do; and under the authority of that Act, and still more in obedience to his conscience and his God, he pronounced this to be a most impious and profane libel.'[19] But the jury found Hone not guilty.

So the government changed the law and toughened up the juries. In October 1819, the publisher Richard Carlile was prosecuted for publishing Tom Paine's *Age of Reason* and Palmer's *Principles of Nature*. The new Acts gave him no chance, despite an eleven-hour speech to the jury. He went to prison for three years. So did Joseph Harrison, for saying in the street in August 1819: 'The government has starved the people, and now it is right for the people to starve the goverment.' In August 1829 the government got its own back on Wooler of the *Black Dwarf* under one of the 'Six Acts' for helping to arrange a mass meeting in Birmingham. In 1821, Richard Carlile's wife was sent down for a year and fined £500 for libel for criticizing the government; three publishers were sent down for attacking Lady Caroline Wrottesley in *John Bull*; and a Manchester bookseller was convicted and imprisoned for selling a book by Richard Carlile to a government spy who had asked him to get the book specially for him.

These appalling laws had to be enforced. And since there was no general consent for any of them, they had to be enforced by violence.

Throughout almost all the twelve years of Shelley's adult life, the government maintained a standing army in Britain which was larger and better armed even than the army in France, Spain or the West Indies. In the twenty-three years of the Napoleonic Wars, 155 barracks were built for armies in the 'disaffected' towns and cities of Britain. In 1812, Parliament gave the go-ahead for the biggest burst of barrack-building in British history. Barracks were built at Regents Park, London (for 138,000 soldiers), Liverpool (82,000), Bristol (60,000) and Brighton (20,000).[20] Sir Francis Burdett, M.P. for Westminster, complained: 'Ministers are intending to establish a military despotism in this country.'[21]

Where the barracks were no longer large enough, other arrangements were made. During the Luddite uprising in 1812 there were seventy-one companies of infantry and twenty-seven troops of Horse Guards and Dragoons in Lancashire.[22] A letter from Huddersfield in August of that year reported: 'We now have upwards of 1,000 soldiers in the town and the publicans are very much distressed to accommodate them.' There were only 33 pubs – and 30 soldiers billeted in each of them![23] These troops were reinforced by an army of spies, and by systematic torture. Spies frustrated what could have been the first ever working class insurrection in 1817; they provoked and exposed a conspiracy to murder the Cabinet in 1820; they dogged the movements of all political societies and associations throughout the period. As for torture, a letter from Manchester at the height of the Luddite uprising in 1812 declared: 'All possible means have been tried to induce the Luddites in prison to divulge the whole extent of their plan and to impeach their ringleaders – but without effect.'[24]

As if army, spies and torture were not enough, the government encouraged their middle class supporters to arm themselves against the working people. Gentlemen organized and drilled themselves into the yeomanry. Only people of some substance – shopkeepers, wine merchants, employers and of course landed gentry – were admitted to the yeomanry, whose horses, uniforms and weapons were subsidized by the Exchequer. The powers of this yeomanry were not defined or limited. In most cases their actions were subject to the magistracy, and since almost all magistrates were leading yeomen there was every scope for 'rough justice'. Strikes and processions were a familiar target for these yeomen, and strikees and demonstrators would be lucky not to feel the steel of the yeoman's sabres.

The years 1810–22 were twelve years of dictatorial laws, prejudiced judges and packed juries, the suppression of free expression, the Combination Acts and inhuman punishments – all backed up with organized military power barracked in every major town and city. Edward Thompson sums it up: 'The British people were held down by force.'[25]

Yet still, whether in spite of the oppression or because of it, there was resistance. Only a small part of that resistance showed itself in Parliament. Parliament during these years was not a representative body at all. The House of Commons was only marginally more representative than the

House of Lords. Indeed the more powerful Lords controlled a great bulk of the so-called Commons. Eight senior peers owned fifty-one of the seats in the Commons. Their nominees were selected unopposed. Two hundred and ninety-two of the 513 seats in Parliament were in the gift of the aristocracy. Even in the few seats where anything remotely like a genuine election took place, the franchise was restricted to the rich.

In Penryn, Cornwall, in the 1818 general election, the mayor shocked the voters by declaring his intention to enforce the voters' oath against bribery. The voters collected in a mob outside his house shouting in gentlemanly accents, 'We want bribes!' They got the bribes and a man called Swann was duly 'elected'. A Parliamentary Commission eventually expelled Swann, despite his justifiable complaints that he was only following the 'normal practice'. The real objection to Swann was that he was not the nominee of a recognized 'borough-maker' or nobleman.

The French Revolution had irrevocably split the Whig Party, the party of the landed gentry which controlled the House of Commons for most of the eighteenth century. Many left the party with Burke to fulminate with the Tories against the revolution. Others, like Charles James Fox, stayed on to campaign for Parliamentary reform. But by the end of the century many of these had given up politics and gone home to their country mansions. Fox himself wrote: 'Why should one not consider one's own ease, and do nothing? . . . While what we used to call the *exploded* principles of tyranny seem [to be] acquiring even a sort of popularity, and no countenance is given in any one part of the world to sentiments of moderation, liberty and justice, I own I completely despair, and feel myself quite excusable in giving more attention to Euripides than to either House of Parliament.'[26]

With the Foxites gone, the field was left almost entirely to the Tories. The few 'reforming Whigs' left – men like Sir Samuel Romilly and Henry Brougham – were content to make occasional interventions on behalf of penal reform or against the war. But most of their time was spent making their fortunes.

Consistent attack and opposition in Parliament was left, in effect, to one man: Sir Francis Burdett, himself enormously rich with a great house in Piccadilly. Burdett was elected throughout the period by the relatively widely enfranchized Westminster constituency, and he kept up a heroic campaign against the government, sometimes without any support. When, in 1812, he moved the reference back of the Prince Regent's speech, attacking the government's war policy and denouncing the government as 'a rapacious and haughty oligarchy', he was supported by one teller (Lord Cochrane, the admiral who later fought for the freedom of the people of Chile) and one other voter. Burdett's attacks got him into trouble more than once. In 1810 his defence, in Cobbett's *Register*, of John Jones, a former member of the Corresponding Society, who was imprisoned for contempt of Parliament for daring to criticize its proceedings, landed him in the Tower of London. In 1819 a spirited attack on the Peterloo massacre again landed him in prison for libel for several months.

One story about Burdett is enough to expose his limitations, however. When he was arrested for supporting John Jones, feeling ran high in the city. Crowds collected in the streets and the sergeant-at-arms, to effect the arrest, had to break down Burdett's front door. In July 1810, Parliament was prorogued, and Burdett was due to be freed. An enormous demonstration was arranged by the Westminster Committee to meet him. The whole of working London seemed to respond to the call.

'The line of streets from Stratton Street to Piccadilly was thickly lined with people,' wrote a contemporary reporter, 'and a huge march went to the Tower carrying placards: "THE CONSTITUTION! TRIAL BY JURY! BURDETT FOR EVER!" ' [27] The march arrived at the Tower at midday. At three in the afternoon it was still there. Finally a notice went up outside the Tower saying: 'He is gone by the water.' The crowd didn't believe it, but Sir Francis had

indeed left the Tower by the river on the other side of the
crowd. The procession wandered disconsolately back to Piccadilly, but Sir Francis was not at home. The crowd dis-
persed. When the Westminster Committee remonstrated
with him for destroying the enthusiasm of their demonstration, Sir Francis explained: 'I did not want to cause a single
accident.'[28]

This patrician opposition was supported to the hilt by the
Examiner and the Hunt brothers. They too went to prison
for their views; on occasion the ferocity of their attacks on
the war, the government, the King and the corrupt Parliament knew no bounds. But the Hunts were not even republicans, much less levellers. They strove all the time to
keep opposition to the government in the hands of Parliament and out of the hands of the 'mob'.

One of Burdett's closest friends was William Cobbett,
perhaps the most influential journalist of his age, if not of
any age.

Cobbett wrote clear, simple English. His *Register* was
addressed not just to the upper classes, but to the masses.
He kept up a relentless war on the government, particularly
on corruption, placemen, pensioners and sinecures. He was
a passionate reformer, for the common people against their
governors. But his practical reform measures harked back
to a mythical golden age of free husbandry, with each man
tilling his piece of land in freedom and equality with the
next. Although he castigated the horrors of the factory system and strongly supported victimized and imprisoned trade
unionists, Cobbett was opposed to societies, political parties
or concerted strike action. And his books of 'advice' – to
young men, to women, and so on – are full of the bombast
of someone who feels he has all the moral answers but none
of the political ones.

The most important resistance came not from Parliament
or journalists. It came from the 'mob' itself, from the working people, who for the first time in British history started
to feel their collective strength. In spite of the Combination
Acts, there were strikes in almost every industry. Coal-

miners struck against cuts in wages in Wolverhampton and
Coseley in November 1815 and in Newcastle in May 1816.
In March 1817, the miners at Radstock, Somerset, and the
surrounding country went on strike and came together to
defy the oncoming yeomanry.

They made a stand, according to one report, well-fur-
nished with immense bludgeons; seeing the cavalry approaching, they gave three cheers and called out, 'Bread or
Blood!'

Sir John Hippisley, a local yeoman and chairman of the
magistrates, called out, 'What do you want?'

Back came the reply: 'Full wages. We are starving.'

Sir John Hippisley replied with all the passionate logic of
his class: 'Your minds are inflamed by parodies on the liturgy
of the church, seducing you not only from your King but
from your God.'[29]

The cavalry charged, and four men were arrested.

The magistrates had more success in stopping what must
have been the first ever 'Right to Work' march – the march
of the miners from Bilston, Staffordshire, all of whom were
thrown out of work by the postwar depression of 1816. The
coal owners gave groups of miners wagons of coal; they
decided to push these to London taking a number of different
routes and ask the Prince Regent to find work for them.

These Bilston miners had no experience of struggle. They
were meek in the extreme. Yet their pathetic demonstrations
aroused passionate feeling in the towns and villages through
which they passed. The processions swelled. Terrified of the
effect the march might have among the London poor, the
magistrates took action. The marches were stopped at
Leicester, at St Albans, and at Maidenhead and sent back.
Miners from Wolverhampton marching to Liverpool were
stopped at Chester. 'The men immediately pulled off their
hats and paid great and respectful attention while the magistrates addressed them on the illegality and dangerous tend-
ency of their proceedings.'[30]

This difference between the attitude of the miners from
Somerset and from Bilston was reflected across the country.

In some areas and workplaces, workers acted out the subservient role expected of them. But in others, as they saw
their livelihoods destroyed, the workers took action. In the
twelve years from 1810 to 1822 there were three waves of
working class action, each one of which bordered on
insurrection.

The first was the agitation known as the Luddite uprising,
which took place in 1812. It started in the East Midlands –
Nottinghamshire and Leicestershire – but quickly spread
through Yorkshire and Lancashire. It was sparked off by the
lowering of wages and the mass unemployment caused by
the introduction of new machinery for making clothes and
stockings. Gangs of men would 'visit' employers who had
machines in their houses and shops, smash the machines,
and vanish. These raids were not, as official history has it,
the work of unorganized hooligans. The Luddites were well
drilled. For the most part, they escaped the network of
troops and spies that was marshalled against them. An attack
on a mill at Rawfolds near Leeds resulted in the arrest of
fifteen Luddites and their execution at York. Thirteen others
were hanged at Chester. But for the most part the Luddites
were never caught, despite the constant success of their
operations.

Nor was the Luddite movement directed only at machinery. As the year went on, and the organization of the gangs
grew stronger, they collected arms and organized food riots
with the specific intention of lowering food prices.

A letter from Sheffield on 13 August 1812 ran: 'The populace has drawn up a paper which they have called upon the
flour dealers to sign, fixing flour price at 3/- a stone. Many
complied. The selling price is now 7/-.'[31] Lord Milton, the
chairman of the magistrates, made a speech telling the people
they must wait for low prices until the harvest – 'at which
they were much infuriated'. These 'mobs' met every night
in many Yorkshire, Lancashire and Midlands towns. In Nottingham one night they placarded the town offering a reward
for the body of the mayor, 'dead or alive'.

The movement died as silently as it had started, but the
organizers were still there for the next wave of agitation,

during the postwar depression of 1816–17. The 'Pentridge rising' of 1817, the culmination of a year's strikes, riots and demonstrations, was, in the event, a disaster. Jerry Brandreth, who was probably a Luddite in 1812, organized a march of farm labourers and local workers on Nottingham, where they planned to start an insurrection. An insurrectionary organization of a skeleton kind already existed across Yorkshire, and feelings were running so high that the Brandreth spark could well have lit a bonfire. But government spies had penetrated his organization and skilfully organized the 'rising' so that it could not be co-ordinated. Brandreth's small force was routed by cavalry at Pentridge, Derbyshire. Brandreth and two colleagues were captured and hanged.

But the real meaning of the rising was well appreciated by the government. On 24 February 1817, Castlereagh told the House of Commons: 'Looking to the history of the revolutionary spirit of this country, it appears to have descended from the higher and better-informed ranks in which it formerly betrayed itself, to those lower reaches in which it is now principally to be found.'[32]

Encouraged by the success at Pentridge, the government threw itself into the oppression of these 'lower reaches'. Wages were held firmly down. In the summer of 1818 a great strike broke out among the spinners of Manchester who were paid, on average, £47 13s. 4d. a year, out of which they had to pay for their own piecers, or helpers (usually children), and their own candles. The small master spinner or employer (with less than fourteen workers employed) earned £3,033 5s. 4d.[33] a year.

The strike was conducted with much enthusiasm; 15,000 spinners paraded thrice weekly through the Manchester streets. But it was broken with great brutality. Two hundred and fifty spinners went on the black list – to permanent unemployment.[34] Several others were imprisoned.

Yet this oppression could not stop the outcry for reform, which rose to a crescendo in the summer of 1819.

In June, at Hunslett Moor, Leeds, 35,000 people met to demand universal suffrage. In July another monster meeting unanimously elected Sir Charles Wolsely as the 'legislative attorney' for Birmingham. (Birmingham, with 150,000 inhabitants, had no M.P. Nor, for that matter, had Manchester, Sheffield, or Leeds.)

The organizers called for two more meetings, even larger, one at Leeds and one at Manchester, both for August. The government replied with a proclamation on 30 July against all 'seditious meetings'. The Leeds organizers complied but in Manchester they decided to go ahead with the meeting. Some 80,000 working people turned out at St Peter's Field on 18 August, to be met by cavalry charges from yeomanry. The yeomen used their sabres with reckless abandon against unarmed men, women and children. Eleven people died, including a child.

The horror throughout the country was instantaneous. Huge meetings were held, attended by many of the liberal gentry. The Earl of Fitzwilliam and the Duke of Norfolk addressed a meeting of 20,000 in York. Fitzwilliam was sacked as Lord Lieutenant of Yorkshire. Strikes and demonstrations continued thoughout the rest of the year. But the government, safe behind their 'Six Acts' of repression, found it easy to contain the reform leaders in the Commons and the Lords.

The 'lower reaches', the masses – much more difficult to contain – had, as so often since, handed over the reins of reform to the 'higher and better-informed ranks'. The immediate beneficiaries were Castlereagh, Eldon, Sidmouth and the rest of the 'ghastly masquerade'.

The industrial revolution was conducted under the most monstrous and corrupt government the country has ever seen. But it also created a new opposition, less organized, less well-endowed yet much more resolute than anything Charles James Fox or the Duke of Norfolk could muster. These two branches of the same tree – the tyranny of property and the growing working class opposition to it – overshadowed British politics during the twelve years in which the adult Percy Bysshe Shelley was alive and thinking about them.

2

Republican

Oh, that the free would stamp the impious name
Of KING into the dust!

'Ode to Liberty', 1820[1]

The family into which Percy Bysshe Shelley was born in the
third year of the French Revolution was typical of the
English upper classes of the time. His rather absurd second
name – by which he was known in boyhood, though from
early on most of his friends and intimates called him 'Shelley'
– was taken from his grandfather, Bysshe Shelley, who had
made himself a fortune by the two most time-honoured
methods of the well-bred English male: deceiving rich wom-
en into marriage, and inheritance. The old rascal had inherited a vask hunk of Sussex, several thousand sheep and a
lovely house at Field Place near Horsham. Ambitious Sussex
sheep farmers of the period found it useful, if not manda-
tory, to cultivate the biggest sheep farmer of them all, the
Duke of Norfolk. The Duke, as we have seen, was playing
at being a liberal and a radical, so Bysshe Shelley the elder
became a liberal and a radical. He was rewarded by the short
coalition administration of 1806 with a baronetcy.

Old Bysshe was such a miser that he couldn't bear to live
in his country mansion, and stayed instead in a small house
at Horsham. Field Place he handed over to the next in line
for the baronetcy, his son Timothy.

Timothy found out early on how important it was for
country gentlemen to mix business with politics. He courted

the Duke of Norfolk, and became the Whig M.P. for the Duke's pocket borough at Shoreham-on-Sea, which boasted fifteen electors, all owned by the Duke. Sir Timothy sat in Parliament for a quarter of a century without making a single speech. He was good-natured, except where his property was threatened (which it seldom was), narrow-minded and deeply suspicious of knowledge. 'Never read a book,' he warned his son John, Shelley's younger brother, 'and you will be a rich man.'[2]

Upper-crust political families, then as now, were intensely proud of their sons, especially their eldest sons. Sir Timothy was no exception. He got on well with his son and heir, even if he had cause to be apprehensive about him. Young Bysshe, it seemed to him, was rather odd. He set off fires and explosions in the grounds. He wrote verses to the cat. And sometimes he went on long midnight walks with his younger sisters, whom he terrified with ghastly and ghostly lamentations.

Sir Timothy also received disturbing reports from the expensive schools to which he sent his heir. At Syon House, a barbarous place even by the barbarous standards of British 'preparatory schools' (in which young boys of the aristocracy, often from the age of six, were trained to behave like their parents), the lad had been reported 'out of step'. At Eton the boy was obviously unhappy. He was outlawed by his schoolmates for refusing to 'fag' – that is, to act as servant to an older boy. Yet there were compensations for Sir Timothy. No one could deny that the boy was bright. Indeed, he could hardly have been brighter. Sir Timothy, who believed strongly that personal characteristics were inherited, did not know where the devil his son had got his brightness from. By the time the lad was eighteen he had read more books than the bumbling baronet read in a lifetime.

Young Bysshe, mused Sir Timothy, would do well at Oxford, and would certainly make a fine Whig M.P. The jaded, defeated Progressive Whigs desperately wanted young blood in the House of Commons. The Duke of

Norfolk and the other Whigs, when they came to dinner at Field Place, would make a fuss of the young lad, and talk politics often for his benefit. 'Politics,' the Duke once told Shelley, 'are the proper career for a young man of ability and of your station in life.' In the school holidays, a proud Sir Timothy took the youngster up to the House of Commons and proudly introduced him to lords, M.P.s and ministers. The boy seemed strangely silent about it all, but was clearly interested in the political issues, which Sir Timothy could not understand.

What sort of politics were talked at those dinner parties and weekend sojourns at Field Place? The guests came mainly from the rump of the Progressive Whigs. Their politics were uniformly anti-Tory and anti-government. In the safe atmosphere of the great country houses, these aristocratic Whigs would let slip radical and republican ideas far more challenging than anything they would say in Parliament or at election meetings. When in 1798 the Duke of Norfolk toasted the 'Majesty of the People' he was only doing in public what many of his protégés did in private at almost every dinner party. Although most of these Whigs were instinctive royalists, most of them loathed King George III. As the Prince Regent depended increasingly on the Tory administration to pay his gambling debts, the Whigs turned against him too. At any rate, the idea that there was nothing divine or sacrosanct about the King and the court was one which Shelley must have heard expounded regularly throughout his youth.

To a young aristocrat who had been to Syon House and Eton that idea was shocking. The entire educational system at both establishments, then as now, depended on unquestioning obedience to and belief in king and country. The King, the Prince Regent, and all the princes and princesses were daily described as divinities who could do no wrong.

Partly from his father's association with the Whigs, partly from his own observation, Shelley discovered very early in life that the royal family were nothing of the kind. On the contrary they – and all the other royal families – were

brigands, hypocrites, libertines and liars. This discovery hit
Shelley like a thunderclap; it affected his thinking and writing all his life.

In 1810, his first year at Oxford, he published his first
poems, anonymously. He chose the pseudonym Margaret
Nicholson, after a washerwoman who had attempted to
assassinate George III in 1786. The poems published in the
collection, and in letters which he wrote to his friends at
that time, ring with his outrage against the imposters at
court:

> Yes! smooth-faced tyrants chartered by a Power
> Called King, who in the castellated keep
> Of a far distant land wears out his days
> Of miserable dotage, pace the quay
> And by the magic of a dreadful word,
> Hated though dreadful, shield their impotence,
> Their lies, their murders and their robberies.[3]

In the year he left Oxford, he started on his first great
poem, *Queen Mab* (1812). In the poem, a spirit of a young
girl is wafted into the stratosphere by a Fairy Queen. The
Fairy Queen shows her the earth with all its horrors, and its
potential. Chief among the horrors is:

> The King, the wearer of a gilded chain
> That binds his soul to abjectness, the fool
> Whom courtiers nickname monarch, whilst a slave
> Even to the basest appetite—that man
> Heeds not the shriek of penury; he smiles
> At the deep curses which the destitute
> Mutter in secret, and a sullen joy
> Pervades his bloodless heart when thousands groan . . .[4]

Around the King is the aristocracy:

> Those gilded flies
> That, basking in the sunshine of a court,
> Fatten on its corruption![5]

The Fairy Queen goes on to anticipate the question her charge will ask, and to answer it, if not quite accurately, at least furiously:

> Whence, think'st thou, kings and parasites arose?
> Whence that unnatural line of drones, who heap
> Toil and unvanquishable penury
> On those who build their palaces, and bring
> Their daily bread?—From vice, black loathsome vice;
> From rapine, madness, treachery, and wrong;
> From all that 'genders misery, and makes
> Of earth this thorny wilderness; from lust
> Revenge, and murder. . . .[6]

This fury stayed with Shelley and gathered momentum. Almost all his narrative poetry has at its centre a king or a tyrant. They vary in their brutishness. Count Cenci in *The Cenci* is an undiluted monster, a Castlereagh. Mahmud in *Hellas* is more sympathetic. Othman in *The Revolt of Islam* is, at times, almost pitiable. Even Jupiter in *Prometheus Unbound* has a soft side. But they are all anti-heroes, all to be challenged, hunted down and overthrown.

With the same fury, Shelley pursued the English monarchs of his day. George III was accurately described at the beginning of a sonnet called 'England in 1819' as 'An old, mad, blind, despised, and dying king'.[7] But he reserved his spiciest venom for the Prince Regent, later George IV. When he read about the fantastic fête in 1811 to celebrate the Prince's accession to power, Shelley wrote to his confidante, Elizabeth Hitchener:

What think you of the bubbl[ing] *brooks, & mossy banks* at Carlton House—the allee-verts &c—it is said that this entertainment will cost 120,000£; nor will it be the last bauble which the nation must buy to amuse this overgrown bantling of regency. How admirably this growing spirit of ludicrous magnificence tallies with the disgusting splendors of the stage of the Roman Empire, which preceded its destruction![8]

Shelley returned to this theme in a poem called 'The

Devil's Walk', which he wrote at about the same time, in 1812, and later had pasted up on walls in North Devon (the servant who pasted it up was arrested and sent to prison for six months):

> Fat as that Prince's maudlin brain
>   Which, addled by some gilded toy,
> Tired, gives his sweetmeat, and again
>   Cries for it, like a humoured boy.
>
> For he is fat, his waistcoat gay,
> When strained upon a levee day,
>   Scarce meets across his princely paunch;
>   And pantaloons are like half moons
> Upon each brawny haunch.[9]

In *Oedipus Tyrranus*, or *Swellfoot the Tyrant* (1820), George IV appears again, still fat, and still fattening as thousands starved to death. He appears as Swellfoot, the Tyrant of Thebes, surrounded by fawning ministers. The people are the Pigs – Burke's 'swinish multitude'.

> *Mammon* [Prime Minister Liverpool]. I fear your sacred
>   Majesty has lost
> The appetite which you were used to have.
> Allow me now to recommend this dish—
> A simple kickshaw by your Persian cook,
> Such as is served at the great King's second table.
> The price and pains which its ingredients cost
> Might have maintained some dozen families
> A winter or two—not more—so plain a dish
> Could scarcely disagree.—
>
> *Swellfoot* [George IV]. After the trial,
> And these fastidious Pigs are gone, perhaps
> I may recover my lost appetite,—
> I feel the gout flying about my stomach—
> Give me a glass of Maraschino punch.
>
> *Purganax* [Castlereagh] (filling his glass, and standing up).
>   The glorious Constitution of the Pigs! . . .
>
> *Laoctonos* [Wellington]. Claret, somehow,
> Puts me in mind of blood, and blood of claret!

> *Swellfoot.* Laoctonos is fishing for a compliment,
> But 'tis his due. Yes, you have drunk more wine,
> And shed more blood, than any man in Thebes.
> For God's sake stop the grunting of those Pigs!
>
> *Purganax.* We dare not, Sire, 'tis Famine's privilege.[10]

George IV had married Caroline, Princess of Saxe Co-
burg, while he was still Prince Regent. He locked her up in
a castle in Kent for the early years of their marriage, and
then allowed her to travel on her own in Europe while he
amused himself with other women of the court. When he
became king, Caroline returned to claim the throne. George
and the Tory Ministry tried to get a Bill through Parliament
to disqualify her as queen. The opposition, with a lot of
popular support, resisted the measure, which foundered and
failed.

The theme of *Swellfoot the Tyrant* is the return of Caroline
and her rousing of the people (the Pigs) to a revolt against
Swellfoot and the Ministry. It reads in parts as though Shelley saw the Queen as a likely leader of rebellion, as though
revolt could spring from a royalist source. If that were so,
of course, the main argument against kings would founder.
If there can be 'good' kings, surely they can put right any
harm which is done by 'bad' kings.

Shelley answered this point directly, in a letter to his
friend Thomas Love Peacock on the Queen Caroline affair:

I cannot help adverting to it as one of the absurdities of royalty,
that a vulgar woman, with all those low tastes which prejudice
considers as vices, and a person whose habits and manners everyone would shun in private life, without any redeeming virtues
should be turned into a heroine, because she is a queen, or, as a
collateral reason, because her husband is a king; and he, no less
than his ministers, are so odious that everything, however disgusting, which is opposed to them, is admirable.[11]

But Caroline, empty and vain, had to be supported against
George, because if she could discredit George all monarchy
would suffer. At the end of *Swellfoot the Tyrant* there is a
small clue to Shelley's real attitude to the Caroline crisis.

The Queen triumphs; the Pigs are turned into Bulls, and the Ministers into Pigs. The hunt is on. One of the Bulls, a Minotaur, turns to the Queen and bids her get on with the hunt:

> And if your Majesty will deign to mount me,
> *At least till you have hunted down your game,*
> I will not throw you.[Author's italics.][12]

The Queen was useful until the King and his ministers were discredited – but no further.

Shelley's hatred of *all* kings, however much he might support one against the other, extended even to Napoleon Bonaparte. To many, Bonaparte still represented the flame of the French Revolution, and most republicans who, like Shelley, secretly supported the French armies against the English were inclined to worship Bonaparte. But when Shelley's Tory friend Hogg wrote to rib him for his partiality to Bonaparte, Shelley wrote back angrily: 'Excepting Lord Castlereagh you could not have mentioned any character but Buonaparte whom I condemn & abhor more vehemently.'[13]

When Napoleon fell, Shelley wrote a sonnet, 'Feelings of a Republican on the Fall of Bonaparte'(1815).

> I hated thee, fallen tyrant ! I did groan
> To think that a most unambitious slave,
> Like thou, shouldst dance and revel on the grave
> Of Liberty. Thou mightst have built thy throne
> Where it had stood even now: thou didst prefer
> A frail and bloody pomp . . .'[14]

The spectacle of Napoleon, the once-populist corporal, making himself emperor and clothing himself with the pageantry of the old imperial order disgusted Shelley.

Shelley's hatred for monarchy was not founded only on the waste of luxury in the middle of poverty. His argument went deeper. Kings, he argued, had no right to govern. They were not chosen by the governed, and the governed had therefore no redress against their rulers. This idea – that *representative* government is the only justifiable government – came directly from Tom Paine, whose works Shelley read while still at Eton, and revered all his life. 'Government,' Shelley wrote in his 'Proposals for an Association' in 1812, 'can have no rights, it is a delegation for the purpose of securing them to others. . . . The strength of government is the happiness of the governed.'[15] Still with Paine, he argued in 'A Philosophical View of Reform' (1820) that any government that was not representative had no right to a day in power: 'A government that is founded on any other basis is a government of fraud or force and ought on the first convenient occasion to be overthrown.'[16]

The argument applies only where monarchs *do* have power. Already, even in Shelley's day, there were people who defended the monarchy on the curious grounds that their power had been dwindling ever since the American War of Independence.

Shelley agreed that the political power of the monarchy was declining. In its place, he wrote, again in 'A Philosophical View of Reform': 'The power which has increased . . . is the [pow]er of the rich. The name and office of king is merely the mask of this power, and is a kind of stalking-horse used to conceal those "catchers of men", whilst they lay their nets. Monarchy is only the string which ties the robber's bundle.'[17]

Power was passing to the landlords and capitalists, but the king still had a vital role to play. Apart from acting as a 'stalking horse', the monarchy had, and still has, an enervating effect on society. Shelley understood this phenomenon very well, and wrote of it several times. The common people lived their lives through royalty; they glorified the passions, loves and griefs of royalty, and as a result devalued the passions, loves and griefs of 'ordinary' people. Through adulation of royalty, people lost confidence, not merely in their own abilities – a divisive educational system took care of that – but even in their own passions. What did 'ordinary' love and grief matter compared to those of the royal family?

In those days there was no popular press to regurgitate
banalities about royalty. But there was a press, a literary set,
town-criers and newshounds who concentrated, often exclusively, on impressing the common people with the wonders of the court. Every royal marriage and birth was
heralded as a miracle, every royal death as a calamity.

About George III and the Prince Regent there was little
for the scribblers to get excited, so they devoted most of
their attention to the Princess Charlotte, the Prince's daughter, a pretty and harmless girl of seventeen. In the royalist
press, she became an angel. In 1817, a year after her marriage, the Princess died while giving birth to her first child.
A torrent of lamentation flowed out of the palace into the
gutters of the royalist propaganda machine. All over the
country people wept in the streets for their 'beloved princess'. Churches were packed to standing room for Charlotte
funeral services.

Shelley's response was to write his 'Address to the People
on the Death of Princess Charlotte' (1817), subtitled, in a
quotation from Tom Paine's *Rights of Man*: 'We pity the
plumage, but forget the dying bird.'

The pamphlet compared the public reaction to the death
of the princess to that which greeted the execution the following day of Brandreth, Ludlam and Turner, for their part
in the Pentridge uprising. The execution, the pamphlet
argued, was a far more serious matter than the Princess's
death. In a striking passage, the pamphlet exposed the dead-
liest effect of the monarchy: its ability to unleash grief for
a royal tragedy *in order to bottle up the grief* for thousands of
other human tragedies. The passage rings with Shelley's
sympathy for the poverty-stricken masses, and his concern
that that sympathy should be universally appreciated and
shared.

This much the death of the Princess Charlotte has in common
with the death of thousands. How many women die in childbed
and leave their families of motherless children and their husbands
to live on, blighted by the remembrance of that heavy loss? . . .

You walk with a merry heart through the streets of this great city, and think not that such are the scenes acting all round you. You do not number in your thought the mothers who die in childbed. It is the most horrible of ruins:—In sickness, in old age, in battle, death comes as to his own home; but in the season of joy and hope, when life should succeed to life, and the assembled family expects one more, the youngest and the best beloved, that the wife, the mother—she for whom each member of the family was so dear to one another, should die!— Yet thousands of the poorest poor, whose misery is aggravated by what cannot be spoken now, suffer this. And have they no affections? Do not their hearts beat in their bosoms, and the tears gush from their eyes? Are they not human flesh and blood? Yet none weep for them—none mourn for them—none when their coffins are carried to the grave (if indeed the parish furnishes a coffin for all) turn aside and moralize upon the sadness they have left behind.[18]

It was only natural that Shelley's republicanism should quickly blossom into a fierce anti-militarism. From an early age he was writing poetry against the Napoleonic Wars. In 'Falsehood and Vice, a Dialogue', included in the Notes on *Queen Mab*, Vice argues with Falsehood as to which has done the greatest damage to humanity. Vice says:

> I have extinguished the noonday sun,
> In the carnage-smoke of battles won:
> Famine, Murder, Hell and Power
> Were glutted in that glorious hour
> Which searchless fate had stamped for me
> With the seal of her security. . . .
> For the bloated wretch on yonder throne
> Commanded the bloody fray to rise.[19]

In *Queen Mab*, as usual, Shelley cannot contain his fury:

> War is the statesman's game, the priest's delight,
> The lawyer's jest, the hired assassin's trade,
> And, to those royal murderers, whose mean thrones
> Are bought by crimes of treachery and gore,
> The bread they eat, the staff on which they lean.[20]

Queen Mab goes on to describe the generals who carry out their royal master's wishes in the field – men like Wellington who were regarded throughout high society as flawless champions of virtue.

> These are the hired bravos who defend
> The tyrant's throne—the bullies of his fear:
> These are the sinks and channels of worst vice,
> The refuse of society, the dregs
> Of all that is most vile: . . .[21]

The Peninsular War, which the court and the government hailed as a glorious British triumph, was for Shelley 'that prodigal waste of human blood to aggrandise the fame of Statesmen'.[22] He was outraged by Castlereagh's expedition to the Walcheren. A batch of his early poems was published to raise funds for the Irish journalist, Peter Finnerty, imprisoned for criticizing the expedition in a Dublin newspaper. He lambasted the pressgang whereby unemployed men could be seized by force and dragooned into military service. The best of his early poems, 'A Tale of Society as it is' (1811), is the story of a lonely and impoverished old woman whose only source of revenue and comfort – her son – is taken from her by the pressgang:

> But, when the tyrant's bloodhounds forced the child
>   For his cursed power unhallowed arms to wield—
>   Bend to another's will—become a thing
> More senseless than the sword of battlefield—
> Then did she feel keen sorrow's keenest sting, . . .[23]

When Shelley went to Ireland in 1812, he took up the case of a young Irishman called Redfern who had been pressganged into the war, and whose family was left to rot in poverty. He bullied Burdett, the radical M.P. for Westminster, to agitate on Redfern's behalf, and attempted (unsuccessfully) to publish the facts of Redfern's case in the press.

The supposed gains from conquest, promised to the people by kings and generals, were, Shelley wrote, always illusory. 'Is war necessary to your happiness and safety?' he asked in his 'Address to the Irish People'.

The interests of the poor gain nothing from the wealth or extension of a nation's boundaries, they gain nothing from glory, a word that has often served as a cloak to the ambition or avarice of Statesmen. The barren victories of Spain, gained in behalf of a bigoted and tyrannical Government, are nothing to them. The conquests in India, by which England has gained glory indeed, but a glory which is not more honourable than that of Buonaparte, are nothing to them. The poor purchase this glory and this wealth, at the expense of their blood and labor, and happiness, and virtue. They die in battle for this infernal cause.[24]

The trappings of nationalism and jingoism were anathema to him. In one passage, for the publishing of which he was extremely fortunate not to be prosecuted, he wrote:

I call expressions . . . political cant, which, like the songs of Rule Britannia and God save the king, are but abstracts of the caterpillar creed of courtiers, cut down to the taste and comprehension of a mob; the one to disguise to an alehouse politician the evils of that devilish practice of war, and the other to inspire among clubs of all descriptions a certain feeling which some call loyalty and others servility.[25]

That was in 'Proposals for An Association', also addressed to the Irish. In these two pamphlets Shelley identified the true reasons for the oldest and most despicable of British conquests – the conquest of Ireland:

There are many Englishmen who cry down the Irish, and think it answers their ends to revile all that belongs to Ireland; but it is not because these men are Englishmen that they maintain such opinions, but because they wish to get money, and titles, and power.[26]

Colonial conquest, especially in Ireland, had led to specialization in torture, which Shelley also abhorred. The 'obtaining of information' from an enemy or a dissenter by torture was, for him, the ultimate obscenity of the times in which he lived, and his writings are full of anger about it. In his play, *The Cenci*, written in Italy in 1819, the tyrant, Count Cenci, is murdered on the instructions of his daughter Beatrice, after he has raped her. The papal authorities, who have been well paid during Cenci's lifetime to 'absolve' and 'hush up' his innumerable crimes, are determined to get to the root of his killing. They capture Beatrice, her mother and the murderer, Marzio, who is tortured and 'confesses'.

As judge and cardinal congratulate themselves on thus 'solving' the crime, Beatrice rounds on them with a speech which should be pasted up in torture chambers all over the world:

> Cardinal Camillo,
> You have a good repute for gentleness
> And wisdom: can it be that you sit here
> To countenance a wicked farce like this?
> When some obscure and trembling slave is dragged
> From sufferings which might shake the sternest heart
> And bade to answer, not as he believes,
> But as those may suspect or do desire
> Whose questions then suggest their own reply:
> And that in peril of sudden hideous torments
> As merciful God spares even the damned. Speak now
> The thing you surely know, which is that you,
> If your fine frame were stretched upon that wheel,
> And you were told: 'Confess that you did poison
> Your little nephew; that fair blue-eyed child
> Who was the lodestar of your life:'—and though
> All see, since his most swift and piteous death,
> That day and night, and heaven and earth, and time,
> And all the things hoped for or done therein
> Are changed to you, through your exceeding grief,
> Yet you would say 'I confess anything:'
> And beg from your tormentors, like that slave,
> The refuge of dishonourable death. [27]

Camillo is 'much moved' by this speech. But the judge remarks; 'Yet she must be tortured.' Shelley had as much contempt for judges as he had for the kings, their masters. As Queen Mab puts it:

> Those too the tyrant serve, who, skilled to snare
> The feet of Justice in the toils of law,
> Stand, ready to oppress the weaker still;
> And right or wrong will vindicate for gold, . . .[28]

Kings, queens, aristocrats, wars, torturers and judges –
Shelley hated them all. He was all his life an uncompromis-
ing republican and anti-militarist.

His politics, as we shall see, went deeper. He penetrated
closer to the source of the social evils around him than did
most republicans and anti-militarists of the day. He saw that
there were darker and more dangerous forces at work to
exploit and injure humanity. But, however sophisticated his
political philosophy, he never lost his sense of outrage at the
effrontery and barbarism of monarchs and those who served
them.

His most famous sonnet, 'Ozymandias', written in 1817,
whose words are so well known and whose meaning so
conspiciously ignored, is about that effrontery, that barbarism, and the human wilderness to which they lead:

> I met a traveller from an antique land
> Who said: 'Two vast and trunkless legs of stone
> Stand in the desert . . . Near them, on the sand,
> Half sunk, a shattered visage lies, whose frown,
> And wrinkled lip, and sneer of cold command,
> Tell that its sculptor well those passions read
> Which yet survive, stamped on those lifeless things,
> The hand that mocked them, and the heart that fed:
> And on the pedestal these words appear:
> "My name is Ozymandias, king of kings:
> Look on my works, ye Mighty, and despair!"
> Nothing beside remains. Round the decay
> Of that colossal wreck, boundless and bare
> The lone and level sands stretch far away.'[29]

3

Atheist

Men say they have seen God, and heard from God,
   Or known from others who have known such things,
And that his will is all our law, a rod
   To scourge us into slaves—that Priests and Kings,
   Custom, domestic sway, ay, all that brings
Man's freeborn soul beneath the oppressor's heel,
   Are his strong ministers, . . .

Laon and Cythna, 1817[1]

'Expelled! Expelled – for atheism!'[2] Half anxiously, half triumphantly, Shelley blurted out his news to his cousin Tom Medwin. It was 27 March 1811. Shelley and his friend Hogg had been at Oxford less than six months. They were both prodigiously clever. Yet they were both expelled – for a sin which shocked the High Tory gentlemen who ran the college to the very core of their bones.

Hogg and Shelley had written, and published, a defence of atheism, the first ever to appear in print in the English language. A few copies of their pamphlet, 'The Necessity of Atheism', could be seen for about twenty minutes at Slatters bookshop in Oxford High Street. It is very unlikely that anyone bought it. But Shelley had sent it by post to a mischievous selection of bigots, bishops and religious scholars. Almost as soon as the post was opened, he was summoned to the master's lodgings and asked if he had written the pamphlet. He refused to answer, and was expelled. Hogg followed him soon afterwards.

When Sir Timothy Shelley heard the news, he was furious. He knew about his son's rather distasteful fancies, but had never imagined that they would bring such disgrace

on the Shelley family. He wrote to his son, who had moved
to digs in London, ordering him to recant. After a few
months, he suggested, the college authorities would accept
an apology and allow the hothead back. But there was no
apology, and no recantation. As Shelley explained in letters
to his father, his atheism was not a passing fancy or an
undergraduate prank. It was essential to everything he believed in. To recant his atheism was to recant all his ideas,
and that he could not and would not do.

Sir Timothy replied by cutting off his son's allowance and
shutting him forever out of the comfortable aristocratic
circle in which he had been born and bred.

Shelley's formal education, like that of every other well-
bred boy of his time, was founded on the reading of the
New and Old Testaments, probably in that order. The New
Testament was full of stories about a man called Jesus Christ.
According to the 'gospels', ascribed to four men who had
been Christ's disciples, Jesus was born as the result of a
union between a virgin and a ghost. When he died he rose
again, and was apparently seen by many of his disciples in
different places. During his lifetime, he performed many
miracles. He fed 5,000 people with five loaves and two fishes. He
turned water into wine, and even raised someone from the dead.

These stories were then matched up with a number of
'prophecies' which were made by Hebrew prophets in the
Old Testament. They predicted the 'coming' of the 'son of
God', who would do a number of amazing things – some
of which, as the New Testament showed, he did do.

Grown men who seemed to Shelley to be otherwise perfectly sensible urged him and his schoolmates not just to
believe all this, but to worship it. They insisted that Jesus
Christ really *had* been born the son of God, and therefore
had to be worshipped – all the time: in grace before meals;
at church once a day, and twice if not three times on Sunday.
Young boys were 'confirmed' in the faith by a bishop laying
his hands on their heads. This entitled them to drink wine
and eat bread in church and imagine while doing so that

they were eating the body and drinking the blood of Jesus himself.

Shelley kept asking himself: 'Why should I believe all this?' The only proof of it all was the say-so of the gospel-writers. And they had not written the gospels themselves. Indeed, they had been ghost-written some sixty years after the youngest of the four saints had died. Should you believe something which seems unlikely just because someone says that they saw or experienced it? Shelley was dubious. As he argued in a letter to his father only seven weeks before his expulsion:

Supposing twelve men were to make an affidavit before you that they had seen in Africa, a vast snake three miles long, suppose they swore that this snake eat nothing but Elephants, & that you knew from all the laws of nature, that enough Elephants cd. not exist to sustain the snake—wd. you believe them?[3]

No. Few people would. And Shelley was inclined not to believe the far more preposterous and unnatural stories in the Bible. 'The Necessity of Atheism' was reprinted and expanded in the Notes on *Queen Mab*. In these Notes Shelley also wrote under the heading 'I will beget a Son, and He shall bear the sins of all the world':

Christianity, like all other religions, rests upon miracles, prophecies, and martyrdoms. . . .

Miracles resolve themselves into the following question:—Whether it is more probable the laws of nature, hitherto so immutably harmonious, should have undergone violation, or that a man should have told a lie? . . .

We have many instances of men telling lies;—none of an infraction of nature's laws, . . . The records of all nations afford innumerable instances of men deceiving others either from vanity or interest, or themselves being deceived by the limitedness of their views and their ignorance of natural causes: but where is the accredited case of God having come upon earth, to give the lie to His own creations? There would be something truly wonderful in the appearance of a ghost; but the assertion of a child that he saw one as he passed through the churchyard is universally admitted to be less miraculous.[4]

The same argument applied to the prophecies: 'It is more probable that writings, pretending to divine inspiration, should have been fabricated after the fulfilment of their pretended prediction than that they should have really been divinely inspired, . . .'[5] And, as he wrote in 'A Refutation of Deism' (1814), to the virgin birth:

It seems less credible that the God whose immensity is uncircumscribed by space, should have committed adultery with a carpenter's wife, than that some bold knaves or insane dupes had deceived the credulous multitude. We have perpetual and mournful experience of the latter: the former is yet under dispute. History affords us innumerable examples of the possibility of the one: Philosophy has in all ages protested against the probability of the other.[6]

The balance of probabilities, then, was overwhelmingly weighted against the miracles, the prophecies, the virgin birth, the resurrection and all the other extraordinary things which are meant to have happened to Christ. But were all those things necessary to a belief in God? Wasn't it possible to believe in God without the Old Testament prophecies, the gospels and the miracles?

Shelley rejected Christianity from a very early age. But when he first went to Oxford, he flirted with the idea that there might be a God, a supernatural being who had created the universe and was responsible for the 'spirit' which breathed through life. This belief in God but rejection of all forms of religion which depended on 'revelation' on earth was known as deism.

Curiously, it was Shelley's friend Hogg, the son of a Tory property lawyer from Durham, who introduced him to the writings of the French anti-religious writers of the mid- and late-eighteenth century – particularly to D'Holbach, who believed that all religion was a sign of ignorance. These writers, and Hogg's persistent arguments, turned Shelley from a deist to an atheist.

As he grew older, he found that many established liberals and radicals, including his friend Leigh Hunt, while opposing Christianity and the fables in the Bible, clung to deism.

To answer them, Shelley wrote a carefully argued pamphlet, 'The Refutation of Deism' (1814).

The pamphlet was written with half an eye on the censor and the blasphemy laws. It is a dialogue between Theosophus (a deist) and Eusebes (a Christian). Eusebes starts with a conventional declaration of faith in Christianity and the Bible. Theosophus, using the arguments against miracles and the testaments from 'The Necessity of Atheism', destroys him utterly.

Eusebes, instead of continuing his argument, asks Theosophus whether he believes in any god. Yes, says Theosophus, he believes in a creator of the universe, a supernatural deity; belief in such a god can be justified by reason, as belief in the miracles and the testaments cannot be.

Eusebes pounces. It is, he says, impossible to sustain any god by reason. If the universe was created by a creator, then the reasonable man must ask *who created the creator*? The very argument which deists used against miracles – the argument about the balance of probabilities – can be used just as powerfully against the existence of a divine creator.

Until it is clearly proved that the Universe was created, we may reasonably suppose that it has endured from all eternity. In a case where two propositions are diametrically opposite, the mind believes that which is less incomprehensible: it is easier to suppose that the Universe has existed from all eternity, than to conceive an eternal being capable of creating it. If the mind sinks beneath the weight of one, is it an alleviation to increase the intolerability of the burden?[7]

The pressure of the argument is irresistible. Theosophus, the deist, admits that there is no rational basis for believing in the existence of any god, not even his sublime, unestablished and unrevealed deity. Eusebes, the Christian, wins the argument – even though his defence of the gospels and the miracles has been transparently destroyed.

No thinking person can read 'The Refutation' without drawing the obvious conclusions. First, that the process of reason destroys belief in *all* gods.

Second, that defenders of religions realize this. They do not argue for their gods by the process of reason. Indeed, they cannot allow reason to enter religious discussion, for fear that it will undermine religion at its base. They are obliged to establish their religion by means of fantasy: by the 'revelation' of divine beings on earth, by sons of God and virgin births, by moving stars in the east, resurrections and so on. The more preposterous the miracle, the more it assists the defenders of religion. The miracles are not just the trappings of religion. They are essential to its mass appeal.

The third conclusion is the most important. The deists, Shelley argued, by conceding the major point – the existence of a sublime and supernatural creator – were letting established religion off the hook. They allowed the Christians, as Eusebes did in 'The Refutation', to turn the argument away from the absurdities of miracles and communions to the irrationality of the deists' case.

This was not just academic. For religion was not a matter of personal belief, a hobby which men and women kept to themselves. It shaped and guided their behaviour in society. Those who believed in a 'supernatural power' could easily be persuaded that that power determined what was right and what was wrong, what should be done and what should not.

Under pressure of their religious beliefs men and women superceded their own ability to decide on these things. And here Shelley saw the danger. Religion, he noticed, had almost everywhere in the world become *established*, that is, adopted and enforced by governments. These governments, none of which were elected, were then able to determine the moral and social behaviour of their subjects.

Very often the morality laid down by governments in the name of the religion which they had established bore no relation to the morality of the founder of the religion. The best example was that of Jesus Christ and Christianity.

Shelley had read almost all there was to read about the life of Christ. He was fascinated by Christ, and admired him as a reforming leader. In all his writings on the subject, Shelley generously, sometimes too generously, paid tribute to Christ's qualities: his interest in the common people, his contempt for wealth and sycophancy, his humanitarian philosophy arrived at by observation and by thought. And here was the paradox which excited Shelley's interest. Christ's teachings, sayings and life-style seemed to contradict everything taught, said and done in the name of Christianity. Christ, the challenger of authority, was cited in the name of authority. According to the Magnificat, Christ's God would 'put down the mighty from their seats and the rich he would send empty away'. Yet the same Christ was glorified by the mighty and the rich.

St Luke, Chapter 4, verse 18, has: 'The spirit of the Lord is upon me, because he hath chosen me to preach the gospel to the poor: he hath sent me to heal the broken-hearted, to preach deliverance to the captives and recovery of sight to the blind and to set at liberty them that are bruised.' Yet Shelley observed that, throughout the ages, the established Christian church had treated the broken-hearted, the blind and the bruised with the most unspeakable cruelty and neglect.

In a glorious passage in his 'Letter to Lord Ellenborough', written in 1812, Shelley applied himself to this paradox:

Jesus Christ was crucified because he attempted to supersede the ritual of Moses with regulations more moral and humane—his very judge made public acknowledgment of his innocence, but a bigotted and ignorant mob demanded the deed of horror.— Barabbas the murderer and traitor was released. The meek reformer Jesus was immolated to the sanguinary Deity of the Jews. Time rolled on, time changed the situations, and with them, the opinions of men.

The vulgar, ever in extremes, became persuaded the crucifixion of Jesus was a supernatural event, and testimonies of miracles, so frequent in unenlightened ages, were not wanting to prove that he was something divine. This belief, rolling through the lapse of ages, acquired force and extent, until the divinity of Jesus became a dogma, which to dispute was death, which to doubt was infamy.

Christianity is now the established religion; he who attempts to disprove it must behold murderers and traitors take precedence of him in public opinion, tho', if his genius be equal to his courage, and assisted by a peculair coalition of circumstances, future ages may exalt him to a divinity, and persecute others in his name, as he was persecuted in the name of his predecessor in the homage of the world.[8]

Making Christianity into an *established religion* made nonsense of the life and teachings of Christ. But it did much more than that. For Shelley the most horrible crime of established religion was that it restrained the human mind with the halter of superstition. In a tiny prose fragment which he wrote, probably in 1819, called 'On the Revival of Literature', Shelley wrote of the Middle Ages:

Superstition, of whatever kind, whether earthly or divine, has hitherto been the weight which clogged man to earth, and prevented his genius from soaring aloft amid its native skies. . . . To the mind both humane and philosophical, there cannot exist a greater subject of grief, than the reflection of how much superstition has retarded the progress of intellect, and consequently the happiness of man.[9]

Established religions, Shelley noticed, had always been friendly to tyranny. By dulling men's minds and by fixing them on a life *hereafter*, religion had always discouraged dissent and welcomed subservience in life here and now. The harsher the punishments for sinning, the more desperately people knuckled under. And a crowd of well-educated gentlemen, called parsons, vicars or priests, were well paid to convince their congregations that 'sinning' included opposition to the government, the war and the squire.

Queen Mab had been harsh enough on the government, the war and the squire. But when it came to the priests who defended all three, she could not control her temper:

> Then grave and hoary-headed hypocrites,
> Without a hope, a passion, or a love,
> Have crept by flattery to the seats of power,
> Support the system whence their honours flow. . . .

> They have three words:—well tyrants know their use,
> Well pay them for the loan, with usury.
> Torn from a bleeding world!—God, Hell, and Heaven.
> A vengeful, pitiless, and almighty fiend,
> Whose mercy is a nickname for the rage
> Of tameless tigers hungering for blood.
> Hell, a red gulf of everlasting fire,
> Whose poisonous and undying worms prolong
> Eternal misery to those hapless slaves
> Whose life has been a penance for its crimes;
> And Heaven, a meed for those who dare belie
> Their human nature, quake, believe, and cringe
> Before the mockeries of earthly power.[10]

The notion that the chief function of religion is to serve as a prop for tyranny comes again and again in Shelley. In *The Revolt of Islam* (1817) he wrote:

> The will of strength is right—this human state
> Tyrants, that they may rule, with lies thus desolate.[11]

'The will of strength is right'. That was, for Shelley, the only clear, consistent morality in all established religions.

Different creeds spurred the masses of one country to war with another. Hundreds of thousands of people had been and were being slaughtered in the name of different religions, whose founders had proclaimed the maxim *in terra pax* (peace on earth). Nowhere was the cynical use of religion to encourage conflict more obvious than in Ireland. While Protestants and Catholics exhausted themselves in a holy war, the landlords, most of them British, plundered at will. Shelley was quick to join the movement for Catholic emancipation in Ireland. His pamphlet, 'An Address to the Irish People' (1812), starts with a direct assault on religious government and the religious discrimination which it breeds:

> . . . they [the Protestants] trust the reins of earthly government only to the hands of their own sect; in spite of this, I never found one of them impudent enough to say that a Roman Catholic, or

a Quaker, or a Jew, or a Mahometan, if he was a virtuous man, and did all the good in his power, would go to Heaven a bit the slower for not subscribing to the thirty-nine articles – and if he should say so, how ridiculous in a foppish courtier not six feet high to direct the spirit of universal harmony, in what manner to conduct the affairs of the universe![12]

While arguing passionately for equal rights for Catholics, Shelley was quick to point out that the Roman Catholic church when in the ascendancy had been guilty of the most hideous atrocities. Thirty thousand people had been burned in Italy and Spain under the Inquisition 'for entertaining different opinions from those of the Pope and the Priests'.[13] In France the Catholic monks, by order of the Pope, had massacred 80,000 Protestants. All religions had been used by the political rulers of the time to stamp on their critics and to slaughter their enemies. As long as people put religion above free thought, this would continue, with Protestants, Catholics, Jews, Methodists and Muslims taking it in turns to be oppressors and oppressed.

The Protestant ascendancy in Ireland, Shelley continued, was inextricably linked to the ascendancy of the landlords over the tenantry. The two went together, and had to be ended together. Here Shelley made a leap forward from the philosophers like Spinoza and D'Holbach who had inspired his atheism. They had argued that if men's ability to reason were freed from the harness of superstition, if the church were disestablished and free thought encouraged, then tyranny would automatically crumble. The 'free play of opinions' would of itself ensure the downfall of tyranny. Shelley pushed the argument further.

Different religions, he suggested, answered the needs of different tyrannies. The key was property. Who had the property, how did they get it, and how could they hold on to it against the interests of the people who produced it? The answers to these questions determined what sort of religion was established and shoved down people's throats. They determined who fought whom and when. They also united different tyrannies and different creeds in the event

of popular revolt.   A striking example of such unity comes
in *The Revolt of Islam*, which is, as Shelley tells us, a poem
about the French Revolution. After Napoleon had been defeated at Waterloo, the different factions in the victorious
Grand Alliance started to squabble over the spoils. The
squabble was conducted in religious terms. Each creed or
denomination – Russian Orthodox, Protestant, Catholic,
etc. – argued that they were the only true Christians, and
were therefore solely entitled to the territory and treasure of
defeated France.

Presiding over all this squabbling is 'a zealous man who
led the legioned west'. This was Lord Castlereagh.

> He loathed all faith beside his own, and pined
> To wreak his fear of Heaven in vengeance on mankind.[14]

But deeper than his loathing of all the other religions was
his terror of free thought:

> But more he loathed and hated the clear light
>   Of wisdom and free thought, and more did fear,
> Lest, kindled once, its beams might pierce the night, . . .[15]

The end of the Napoleonic Wars brought with them
popular demands for liberty and a revival of religious scepticism, which Castlereagh saw as a more 'subtle' enemy than
the different religions. In the poem he calms the warring
factions, just as in life Castlereagh persuaded the rulers of
Russia and Austria to shelve their religious faction-fighting
until the rebels in their own countries had been dealt with.

> 'Peace! Peace!' he cried, 'when we are dead, the Day
>   Of Judgement comes, and all shall surely know
> Whose God is God, each fearfully shall pay
>   The errors of his faith in endless woe!
>   But there is sent a mortal vengeance now
> On earth, because an impious race had spurned
>   Him whom we all adore,—a subtle foe,
> By whom for ye this dread reward was earned,
> And kingly thrones, which rest on faith nigh overturned.'[16]

The quarrelling kings shelve their differences and the revolutionaries are burned at the stake.

There was a bond which united all tyrants: the bond of property. They would fight over property, and by whipping up sectarian religious hysteria would persuade the people to fight for them in such wars. But if ever the people of any country started to make demands on that property, then both kings and churches would unite to defend it.

The churches played as vital a role in the unification of different religions against atheism as they did in the sectarianism of the 'holy wars'. The explanation of their behaviour was rooted in the determination of the ruling minority to hang on to its wealth. The priesthood, Shelley concluded, was an essential part of 'the system whence their honours flow' – a system of exploitation. They supported the rich because they were part of the rich.

In Shelley's most desperate expression of fury against the poverty of the mass of British working people, written in 1819, the character who personifies the idle heartless rich is not a landowner, industrialist, lawyer or king, but:

> Young Parson Richards stood at his gate
> Feeding his hound with bread;
> Hunch after hunch the mere beast ate
> Moving his tail and his head.[17]

As the parson feeds his dog, a starving woman with her dying child in her arms comes to plead for a crust. She is a believer, and she reminds Richards that he is the father of the child – and of his sacred claims:

> Priest, consider that God who created us
> Meant this for a world of love—
> Remember the story of Lazarus
> You preach to the people of— . . .
>
> And yet I cannot imagine how we
> Can call him just and good,
> When he sends a wretched woman like me
> To a man like you for food.

> Oh God! This poor dear child did I
> At thy command bear and cherish!—
> Thou bads't us increase and multiply.
> And our tyrants bid us perish![18]

The parson pays no attention, and goes on feeding his dog. The woman and her child die at the garden gate. The priest turns away. The image of the well-fed churchman turning away from his starving flock captures all Shelley's disgust and loathing for the established church of his day.

It also explained why established religion was intolerant even of other religions: how it was prepared to persecute any form of belief which did not fit the tangible interests of the propertied class which it represented. This *explanation* – that property was the key to religious superstition – was Shelley's most striking contribution to the argument about religion. It was brilliantly expressed in his letter to the *Examiner* about the prosecution of Carlile, written in 1819, at the peak of his genius:

And the prosecutors care little for religion, or care for it only as it is the mask & the garment by which they are invested with the symbols of worldly power. In prosecuting Carlile they have used the superstition of the Jury as their instrument for crushing a political enemy, or rather they strike in his person at all their political enemies. They know that the Established Church is based upon the belief in certain events of a supernatural character having occurred in Judaea eighteen centuries ago; that but for this belief the farmer would refuse to pay the tenth of the produce of his labours to maintain its numbers in idleness; that this class of persons if not maintained in idleness would have something else to do than to divert the attention of the people from obtaining a Reform in their oppressive government, & that consequently the government would be reformed, & that the people would receive a just price for their labours, a consummation incompatible with the luxurious idleness in which their rulers esteem it their interest to live.[19]

Gleams of godlike light have been detected in Shelley's later work by biographers and essayists who wanted to prove that god almost always catches up with errant and

youthful atheists. This is all nonsense. In 1819 Shelley wrote
to Hunt: 'Added days and years and hours add to my disapprobation of this odius superstition [religion].'[20] And so he
continued to his death.

In January 1821, for instance, he read an essay by a young
English Christian called Julius Hare. Hare argued that atheists like Shelley directed their scepticism first towards the
devil. Once people's belief in the devil had been undermined,
Hare went on, there was nothing to sustain their faith in
God, still less in the Holy Ghost. This theory (in his own
words) 'immeasurably amused' Shelley, and he set straight
to work on an essay 'On the Devil and Devils', which,
unhappily, he never finished. There is enough left of it,
however, to show that his attitude to religion was even
more hostile then than it had been when he wrote *Queen
Mab* eight years earlier. It is not just an onslaught on the
story of the fall from heaven. It binds that story to the wills
and passions of earthly rulers. The devil becomes

. . . at once the Informer, the Attorney General, and the Jailor of
the Celestial tribunal. . . .
   . . . The dirty work is done by the Devil, in the same manner
as some starving wretch will hire himself out to a King or Minister
to work with a stipulation that he shall have some portion of the
public spoil, as an instrument to betray a certain number of other
starving wretches into circumstances of capital punishment, when
they may think it convenient to edify the rest, by hanging up a
few of those whose murmurs are too loud.[21]

The devil's job is to poison people's minds by attacking
their self-confidence. He serves as a scapegoat for crime and
violence in society, a creature of the disgusting imaginations
of people who rule by disgusting methods. The fragment
ends with some satirical questions about where the devil
really lives, where are packed all the evil souls condemned
to hell fire, whether there is a devil on every planet, and so
on. Not an iota of the sharp, atheist conviction which inspired *Queen Mab* has been lost.

Stories from Shelley's life at the time confirm his continuing atheism. In Austin Gray's biography (1948) of Byron's

lover, the Countess Guiccioli, there is this account of an afternoon discussion in Byron's house in Pisa in the summer of 1821:

Byron told with some humour the story of a miracle that was said to have taken place in Lucca recently. Shelley's voice grew shrill with scorn as he denounced all belief in miracles as a deplorable superstition . . . Teresa showed her displeasure by keeping silence. Byron turned to her with a smile:

'Do you, then, believe in a miracle?' he asked.

'I believe in miracles,' she answered bravely, 'because I believe in God.'

There were smiles all around the room, and Shelley's jaw was thrust out in defiance. But the fair theologian went her way. The law of Nature, she said, was a law only and might be amended or repealed. God had made the law of nature, and in his wisdom he might change his own handiwork. Shelley was on his feet muttering something about irresponsible despots, but she bore him down. All these *signore* in her salon were lovers of liberty for themselves and for the human race – what right had they, even if they had the power, to deny liberty to God? Was God alone to be stultified by his own works? 'I believe in miracles because I believe in God, and I could not believe in God if I did not know him to be omnipotent.'

'God!' cried Shelley, 'God! *That*—', but Byron tactfully closed the argument on Teresa's side.[22]

Soon afterwards Shelley began his poem on the struggle of the Greek people against the Turkish empire, *Hellas* (1821). *Hellas* has furnished a lot of Christian Shelley-lovers with 'proof' that Shelley was by this stage becoming converted to Christianity. Walter Peck, in his huge biography of Shelley (1927), writes: 'He had now reached the point where Christ could be a source not only of a sympathetic and understanding prose essay, but even of his lyric muse. And this, it seems to me, certainly indicates a deepening conviction of the beauty and strength of the Master.'[23] The 'Master', of course, is Jesus Christ, and Mr Peck goes on to argue that *Hellas* placed Shelley 'in entire accord, today, with a large number of recognized Protestant churches laying title to the name of "Christian".' *Hellas*, Peck concludes, would even have admitted Shelley to Holy Communion![24]

What is the evidence for this?

Peck quotes the chorus of female Greek slaves in *Hellas*, who speak up for Christianity:

> The moon of Mahomet
> Arose, and it shall set:
> While blazoned as on Heaven's immortal noon
> The cross leads generations on.[25]

This and other hallelujahs to Christianity are cited by Peck as proof of Shelley's own belief in the power of the cross.

But the chorus of Greek slaves are characters in a drama. The Greeks were Christians, the Turks Mohammedans. Naturally, the Greek slaves praised Christianity. They were not reflecting Shelley's view. In case there is any doubt about that, Shelley adds a note to the chorus: 'The popular notions of Christianity are represented in this chorus as true in their realtion to the worship they superseded, and that which in all probability they will supersede, *without considering their merits in a relation more universal.*'[26] (Author's italics.)

He then goes on to restate his familiar position on gods of every description: 'The received hypothesis of a Being resembling men in the moral attributes of His nature, having called us out of non-existence, and after inflicting on us the misery of the commission of error, should superadd that of the punishment and the privations consequent upon it, still would remain inexplicable and incredible.'[27]

Hellas is chiefly a poem about the struggle for Greek freedom. In the process it is also about 'the punishment and the privations' which flow from established religion. The choruses tell how the radicalism of Jesus Christ became polluted by the savagery of the religion which stole his name; how the reason and thought which gave rise to democratic Athens was destroyed by religious oligarchy; how the war between the Greeks and the Turkish empire, *if seen only as a battle between religions*, would continue forever.

Towards the end of the poem, Mahmud, the Turkish tyrant, who is tortured by religious doubt and, as a result,

by lack of confidence in the armed might of his empire, calls
in a 'wandering Jew', Ahasuerus, and asks for his guidance.
The Jew replies first with a contemptuous dismissal of the
apparent realities of the conflict, and of the world, including
the power of God, and then with a statement of what *is*
eternal and what *does* last forever:

> Thought
> Alone, and its quick elements, Will, Passion,
> Reason, Imagination, cannot die;
> They are, what that which they regard appears,
> The stuff whence mutability can weave
> All that it hath dominion o'er, worlds, worms,
> Empires and superstitions. . . .
> Wouldst thou behold the Future?—ask and have!
> Knock and it shall be opened—[28]

It is thought which provokes change, and in consequence
has power over everything else. Knock and it shall be
opened. No wonder Ahasuerus terrified Mahmud, even in
the middle of a string of Turkish victories. Once the power
of Mahomet (or, on the other side, the power of Christianity) was subverted, what chance would be left for kings
and tyrants? Richard Holmes describes *Hellas* as 'one of the
most sophisticated and historically mature statements of
Shelley's atheism'.[29]

That atheism stayed with Shelley until he died (only nine
months after *Hellas* was written). On 11 April 1822, he
wrote to his friend Horace Smith, jocularly referring to
Tom Moore's complaint that he (Shelley) was subverting Byron's
Christian faith.

I think you know Moore.—Pray assure him that I have not the
smallest influence over Lord Byron in this particular; if I had I
certainly should employ it to eradicate from his great mind the
delusions of Christianity, which in spite of his reason, seem perpetually to recur, . . . I differ with Moore in thinking Xtianity
useful to the world: no man of sense can think it true: and the
alliance of the monstrous superstitions of the popular worship
with the pure doctrines of the Theism of such men as Moore,

turns to the profit of the former, & makes the latter the fountain of its own pollution.[30]

Finally, there is the evidence of Edward Trelawney, who was with Shelley in the last weeks of his life and recorded many of his conversations. When Trelawney asked Shelley why he called himself an atheist, he replied: 'I took up the word, as a knight took up a gauntlet, in defiance of an injustice. The delusions of Christianity are fatal to genius and originality; they limit thought.'[31]

Another conversation 'within a month of Shelley's death' went like this:

SHELLEY: 'Religion itself means intolerance. The various sects tolerate nothing but their own dogmas. The priests call themselves shepherds. The passive they drive into their folds. When they have folded you, then they are satisfied. They know you fear them; but if you stand aloof, they fear you. Those who resist they consider as wolves, and, when they have the power, stone them to death.'

I said: 'You are one of the wolves.'

SHELLEY: 'I am not in sheep's clothing.'[32]

This is how he felt about religion right up to his death. As Trelawney concluded, 'There could have been no wavering in his antipathy to all religion.' How then have so many commentators pretended otherwise?

The answer is that in a lot of his later poems there are references to 'God', 'Heaven', and 'The Eternal' which seem at first sight to have a formal religious meaning. In his most-quoted poem, *Adonais*, the elegy to John Keats written in 1821, there are lots of these. For instance:

> The One remains, the many change and pass;
> Heaven's light forever shines, Earth's shadows fly; . . .[33]

Or:

> The soul of Adonais, like a star,
> Beacons from the abode where the Eternal are.[34]

It is quite obvious from his conversations and writings

that these, and other references, especially in his most ab-
struse poem, *The Triumph of Life* (1822), are not translatable
into simple religious beliefs. Shelley used the words of
religion to convey quite irreligious ideas.

The 'eternal' values were the ones which lasted forever,
not through divine intervention, but as a result of human
endeavour. Keats beaconed from the abode where the eternal
are, not because he had gone to a Christian heaven, but
because of the wonderful contribution he had made to the
human race. Though human life was not superseded by
something superstitious, like a heaven, it did not end with
death, because the contributions made by human beings to
their fellow humans lived on after them. *That* was the difference between Adonais' heaven and the earth, whose
shadows fly.

When Shelley was depressed, as he certainly was when he
wrote *Adonais* and *The Triumph of Life*, he was inclined to
rhapsodize about the glories of this 'eternity'. The result is
sometimes pessimistic and vague.

Pessimism and vagueness, however, were not typical
Shelleyan characteristics, and only very rarely overcame
him. He remained to the end a confirmed atheist, but he
was never a cynic. He refused to believe in God but he
believed, perhaps more passionately than all the Christians
of his time, in humanity. The servants of God, especially
the established churches, divided people from one another
and destroyed their faith in one another. Gods, heavens and
hells increased people's awe of death. They encouraged
introspection and morbidity. Humanity, on the other hand,
was to Shelley 'one harmonious whole', sharing, co-opera-
ting, passing on experiences and abilities from generation to
generation.

The worst thing about religions and superstitions was that
they denied the power of men and women accurately to
answer the questions which religion answered only prepos-
terously. Men and women *could* find out where they came
from and what happened to them after their death. The dark
superstitions of heaven and hell could be replaced by the

clear light of human thought and knowledge. There were no secrets which men and women could not unravel, no fears which they could not overcome.

> The lightning is his slave; heaven's utmost deep
> Gives up her stars, and like a flock of sheep
> They pass before his eye, are numbered, and roll on!
> The tempest is his steed, he strides the air;
> And the abyss shouts from her depth laid bare,
> Heaven, hast thou secrets? Man unveils me; I have none.[35]

4

Leveller

Many and various are the mischiefs flowing from oppression, but this is the representative of them all; namely, that one man is forced to labour for another . . .

'Address to the People on the Death of Princess Charlotte', 1817[1]

'I am,' wrote Shelley, in an early poem, 'the friend of the unfriended poor.'[2] So he was, all his life. No theme occurs more frequently in his writings than his hatred of poverty. In the English countryside, the enclosures and the new farming techniques had made of the farm workers 'a people starved and stabbed in the untilled field.'[3] In the towns and cities, the new industries were creating stockpiles of human squalor. From Cumberland, in 1812, he wrote: 'The manufacturers with their contamination have crept into this peaceful vale. . . . Children are frequently found in the River which the unfortunate women employed at the manufactory destroy. . . .'[4]

The horror of poverty often shook him out of his more extravagant lyrical style. In 'Rosalind and Helen' (1817), which is full of lyrical excesses, the description of poverty is cold and clear:

> Thou knowest what a thing is Poverty
> Among the fallen on evil days:
> 'Tis Crime, and Fear, and Infamy,
> And houseless Want in frozen ways
> Wandering ungarmented, and Pain,
> And, worse than all, that inward stain
> Foul Self-contempt, which drowns in sneers
> Youth's starlight smile, . . .[5]

The poem about the Starving Mother, which he called simply 'A Ballad', is unrecognizable as the work of 'England's greatest lyric poet' (which is perhaps one reason why it was not published for 120 years):

> A woman came up with a babe at her breast
> Which was flaccid with toil and hunger;
> She cried: 'Give me food and give me rest—
> We die if we wait much longer.
>
> The poor thing sucks and no milk will come,
> He would cry but his strength is gone—
> His wasting weakness has left him dumb,
> Ye can hardly hear him moan.
>
> The skin around his eyes is pale and blue;
> His eyes are glazed, not with tears—
> I wish for a little moment that you
> Could know what a mother fears.
>
> Give me a piece of that fine white bread—
> I would give you some blood for it—
> Before I faint and my infant is dead!
> O Give me a little bit!'[6]

Why were people poor? Did they have to be so poor? Shelley noticed how the people among whom he grew up tried to ignore the poor, and, when they could ignore them no longer, to explain them away. 'The poor are always with us' was the rich man's sigh as much in Shelley's time as it is today. Thomas Malthus, a comfortable philosopher, argued not only that the poor were always with us, but that, for the benefit of all mankind, they should remain so. He argued that if the poor got any richer, they would live longer and have more children. The world would be overrun with people, and there wouldn't be enough to go round. Poverty kept the population under control. So did war.

Shelley stripped Malthus of all the trappings. His 'philosophy', he concluded quickly, had one purpose only: to comfort the rich and the warmongers. In 'Proposals for an Association', he wrote (in 1812):

War, vice and misery are undeniably bad, they embrace all that
we can conceive of temporal and eternal evil. Are we to be told
that these are remedyless, because the earth would, in case of
their remedy, be overstocked? That the rich are still to glut, that
the ambitious are still to plan, that the fools whom these knaves
mould, are still to murder their brethren and call it glory, and
that the poor are to pay with their blood, their labor, their
happiness, and their innocence, for the crimes and mistakes which
the hereditary monopolists of earth commit? Rare sophism![7]

What was more, Shelley added later, Malthus and the
population-controllers of his time sought to deny to the
poor the one pleasure that was left to them, the pleasure of
sexual intercourse.

Not satisfied with the argument that poverty was part
of natural or divine law, the rich fell back on another:
that poverty was the fault of the poor. The poor, it was
suggested, were feckless, good-for-nothing. They were
scroungers. They sponged off the wealth of others. Had not
the rich generously granted the Speenhamland dole system,
and were not the poor and unemployed stuffing themselves
on the proceeds?

Shelley replied with 'A Tale of Society as it is'. The poem
tells of an old woman whose son was pressganged into the
war. She waits for him for seven years. When he returns,
both mother and son find there is no work for them. Yet
they still refuse to claim what is due to them from 'the
parish':

> And now cold Charity's unwelcome dole
>   Was insufficient to support the pair;
>   And they would perish rather than would bear
>   The law's stern slavery and the insolent stare
> With which law loves to rend the poor man's soul,—
>   The bitter scorn, the spirit-sinking noise
>   Of heartless mirth, which women, men and boys
> Wake in this scene of legal misery.
>   Oh, William's spirit rather would rejoice
> On some wild heath with his dear charge to die,—

> The death that keenest penury might give
> Were sweeter far than cramped by slavery to live![8]

'The facts,' Shelly wrote in a letter accompanying the poem, 'are real . . . The poor man [whom Shelley had met in Cumberland] said:— "None of my family ever came to *parish*, and I wd. starve first. I am a poor man but I could never hold my head up after that." '[9]

So, as Godwin had done before him, Shelley ticked off the arguments about poverty which were presented to him by his family and his friends. The poor, he concluded, need not always be with us. People were not just mouths to be fed (as the rich described the poor). They produced things, and they could produce enough for all to be happy. People's wealth did not depend on their numbers; it depended on what they produced, and how it was shared out. Moreover, the poor were not feckless, good-for-nothing scroungers. Shelley could see and hear the opposite with his own eyes and ears.

If the rich could not explain why other people were poor, could they explain why they themselves were rich – and could they justify it?

'Surely,' the rich argued – the echo comes up clearly all the way to the 1980s – 'we *must* have rich people, because otherwise "initiative" and "dynamism" won't be properly rewarded. Unless successful people get rich rewards, society will stagnate. Are not the wealthy also the *wealth-creators* and shouldn't they be proud of their wealth, not ashamed of it?'

Shelley replied with some force in *Queen Mab*:

> The harmony and happiness of man
> Yields to the wealth of nations; that which lifts
> His nature to the heaven of its pride,
> Is bartered for the poison of his soul;
> The weight that drags to earth his towering hopes,
> Blighting all prospect but of selfish gain,
> Withering all passion but of slavish fear,
> Extinguishing all free and generous love
> Of enterprise and daring, . . .[10]

'Enterprise and daring' were, in reality, obstructed by the prospect of riches. Invention, scientific inquiry and even exploration were hindered rather than encouraged. Riches encouraged the status quo. 'That's how we're getting the money now. Let's leave it that way', is the automatic refrain of the wealthy. More often than not, the people with 'enterprise and daring' find themselves in conflict with the wealthy. For every act of invention, every genuine entrepreneur, every exploration financed by the rich, there were 10,000 idlers and inheritors suppressing invention and innovation.

The rich did not create wealth at all. They, not the poor, were the scroungers and the spongers. Most of them produced nothing, but consumed a very great deal. Thomas Spence, the Scottish leveller, had written before Shelley was born his great work, *The Constitution of a Perfect Commonwealth*. In the perfect society, he said, there would be 'no lords, no gentlemen . . . no amphibious class between the government and the people. For I did not mean such a nest of wasps to have a place in my Commonwealth, to devour the honey which the working bees had toiled for . . .'[11]

Did Shelley read Spence? There is no evidence either way. But he used the same metaphor about the rich and the poor, over and over again. The worker bees worked; the drones lazed about and consumed what the workers produced. The wretchedness of the workers and the greed of the drones were inexorably bound together. The drones exploited the workers. The result was not simply a disgusting picture of luxury in the middle of poverty; it was a system of exploitation which bound the two together. The engine of exploitation drove society on. It explained every part of production, from the wheat harvest to the coal mine. As Queen Mab put it, in a glorious shout of anger:

> Those gilded flies
> That, basking in the sunshine of a court,
> Fatten on its corruption!—what are they?
> —The drones of the community; they feed

> On the mechanic's labour; the starved hind
> For them compels the stubborn glebe to yield
> Its unshared harvests; and yon squalid form,
> Leaner than fleshless misery, that wastes
> A sunless life in the unwholesome mine,
> Drags out in labour a protracted death,
> To glut their grandeur; many faint with toil,
> That few may know the cares and woe of sloth.[12]

In an agitational poem written seven years later, in 1819, Shelley asked the 'Men of England':

> Wherefore feed, and clothe, and save,
> From the cradle to the grave,
> Those ungrateful drones who would
> Drain your sweat—nay, drink your blood?[13]

In *Swellfoot the Tyrant* (1820), the chorus of priests, in a hymn to famine, sing:

> The earth pours forth its plenteous fruits,
>   Corn, wool, linen, flesh, and roots—
> Those who consume these fruits through thee grow fat;
>   Those who produce these fruits through thee grow
>   lean, . . .[14]

For those who imagine that Shelley abandoned his ideas about exploitation when he got older, the finest passage on the subject comes in *Charles I*, almost the last thing Shelley wrote. The play, of which only a fragment was completed, opens with a royal ceremony which is intended to delight the populace. A youth, properly dazzled, exclaims:

> How glorious! See those thronging chariots
> Rolling, like painted clouds before the wind,
> Behind their solemn steeds: . . .[15]

He goes on for several lines in the reverent tones of a B.B.C. commentator reporting on a jubilee:

>   See how gloriously
> The mettled horses in the torchlight stir

> Their gallant riders, while they check their pride,
> Like shapes of some diviner element
> Than English air, and beings nobler than
> The envious and admiring multitude.[16]

This stings the sceptical Second Citizen into a grand reply, which concentrates on the indissoluble connection between wealth and poverty:

>   Ay, there they are—
> Nobles, and sons of nobles, patentees,
> Monopolists, and stewards of this poor farm,
> On whose lean sheep sit the prophetic crows,
> Here is the pomp that strips the houseless orphan,
> Here is the pride that breaks the desolate heart.
> These are the lilies glorious as Solomon,
> Who toil not, neither do they spin,—unless
> It be the webs they catch poor rogues withal.
> Here is the surfeit which to them who earn
> The niggard wages of the earth, scarce leaves
> The tithe that will support them till they crawl
> Back to her cold hard bosom. Here is health
> Followed by grim disease, glory by shame,
> Waste by lame famine, wealth by squalid want,
> And England's sin by England's punishment.[17]

In the Notes on *Queen Mab*, written in 1812, Shelley explained how exploitation worked. He developed an idea which was then very new – the labour theory of value: 'There is no real wealth but the labour of man. Were the mountains of gold and the valleys of silver, the world would not be one grain of corn the richer; no one comfort would be added to the human race.'[18] The labour of the poor was organized, not to meet their own needs, but to extend the luxury of the rich:

The poor are set to labour,—for what? Not the food for which they famish: not the blankets for want of which their babes are frozen by the cold of their miserable hovels: not those comforts of civilization without which civilized man is far more miserable

than the meanest savage; . . . no; for the pride of power, for the
miserable isolation of pride, for the false pleasures of the hundredth part of society. . . . employments are lucrative in an in-
verse ratio to their usefulness: the jeweller, the toyman, the actor
gains fame and wealth by the exercise of his useless and ridiculous
art; whilst the cultivator of the earth, he without whom society
must cease to exist, struggles through contempt and penury, and
perishes by that famine which but for his unceasing exertions
would annihilate the rest of mankind.[19]

The same idea comes in a letter which Shelley wrote to
Elizabeth Hitchener in December 1811. His family had offered him an income of £2,000 a year if he 'entailed' his own
inheritance to his progeny for ever. Shelley's response was
typical:

Silly dotards! do they think I can be thus bribed and ground into
an act of such contemptible injustice and inutility, . . . That I
should entail 120,000£ of *command over labor* [Author's italics], of
power to remit this, to *employ* it for beneficent purposes on one
whom I know not, who might instead of being the benefactor of
mankind, be its bane, & use this for the worst purposes which
the real delegates of my chance-given property might convert
into a most useful instrument of benevolence.[20]

Inherited wealth, which (then, as now) was far greater
than any wealth earned by inventors or 'men of initiative',
not only originated from someone else's labour, it gave
command over the labour. It determined what, when and
how things were produced, and how they were distributed.
Because that power was vested in the wealthy minority,
working people were continually directed to producing luxuries and absurdities which they did not need and could not
afford.

These theories led Shelley to conclusions which were,
necessarily, very different to those of most other reformers
of his day. 'English reformers,' he wrote – again in the
Notes on *Queen Mab* – 'exclaim against sinecures, – but the
true pension list is the rent-roll of the landed proprietors:
wealth is a power usurped by the few, to compel the many
to labour for their benefit.'[21]

By the same token, 'freedom' and 'liberty' took on, for Shelley, a different meaning to that given them by most reformers and freethinkers. Tom Paine, for instance, hated arbitrary power, but he did not believe that the ownership of property had anything to do with it. This view was shared by most of the radicals and republicans of Shelley's time. Freedom to them meant freedom of thought, freedom of expression and the freedom of the people to choose their government.

To Shelley, property was the key to freedom, as it was to tyranny. Freedom meant little unless it provided for everyone food, warmth and shelter. Shelley was a champion of the right to speak, write, demonstrate and hold political meetings. But these freedoms, he argued, could blossom only when people were free from hunger and cold.

In *The Mask of Anarchy* (1819), he asked the question direct: 'What art thou, freedom?' and answered it as well as anyone before or since:

> Thou art not, as imposters say,
> A shadow soon to pass away,
> A superstition, and a name
> Echoing from the cave of Fame.
>
> For the labourer thou art bread,
> And a comely table spread
> From his daily labour come
> In a neat and happy home.
>
> Thou art clothes, and fire, and food
> For the trampled multitude—
> No—in countries that are free
> Such starvation cannot be
> As in England now we see.[22]

Of the three great demands of the French Revolution – Liberty! Equality! Fraternity! – the first and last depended upon the second. Liberty and Fraternity were meaningless unless they could be shared by all. And they could not be shared by all if a few people were very rich, and most people were very poor. Riches and poverty limited the liberty and the fraternity of both rich and poor, but especially of the poor.

'That state of human society which approaches nearer to an equal partition of its benefits and evils should . . . be preferred,' wrote Shelley in the Notes on *Queen Mab*.[23] Eight years later he was still affirming: 'Equality in possessions must be the last result of the utmost refinements of civilization; it is one of the conditions of that system of society, towards which, with whatever hope of ultimate success, it is our duty to tend.'[24] When Cythna spoke to the masses after the revolt of Islam, she reminded them of the most important of all their aspirations:

> Eldest of things, divine Equality!
> Wisdom and Love are but the slaves of thee, . . .[25]

These ideas about property and equality were central to Shelley's thought, but in his early writings they were vague – often caught up and sometimes lost in an angry tirade or an idealistic vision. He brought them together, drilled them and pushed them forward in his pamphlet, 'A Philosophical View of Reform', which he wrote in 1820.

The pamphlet starts with a historical survey of literature and political thought. The quality of both, it argues, rises and falls in proportion to the resistance to despotism and religion. From the Florentine resistance in the Middle Ages came Dante, Raphael and Michaelangelo. From the Reformation came Montaigne and Shakespeare, Bacon and Spinoza. From the French Revolution came the explosion of literature which had shaken Europe for thirty years.

This was a challenging enough theory for a society which preached the myth that literature and art flourish at a time of 'stability', or uncontested tyranny. But Shelley went further. He developed the idea – almost entirely new at the time – of *class*. The history of feudalism, he wrote, was a history of exploitation by class. In a footnote, clearly intended later to be woven into the text, he said: 'Regular and graduated systems of alternate slavery and tyranny, by which all except the lowest and the largest class were to be gainers in the materials of subsistence and ostentation at the expense of that class, the means being fraud or force, were established in the shape of feudal monarchies . . . '[26]

All this was upset by popular rebellions and revolutions – in Britain against Charles I, in America against George III, and in France. Shelley compared the revolutions, and the results of them: 'France occupies . . . the same situation as was occupied by England at the restoration of Charles the 2nd. It has undergone a revolution . . . which may be paralleled with that in our own country which ended in the death of Charles the 1st.'[27] Neither revolution, Shelley went on, had accomplished what most of their supporters hoped of them. Nevertheless, 'in both cases abuses were abolished which never since have dared to show their face'.[28]

Both revolutions had ushered in a new class, or, as Shelley put it, 'a new aristocracy'[29] which was just as interested in exploiting 'the lowest and the largest class'[30] as its feudal predecessors. Shelley had a name for this 'new aristocracy'. He called them 'capitalists'.[31]

The hunger of these capitalists for more and more wealth was insatiable. They got their wealth by an exploitation every bit as savage as that of the feudal warlords – indeed more savage. 'The aged and the sickly are compelled either to work or starve. Children who were exempted from labour are put in requisition, and the vigorous promise of the coming generation blighted by premature exertion.'[32]

Shelley then expanded his explanation of exploitation by wages – or wage slavery as it later came to be known:

For fourteen hours' labour, which they do perform, they receive—no matter in what nominal mount—the price of seven. They eat less bread, wear worse clothes, are more ignorant, immoral, miserable and desperate. This then is the condition of the lowest and the largest class, from whose labour the whole materials of life are wrought, of which the others are only the receivers or the consumers.[33]

This system of exploitation explained the realities of political power in England. The class which owned property also controlled Parliament. Shelley described graphically how the Parliament of his day was a hundred times less representative than it had been in 1641. The chief reason, he argued, was that democratic political representation – even that envisaged by Oliver Cromwell in 1640 – contradicted the economic needs of the minority who controlled the property. 'The oligarchy of party' was the oligarchy of the rich. 'The power which has increased is the power of the rich.'[34]

For a moment, Shelley dwelt prophetically on the implications of this idea. Propertied power controlled Parliament, but did it follow that popular control of Parliament would bring about popular control of wealth? For Shelley the power of the propertied classes brought the same evils as did the power of an unrepresentative Parliament. There would be no point in abolishing one without abolishing the other. In a passage which showed how far ahead he was of almost all the reformers of his time, he admitted:

I do not understand why those reasoners who propose at any price an immediate appeal to universal suffrage, because it is that which it is injustice to withhold, do not insist, on the same ground, on the immediate abolition, for instance, of monarchy and aristocracy, and the levelling of inordinate wealth, and an agrarian distribution, including the Parks and Chases of the rich, of the uncultivated districts of the country.[35]

But he reassured himself in the next sentence that 'the institution of universal suffrage would by necessary consequence *immediately* tend to the *temporary* abolition of these forms'.[36]

But he was not certain. Alone in his time, he saw a possible distinction between the granting of the vote and the levelling of the property: a distinction which grew into the great political controversies around the extension of the vote in 1832, 1867, and 1918 – which still haunts a British Parliament elected by universal suffrage, but apparently impotent in the face of unelected industrial and financial power.

But all this was speculation. What was true beyond all doubt was that the Parliament and goverment of Shelley's day were corrupt *because* they protected the property of the minority. Shelley then turned to expose what he saw, probably rightly, as the worst of the robberies which the government, in the interests of its class, wrought on the people: the national debt.

The national debt, Shelley explained, had been raised by one set of the propertied class in order to carry out 'two liberticide wars'[37] (against Napoleon and against America). One part of this class, the war manufacturers and ministers, had borrowed from another part, mainly the usurers and banks. By controlling the currency, and proclaiming the national interest, they had devised a scheme for making the working people, who had neither borrowed the money nor benefited from it, pay it back. Shelley proposed that the interest on the debt – which was then costing a fantastic £44 million a year – should be wiped out. The capital, he said, should be repaid by those who had borrowed it to those who had lent it. This would mean 'a mere transfer . . . of property' from one set of rich people to another. 'If the principal of this debt were paid,' he pointed out, '. . . it would be the rich who alone could, as justly they ought to pay it.'[38]

In the final section dealing with the national debt, Shelley breaks off for a discussion about property rights. He disagreed with the levellers when they said that no one had any right to property. The money which was wasted on the national debt could, he wrote, have been wisely spent on 'every peasant's cottage, surrounded with its garden, a little paradise of comfort, with every convenience desirable in civilized life; neat tables and chairs, and good beds, and a nice collection of useful books; . . . '[39]

Despite the patronizing tone, Shelley appreciated that private possessions such as houses, furniture and books can add enormously to human happiness. Shelley did not believe that in a society founded on equality everyone would be forced to share everything. He therefore set down 'two

descriptions of property, which . . . are entitled to two very
different measures of forbearance and regard'.[40] Some property was right and proper, and should be supported by
society; other property was unjust and should be expropri-
ated for the good of society. Shelley's line between the two
was vague.

He defended all property which resulted from labour,
including the property of 'every tradesman who is not a
monopolist, all surgeons and physicians . . . and artists, and
farmers . . .'[41] Unjust property, on the other hand, had 'its
foundation in usurpation, or imposture, or violence, without which, by the nature of things, immense possessions of
gold or land could never have been accumulated'.[42] He
meant, as he put it rather impatiently, the property of 'the
rich'.[43] By and large, the rich had stolen their money, while
most labourers and professional people hadn't. The former
didn't deserve their property; the latter did.

It was a reasonable rough-and-ready guide. But it still
amounted to saying that 'just property' was that which was
'justly earned'; and 'unjust property' that which was 'un-
justly earned'. Shelley had another shot at explaining this
distinction in a little fragment he wrote in 1819:

> What men gain fairly – that they should possess;
> And children may inherit idleness,
> From him who earns it – This is understood;
> Private injustice may be general good.
> But he who gains by base and armèd wrong,
> Or guilty fraud, or base compliances,
> May be despoiled; even as a stolen dress
> Is stripped from a convicted thief, and he
> Left in the nakedness of infamy.[44]

But this doesn't get us much further. The passage justifies
the seizing of private property violently and without compensation. But what property is to be seized isn't at all clear.
The disinction between 'just' and 'unjust' property is clear
– but where to draw the line is not.

The distinction has preoccupied socialist thinkers ever since. A hundred and twenty years later, John Strachey, in his little pamphlet 'Why You Should be a Socialist' – conceivably the most influential socialist pamphlet in British history – put it this way:

The point is that there are two different sorts of private property. The one sort is private property in the means of production: private property in a factory or a mine, or in the land. And the other sort is private property in 'consumers' goods', in food and clothing and furniture, in houses, in motor cars, in gardens, in labour saving devices, in access to amusements, in every sort of thing which we actually use and consume . . .
    It ought to be impossible to mix them up. For there is one rule for distinguishing between them. Private property of the first sort carries an income with it . . . private property of the second sort does not carry an income with it.
    The economic system which is commonly called socialism . . . involves abolishing the first sorts of private property, in order to increase vastly the second sort of property.

It was a clear guide towards which Shelley, 120 years earlier, was groping. He could see plainly enough that 'income' from other people's labour fell into the category of 'unjustifiable property'. He could detect the greatest robbery of his time, the national debt. But the expression 'means of production', together with the idea that factories, mines and fields could be distinguished in the argument about ownership from the things which they produced – these he reached towards, but did not reach.

Similarly with 'the economic system which is commonly called socialism'. In Shelley's time, it was not commonly called anything at all. Even the word 'socialism' was not used until fifteen years after Shelley's death. The idea of the common ownership and democratic control and planning of the *means* of production was not clearly outlined in Shelley's lifetime. In that hectic decade, the means of production were being created in front of people's eyes. Very few thinkers talked about their common ownership or control.

Socialist ideas in that sense started to be talked about and developed soon after Shelley's death – by Robert Owen, the philanthropist from New Lanark, for instance, and, more pungently, by the Irish socialist William Thompson, whose *Principles of the Distribution of Wealth* (1824) anticipated the ideas of class struggle with which Karl Marx and Frederick Engels were to electrify European society twenty years later.

Marx's daughter, Eleanor, and her lover Edward Aveling, gave a lecture to the Shelley Society in 1885 entitled 'Shelley's Socialism'. 'We claim him,' they concluded of Shelley, 'as a socialist.' The lecture shocked the burghers of the Shelley Society. Yet it failed to prove its central point.

Shelley was a socialist only in the broad sense that he advocated a co-operative society. In the specific sense in which socialism means anything at all – the ownership and planning of society's resources by its working people – Shelley was not a socialist. Shelley was a leveller.

His thinking stood firmly in the tradition of the soldiers in Cromwell's army who were fighting for a world where people lived in equality and therefore in peace, the men who were inspired by the famous assertion of Colonel Thomas Rainborough, who fought with them: 'For really I think that the poorest he that is in England hath a life to live as the greatest he.'[45] There were many different strands of that tradition. In Shelley's time there was William Godwin's forthright and unanswerable attack upon inequality in *Political Justice*, and Thomas Spence with his rugged plans for an end to the drones who ran society – and the Spenceans, his followers, who agitated among the common people for rebellion against the government.

Common to all these traditions was a combination of idealism and pessimism. The levellers knew what was wrong, and the best of them were ready to resist it. Most were not so sure about the alternative, however. Levelling, most of them accepted, meant levelling down; levelling down was much better than a system founded on riches and poverty. But, they also had to accept that people would not easily be persuaded to fight for a system under which their living standards were unlikely to improve.

Godwin argued for communities living in equality, in 'simplicity and frugality'. He has been followed by 'bananas and sandals' idealists and environmentalists who call for a 'return to nature' and an end to industrial 'contamination'. The proletarian levellers of Shelley's time called for working class action to achieve a levelled society. But their pessimism about persuading the masses to struggle for an alternative which would not necessarily enrich them turned to impatience, to conspiracies and to individual terrorism, which made them easy prey for the authorities.

But Shelley was fascinated by science, and the astonishing scientific advances of his time. His political idealism was the opposite to that of the 'bananas and sandals' brigade. He thrilled to the wonders of science, not in themselves, but because of what they could do for humanity. His quarrel with a divided society was that scientific advances were corrupted. New methods of producing food were used to increase the starvation of the many and the gluttony of the few; new industries to intensify the labour of the many and the sloth of the few. In 'A Philosophical View of Reform' he complained:

The mechanical sciences attained to a degree of perfection which, though obscurely foreseen by Lord Bacon, it had been accounted madness to have prophesied in a preceding age. Commerce was pursued with a perpetually increasing vigour, and the same area of the Earth was perpetually compelled to furnish more and more subsistence. The means and sources of knowledge were thus increased together with knowledge itself, and the instruments of knowledge. The benefit of this increase of the powers of man became, in consequence of the inartificial forms into which society came to be distributed, an instrument of his additional evil. The capabilities of happiness were increased, and applied to the augmentation of misery. Modern society is thus a[n] engine assumed to be for useful purposes, whose force is by a system of subtle mechanism augmented to the highest pitch, but which, instead of grinding corn or raising water acts against itself and is perpetually wearing away or breaking to pieces the wheels of which it is composed.[46]

From that amazing passage, one conclusion flowed. A levelled society did not simply mean communities of human beings living together as equals. It meant a liberation of all the resources of science and technology. It meant that new inventions, explorations and discoveries could all be matched to people's needs and wants. A levelled society meant a society levelled *up*, a society of plenty.

The key verse in Shelley's 'Ode to Liberty', written in the same year as 'A Philosophical View of Reform', returned to this theme:

> What if earth can clothe and feed
> Amplest millions at their need,
> And power in thought be as the tree within the seed?
> Or what if Art, an ardent intercessor,
> Driving on fiery wings to Nature's throne,
> Checks the great mother stooping to caress her,
> And cries: 'Give me, thy child, dominion
> Over all height and depth'? if Life can breed
> New wants, and wealth from those who toil and groan
> Rend of thy gifts and hers a thousandfold for one![47]

The idea of a society of plenty, which slithers out of Godwin as a half-baked wish, shoots out of Shelley as a certainty. It explains his confidence in his ideas, even though no one was listening to him. People *could be won* to such an alternative. There was no need either for fireside utopias or for individual terrors.

Shelley straddled the gap between the levellers before him and the socialists after him. Those who 'claim him' as a socialist strain the truth about him. And, in straining it, they miss the real value of Shelley to socialists: his fury, his hope, his confidence, and, above all, his revolutionary commitment.

5

Feminist

Can man be free if woman be a slave?
The Revolt of Islam, 1817[1]

IN THEORY

'*La femme*,' wrote the philosopher Rousseau, expressing the central prejudice of his (and Shelley's) time, '*est faite pour plaire et pour être subjugée.*'[2] (Woman was made to give pleasure and to be subservient.) Women were not entitled to any independence. They did not have the vote. Their main job in life was to please their menfolk. If menfolk were not pleased, they took drastic measures. Wife-beating was not only permitted; it was regarded by tasteful philosophers like Rousseau as a duty.

The Protestant church and its missionaries were very much for the subjugation of women, but were more dubious about any 'pleasure' which they might afford. Sexual pleasure in wedlock was regarded as unchristian for men and devilish for women. One result was that London and the cities of the north became world centres of prostitution. In 1812, a letter to the *Examiner* estimated that there were in London 50,000 'public prostitutes' (*Examiner*, 5 January 1812) and Shelley himself in the Notes on *Queen Mab* says that a tenth of the female population of London were prostitutes. Marriage, meanwhile, was sacrosanct. Divorce could only be obtained through Parliament. It was only available (at a minimum of £1,000) to the very rich. No more than a dozen – and usually much less than that – went through every year. Needless to say, divorce was only available on the application of a man.

All this was shaken by the French Revolution. A flood of speeches and pamphlets came out of France preaching a very simple doctrine: 'Either no member of the human race has real rights, or else all have the same; he who votes against the rights of another, whatever his religion, colour or sex, abjures his own . . .'[3]

That was the Marquis de Condorcet, one of the great writers for women's liberation during the French Revolution. Condorcet and others resurrected the ideas of older thinkers whose ideas about sex and marriage had been banned in their lifetime. Denis Diderot, for example, almost an exact contemporary of Rousseau, had discovered that sex was thoroughly enjoyable. Why, he argued, shouldn't people engage in it when and where they pleased? As for children, well, everyone loved children so why couldn't they be brought up in common, regardless of the accident of their parentage?

These ideas carried across the Channel to Britain. William Godwin finished his *Policical Justice* in 1792. 'It is absurd,' he wrote, 'that the inclinations of two human beings should coincide through any long period of time. To oblige them to act and live together is to subject them to some inevitable portion of thwarting, bickering and unhappiness . . . Marriage is law, and the worst of all laws, an affair of property and the worst of all properties . . .'[4]

That men like Diderot, Condorcet and Godwin should openly attack the 'sanctity of marriage' was shocking enough. What was worse was the development of these ideas among women writers – and women writers who did not appear to owe their ideas or their abilities to their husbands or lovers. In Britain, the most remarkable of these women was Mary Wollstonecraft.

Mary Wollstonecraft's political ideas started from a belief in the independent spirit of human beings, and a contempt for a system of society which divided people by birth and wealth. In 1790, the ageing Edmund Burke, his liberalism long since dowsed in the flattery of the Tory gentry, wrote his celebrated attack on democracy and the French Revolu-

tion, *Reflections on the Revolution in France*. Mary Wollstonecraft was the first to counter-attack. Her *Vindication of the
Rights of Men* was written in 1790, before Tom Paine's more
celebrated reply to Burke, *The Rights of Man*. It is not as
complete or as powerful an answer as Paine's, but it spits
with fury at the treatment of *all* poor people. 'Again, Sir, I
must doubt your sincerity or your discernment,' she snapped
at Burke.

You have been behind the curtain . . . You must have seen the
clogged wheels of corruption continually oiled by the sweat of
the laborious poor . . .[a]
    Security of property! Behold, in a few words, the definition of
English liberty . . . But, softly – it is only the property of the rich
that is secure; the man who lives by the sweat of his brow has no
asylum from oppression . . .[b] Your contempt for the poor always
appears conspicuous, and rouses my indignation . . .[c] 'They *must*
respect that property of which they *cannot* partake . . .'[d]
    It is, Sir, *possible* to render the poor happier in this world . . .[e]
Why cannot large estates be divided into small farms? . . .[f] In this
great city . . . how much misery lurks in pestilential corners! . . .
How many mechanics . . . lose their employment![g] [5]

Paine savaged Burke with the famous sentence: 'He pities
the plumage, but forgets the dying bird.' Perhaps Mary
Wollstonecraft gave him the idea with: 'Man preys on man;
and you mourn for the idle tapestry that decorates a gothic
pile.'[6]
    This radical, levelling inspiration runs through Mary
Wollstonecraft's writing. *A Vindication of the Rights of Woman*, written in 1792, makes a series of assaults on the various
fortresses of society: on the standing army ('subordination
and rigour are the very sinews of military discipline'[7]); on
the clergy;[8] on property ('from the respect paid to property
flow, as from a poisoned fountain, most of the evils and
vices which render the world such a dreary scene to the
contemplative mind'[9]). Her appeal to women 'to endeavour
to acquire strength, both of mind and body', to stop behav-
ing to man as 'his toy and rattle',[10] had its root in her

condemnation of a society founded on despotism and submissiveness. She spoke up for 'the numerous class of hardworking mechanics, who pay for the support of royalty when they can scarcely stop their children's mouths with bread' and asked bitterly: 'How are they represented whose very sweat supports the splendid stud of an heir-apparent or varnishes the chariot of some female favourite who looks down on shame?'[11]

Men's patronizing tyranny over women, she concluded, sprang from all this. 'Riches and hereditary honours have made mere ciphers of women, and idleness has produced a mixture of gallantry and despotism into society. The very men who are slaves of their mistresses tyrannise over their sisters and their wives.'[12] It followed that women's *independence* was crucial to any genuine relationship between man and woman. 'It is vain to expect virtue from women till they are in some degree independent of man; nay it is vain to expect that strength of natural affection which would make them good wives and mothers.'[13]

More coolly, she answered the horny throng of masculine philosophers:

I know that libertines will also exclaim that woman would be unsexed by acquiring strength of body and mind, and that beauty (soft bewitching beauty!) would no longer adorn the daughters of men.

I am of a very different opinion, for I think that, on the contrary, we should then see dignified beauty and true grace; to produce which many powerful physical and moral causes would concur. Not relaxed beauty, it is true, or the graces of helplessness; but such as appears to make us respect the human body as a majestic pile fit to receive a noble inhabitant . . .[14]

Parts of the *Vindication*, triumphantly quoted by the prudes and libertines of later generations, play down the sexual aspect. Some of the book, in fact, reads like a governess's lecture (Mary Wollstonecraft, after all, had been a governess, and when she wrote the *Vindication* had had few if any sexual relationships). Later, especially during her years in revolutionary France, her ideas and her writing changed.

She became even sharper in her condemnation of the class divisions of the new industrial society, even sharper in her scorn for masculine superiority – and much more certain that equality for women was necessary not merely for its own, and for society's sake, but also to expand the frontiers of love and passion. In her unfinished novel, *Maria*, one of her main characters says: 'We cannot, without depraving our minds, endeavour to please a lover or a husband, *but in proportion as he pleases us.*'[15]

The pleasure which arises from any relationship for a man, in other words, depends on how much pleasure, including sexual pleasure, the woman gets from it. The structure of that sentence and the passage which surrounds it express what was then almost blasphemous: that women could enjoy sexual pleasure as much as men. These pleasures Mary Wollstonecraft undoubtedly experienced in the course of her affairs with the rogue Gilbert Imlay (to whom she wrote in a letter of 'sensations that are almost too sacred to be alluded to') and with William Godwin, whom she eventually married, and to whom she wrote at the peak of their love affair:

If the felicity of last night has had the same effect on your health as on my countenance, you have no cause to lament your failure of resolution; for I have seldom seen so much live fire running about my features as this morning when recollections very dear called forth the blush of pleasure, as I adjusted my hair.[16]

Freedom, independence of mind and body, equality – all these were essential for women, and without them all the relationships between adults and children, all family life and all sexual passion were distorted and corrupted.

Shelley first stumbled on these ideas in the comparatively dry pages of Godwin's *Political Justice*, which he read while still at Eton. Godwin led inevitably to Mary Wollstonecraft – had they not been comrades, lovers, members of the same radical circle? Shelley's early letters are full of requests for Mary Wollstonecraft's books and letters. By the time he was twenty, he had absorbed them all.

In an early poem of 1812 he underwrote Mary Wollstonecraft's belief that the doctrine of male superiority allowed a
man to overcome the worst excesses of the tyranny of exploitation – by bullying the people 'beneath' him, in particular his wife.

> He bound himself to an unhappy woman;
> Not of those pure and heavenly links that Love
> Twines round a feeling to Freedom dear,
> But of vile gold, cankring the breast it binds;
> Corroding and inflaming every thought
> Till vain desire, remorse and fear
> Envenom all the being.
> Yet did this chain, though rankling in the soul,
> Not bind the grosser body; he was wont
> All means to try of striving.
> To those above him, the most servile cringe
> That ignorance gave to titled Vice
> Was simperingly yielded;
> To those beneath, the frown which commerce darts
> On cast-off friends, unprofitably poor,
> Was less severe than his.[17]

The same idea was pursued more powerfully in *Rosalind
and Helen* (1817), one of Shelley's most neglected longer
poems, probably because it is so overtly feminist. In the
poem two women, meeting again after a childhood friendship, tell each other their life stories. Rosalind's is the experience of battered wives throughout history:

> He was a coward to the strong:
> He was a tyrant to the weak,
> On whom his vengeance he would wreak:
> For scorn, whose arrows search the heart,
> From many a stranger's eye would dart,
> And on his memory cling, and follow
> His soul to its home so cold and hollow.
> He was a tyrant to the weak,
> And we were such, alas the day!
> Oft, when my little ones at play,
> Were in youth's natural lightness gay,
> Of if they listened to some tale

> Of travellers, or of fairy land,—
> When the light from the wood-fire's dying brand
> Flashes on their faces—if they heard
> Or thought they heard upon the stair
> His footstep, the suspended word
> Died on my lips: we all grew pale:
> The babe at my bosom was hushed with fear
> If it thought it heard its father near;
> And my two wild boys would near my knee
> Cling, cowed and cowering fearfully.[18]

The portrait of the coward at work and the bully at home was borrowed from Mary Wollstonecraft. But Shelley expanded what he had learned from her into a more rounded philosophy of free love. In 1812 he wrote a letter to Sir James Lawrence, an author and explorer: 'Your "Empire of the Nairs", which I read this Spring, succeeded in making me a perfect convert to its doctrines. I then retained no doubts of the evils of marriage,—Mrs. Wollstonecraft reasons too well for that; but I had been dull enough not to perceive the greatest argument against it, until developed in the "Nairs", viz., prostitution, both *legal* and *illegal*.'[19]

The *Empire of the Nairs* is a long, rather boring sociological account of the tribal habits of the natives of Malabar. But it opens with an essay proclaiming the principle of free love, and shows, through an extensive account of tribal customs, that there is nothing remotely 'natural' either about monogamous marriage or about male superiority over women. Lawrence argued that monogamy and male superiority within it were no more than legal cloaks for providing men, free, with sex and food. It was prostitution without payment. And it encouraged prostitution with payment.

In an essay attached to Shelley's first great poem, *Queen Mab*, under the heading, 'Even love is sold', he set down his ideas on marriage and prostitution. Many people have written in favour of free love but none with such passion and simplicity.

The first principle is that love must be free, and depends upon freedom: 'Love withers under constraint. Its very essence is liberty: it is compatible neither with obedience, jealousy, nor fear; it is there most pure, perfect, and unlimited, where its votaries live in confidence, equality and unreserve.'[20]

It followed that the decisions about peoples' relationships with one another, when and for how long they live with one another, when and in what way they make love to one another, and so on, are *their business* and no one else's. 'A husband and wife ought to continue so long united as they love each other: any law which should bind them to cohabitation for one moment after the decay of their affection would be a most intolerable tyranny . . . '[21]

There follows Shelley's description of a society where marital relations *are* governed by such laws.

Persons of delicacy and virtue, unhappily united to one whom they find it impossible to love, spend the loveliest season of their life in unproductive efforts to appear otherwise than they are, for the sake of the feelings of their partner or the welfare of their mutual offspring: those of less generosity and refinement openly avow their disappointment, and linger out the remnant of that union, which only death can dissolve, in a state of incurable bickering and hostility. The early education of their children takes its colour from the squabbles of the parents; they are nursed in a systematic school of ill-humour, violence, and falsehood. Had they been suffered to part at the moment when indifference rendered their union irksome, they would have been spared many years of misery: they would have connected themselves more suitably, and would have found that happiness in the society of more congenial partners which is for ever denied them by the despotism of marriage. They would have been separately useful and happy members of society, who, whilst united, were miserable and rendered misanthropical by misery. The conviction that wedlock is indissoluble holds out the strongest of all temptations to the perverse: they indulge without restraint in acrimony, and all the little tyrannies of domestic life, when they know that their victim is without appeal.[22]

To this constrained matrimony, Shelley went on, 'Prostitution is the legitimate offspring'. Women are forced by penury to satisfy the lusts of gentlemen who are unsatisfied by their marriages. Yet the prostitutes, not their clients, are always the ones who take the blame:

Society declares war against her, pitiless and eternal war: she must be the tame slave, she must make no reprisals; theirs is the right of persecution, hers the duty of endurance. She lives a life of infamy: . . . She dies of long and lingering disease: yet *she* is in fault, *she* is the criminal, *she* the forward and untamable child,— and society, forsooth, the pure and virtuous matron . . . ![23]

Prostitution is dreadful for men and women, 'annihilating all genuine passion, and debasing that to a selfish feeling which is the excess of generosity and devotedness'.[24] The chief cause, the essay stresses again and again, is not 'human nature' but laws and religions drawn up by human beings which promote chastity within marriage as the norm.

Chastity is a monkish and evangelical superstition, a greater foe to natural temperance even than unintellectual sensuality; it strikes at the root of all domestic happiness, and consigns more than half of the human race to misery, that some few may monopolize according to law. A system could not well have been devised more studiously hostile to human happiness than marriage.[25]

By this Shelley did *not* mean that people would not or should not join up and live together in long, sometimes lifetime, associations. As he explained, at once:

I conceive that from the abolition of marriage, the fit and natural arrangement of sexual connection would result. I by no means assert that the intercourse would be promiscuous: on the contrary, it appears, from the relation of parent to child, that this union is generally of long duration, and marked above all others with generosity and self-devotion. . . . That which will result from the abolition of marriage will be natural and right; because choice and change will be exempted from restraint.[26]

Natural and right, because people can freely choose – but not perfect. Not even at the height of his idealism did Shelley ever suggest that the abolition of all laws relating to marriage and religious superstition about sex would of itself iron out the fears, jealousies and unevennesses of love and sexual relationships. The freedom of people to break off relationships, for instance, patently does not solve the problem if one partner wants to break it off and the other does not (as Shelley was soon to find out, with the grimmest possible result). Nevertheless the *Queen Mab* essay retains its strength and sparkle over all these years because it speaks up for the right of people to decide on these matters for themselves. The imposition of standards of behaviour by laws or by religion increased the fears, jealousies and unevennesses of human relationships ten thousand-fold.

These ideas never left Shelley. They illuminated all his poetry about human relations. In his most famous love poem, *Epipsychidion*, written in 1820, eight years after *Queen Mab*, he expanded, in more mature and sonorous poetry, on the theme that the laws which command monogamy serve only to stifle love:

> I never was attached to that great sect,
> Whose doctrine is, that each one should select
> Out of the crowd a mistress or a friend,
> And all the rest, though fair and wise, commend
> To cold oblivion, though it is in the code
> Of modern morals, and the beaten road
> Which those poor slaves with weary footsteps tread,
> Who travel to their home among the dead
> By the broad highway of the world, and so
> With one chained friend, perhaps a jealous foe,
> The dreariest and the longest journey go.[27]

That is the famous passage – but immediately afterwards he provided the alternative to monogamy, a wonderful image of kaleidoscopic human relationships, each illuminating the others:

> True Love in this differs from gold and clay,
> That to divide is not to take away.
> Love is like understanding, that grows bright,
> Gazing on many truths; 'tis like thy light,
> Imagination! which from earth and sky,
> And from the depths of human fantasy,

As from a thousand prisms and mirrors, fills
The Universe with glorious beams, and kills
Error, the worm, with many a sun-like arrow
Of its reverberated lightning. Narrow
The heart that loves, the brain that contemplates,
The life that wears, the spirit that creates,
One object, and one form, and builds thereby
A sepulchre for its eternity.[28]

All this, declared the priests and lawmakers, was the philosophy of a libertine. Yet it was the opposite. Shelley attacked the subordination of sex and love to what he described as 'the hyena, lust'. He detested dirty jokes of every description. So bitter were his attacks on the lewd humour of the popular theatre of the time that he earned himself an undeserved reputation for humourlessness. He hated obscenity and pornography. He inveighed against the Roman pornographers from Catullus onwards – and against the idiotic bawdiness of the early English playwrights. All these things seemed to him to debauch what he saw as the 'act which ought always to be the link and type of the highest emotions of our nature'.[29] Dirty songs, dirty jokes and dirty pictures, fashionable, then and now, in an Oxford hall or junior college room, were all driving towards 'the end of social corruption [which] is to destroy all sensibility to pleasure'.[30]

More dangerously, they encouraged men to go out and hunt for sex as the hunter goes out for food. Bribing or bullying a woman into bed became proof of manly achievement, and was therefore tolerated, if not promoted, by society and its laws. 'If there is any enormous and desolating crime, of which I should shudder to be accused,' wrote Shelley to Sir James Lawrence, 'it is seduction.'[31]

From this, some Shelley-idolaters have created an image of Shelley as a prude, who believed in 'love' as an ideal, as something untainted by sex. On the contrary. Shelley wrote openly about sex in a way in which few of the English writers of the time – certainly not the tight Dissenter Godwin, nor even Mary Wollstonecraft – had dared.

One of his most mysterious poems, *Alastor, or the Spirit of Solitude* (1815), is about a young man who had nothing but his ideals. These ideals were perfect. He had a perfect vision of society. He behaved perfectly, never doing any harm to anyone. He devoted himself to knowledge which would perfect that ideal, and deliberately avoided anything which could besmirch it. He turned away from luxury, fame – and sex. Then, suddenly, he had a dream. It was a 'dream of hopes that never yet/Had flushed his cheek'.[32]

In his dream a young woman talked to him. She was not empty-headed, as women were trained to be when talking to young men:

> Her voice was like the voice of his own soul
> Heard in the calm of thought; . . .
> Knowledge and truth and virtue were her theme,
> And lofty hopes of divine liberty,
> Thoughts the most dear to him, and poesy,
> Herself a poet.[33]

That was all right, until things began to take a distinctly physical turn:

> Soon the solemn mood
> Of her pure mind kindled through all her frame
> A permeating fire:[34]

The fire engulfed them both in what must be one of the most tumultous orgasms ever described in poetry:

> Wild numbers then
> She raised, with voice stifled in tremulous sobs
> Subdued by its own pathos: her fair hands
> Were bare alone, sweeping from some strange harp
> Strange symphony, and in their branching veins
> The eloquent blood told an ineffable tale.
> The beating of her heart was heard to fill
> The pauses of her music, and her breath
> Tumultuously accorded with those fits
> Of intermitted song. Sudden she rose,
> As if her heart impatiently endured
> Its bursting burthen: at the sound he turned,

And saw by the warm light of their own life,
Her glowing limbs beneath the sinuous veil
Of woven wind, her outspread arms now bare,
Her dark locks floating in the breath of night,
Her beamy bending eyes, her parted lips
Outstretched, and pale, and quivering eagerly.
His strong heart sunk and sickened with excess
Of love. He reared his shuddering limbs and quelled
His gasping breath, and spread his arms to meet
Her panting bosom: . . . she drew back a while,
Then, yielding to the irresistible joy,
With frantic gesture and short breathless cry
Folded his frame in her dissolving arms.
Now blackness veiled his dizzy eyes, and night
Involved and swallowed up the vision; sleep,
Like a dark flood suspended in its course,
Rolled back its impulse on his vacant brain.[35]

Imagine the shock, after all that, when he discovered that he was dreaming. He was sleeping in a beautiful valley, but when he awoke it looked cold and grey and miserable:

Whither have fled
The hues of heaven that canopied his bower
Of yesternight? The sounds that soothed his sleep,
The mystery and the majesty of the Earth,
The joy, the exultation?[36]

Where had it all gone to? How could he get it back? The sexual dream pursues him through the rest of the poem. It haunts him everywhere he goes. He turns his back on sexual 'temptation' and so, gradually, he loses touch with the source of life:

And now his limbs were lean; his scattered hair
Sered by the autumn of strange suffering
Sung dirges in the wind; his listless hand
Hung like dead bone within its withered skin;
Life, and the lustre that consumed it, shone
As in a furnace burning secretly
From his dark eyes alone.[37]

He was finished. Without real contact, especially sexual contact, with human beings, his ideal could not sustain him. Indeed, all the beautiful things which had ever been produced were quite useless unless they could be shared or enjoyed with other people:

> Let not high verse, mourning the memory
> Of that which is no more, or painting's woe,
> Or sculpture, speak in feeble imagery
> Their own cold powers.[38]

The poet's life was a woe 'too deep for tears'. He had turned his back on 'sobs' and 'groans' and above all 'The passionate tumult of a clinging hope',[39] and so he had nothing to live for.

As Shelley put it in his preface:

The Poet . . . seeks in vain for a prototype of his conception. Blasted by his disappointment, he descends to an untimely grave. . . . They who, deluded by no generous error, instigated by no sacred thirst of doubtful knowledge, duped by no illustrious superstition, loving nothing on this earth, and cherishing no hopes beyond, yet keep aloof from sympathies with their kind, rejoicing neither in human joy nor mourning with human grief; these, and such as they, have their apportioned curse.[40]

But the main lesson is, rather prudishly, left out of the preface. It is that sex is vital to love. Any ideal of love which does not include sex is as lifeless as the young man at the end of *Alastor*. The 'Avenging Spirit of Solitude' catches up with any sexless relationship, with terrible consequences.

All sexual taboos, thought Shelley, were there to be broken by free and equal lovers. In the 'Discourse on the Manners of the Ancient Greeks, Relative to the Subject of Love', he rather shamefacedly admitted his prejudice against the male homosexual act, but asked whether it was in any circumstances as disgusting as a heterosexual act between a man and a prostitute. The love affair between Laon and Cythna in *The Revolt of Islam* is between a brother and sister.

There was one serious objection to unlicensed sexual activity, however: the fact that it resulted, apparently inevitably, in the birth of children. The conservative philosopher, Thomas Malthus, argued that sexual restraint, like poverty, was necessary in order to keep the world's population down. Shelley turned on Malthus in some heat, outraged by a philosophy which denied to the poor not only the things which money could buy but also the pleasures of sexual intercourse.

But Malthus's argument could not be so easily dispensed with, and Shelley knew it. If sexual intercourse always led to childbirth, that *was* an argument for restraint, since it might bring more poverty and distress to the child's family. But, Shelley argued, it was *not* inevitable. He became one of the earliest advocates of birth control.

In the same notebook in which he wrote his 'Philosophical View of Reform', Shelley jotted down his thoughts on the subject under the heading 'Malthus'.

The sexual intercourse by no means presents as has been supposed the alternative of a being to be invested with existence for whom there is no subsistence, or the revolting expedients of infanticide and abortion. Every student of anatomy must be aware of an innocent, small and almost imperceptible precaution by which all consequences of this kind are precluded, and the ends of an union of two persons of the opposite sexes in every other respect fulfilled.

As nothing but evil could result from its partial and unauthorised use, I refrain from explaining myself on a subject with which so much false delicacy is connected . . .

It is curious to remark how few medical men of any considerable science have more children than they can comfortably maintain . . .[41]

This was not published, of course. Indeed it has never been published in any Shelley prose anthology. But if it had been published in 1819 or 1820 when it was written, it would have been the first public argument for birth control in the English language. In 1822 Francis Place, the social reformer and trade unionist, published the first tentative hints about a system of birth control in his *Illustrations and Proofs of the Principle of Population*. In 1823 he advocated it more openly and more publicly. He was followed by Richard Carlile in 1825, who argued that birth control was essential to free love.

These ideas were not new of course. Mary Wollstonecraft had come into contact with them in France after the revolution. They had been argued openly by French emancipators like Condorcet. But when Shelley wrote his fragment, no public advocacy of birth control existed in English.

The 'innocent, small and almost imperceptible precaution' to which Shelley refers could have been the sheath, but was more probably the vaginal sponge which some educated women (and prostitutes) were using, especially if their doctors had advised them that pregnancy would be dangerous to their health.

Effective birth control, which Shelley saw as one of the most emancipating possibilities of science, would remove the fear of sex which stemmed in many women from the belief that every sex act would produce a child. It would restore the sex act to the area of free choice, without which sex and love were meaningless.

But just as sex was vital to love, sex without love was, for Shelley, altogether unsatisfying. Indeed, he argued, in his 'Discourse on the Manners of the Ancients', the deeper the love relationship, the smaller – though the no less indispensable – the part which sex played in it.

It [the gratification of the senses] soon becomes a very small part of that profound and complicated sentiment, which we call love, which is rather the universal thirst for a communion not only of the senses, but of our whole nature, intellectual, imaginative and sensitive; and which, when individualised, becomes an imperious necessity . . .[42]

That is what Shelley meant by love. The extent to which it could be realized for human beings, he argued, depended on the development of civilization. The more civilized society was, the greater the possibility and power of love. 'For man,' the passage above concluded, 'never ceases to be a social being.'

Here was the conclusion which shocked the cultured morality of his age and since far more than his open descriptions of the sex act: that men and women cannot develop full love relationships with each other until society is transformed from top to bottom.

A society founded on unrepresentative power and religious dogma encourages hierarchy in every part of it. Big kings and priests with arbitrary power over society promote little kings and priests with arbitrary power over every house and home. The 'boss man' dictating to his quivering wife and children is a reflection of the 'boss king' dictating to his quivering subjects.

Similarly, a society where the people in power get their enjoyment from the fruits of other people's suffering promotes a morality of enjoyment which depends on suffering. In Shelley's day, the educational establishments of the rich promoted – as they still do – sexual sadism and masochism. The purpose of women, they taught, was to gratify men sexually – just as the purpose of the poor was to provide for the rich. Sex was reduced to a master-servant relationship, because society was organized on a master-servant basis.

There was no hope for Shelley's idea of love unless society was transformed. Such a transformation could not come about until women stirred themselves to revolt against male superiority and against the society which spawned it. Rosalind, in *Rosalind and Helen*, expresses her own subservient intellectual and political role when face to face with her husband:

> Nor my vexed soul had leisure yet
> To doubt the things men say, or deem
> That they are other than they seem.[43]

Doubting, questioning 'the things men say', was vital, Shelley argued, not just for the dignity of women, but for the overthrow of the social order. It was not merely that women should support a revolution; they should lead it. And so it is that in all Shelley's major revolutionary poems, the leading agitators and revolutionaries are women.

In *Queen Mab*, the spirit of a young girl is shown the facts of life by the Fairy Queen. In *Swellfoot the Tyrant*, the Pigs (the people) are agitated to action by the Queen, Iona. In *Prometheus Unbound*, the decisive agitation is carried out by Prometheus's lover, Asia, properly described by Richard Holmes as 'Love Militant'. In *Hellas*, the symbol of liberated Greece is a chorus of female slaves in the Turkish court. In *The Cenci*, it is the tyrant's daughter Beatrice who makes the decision to kill him, and sees that the decision is carried out, even against the will of the male assassins. In *The Mask of Anarchy* the Spirit of Hope 'fled past' in the form of 'a maniac maid'.

But the greatest of all Shelley's revolutionary heroines features in his longest poem, *The Revolt of Islam* (written originally as *Laon and Cythna*), which he wrote in 1817. This poem is difficult to read. The narrative twice doubles back on itself, and is clogged by complicated imagery. Yet it throbs from first to last with energy and excitement. When William Godwin wrote to criticize it, Shelley wrote back cheerfully: 'I listened with deference & self suspicion to your censures of "Laon & Cythna"; but the productions of mine which you commend hold a very low place in my own esteem; & this reassured me, in some degree at least. The Poem was produced by a series of thoughts which filled my mind with an unbounded & sustained enthusiasm.'[44]

No idea shines through the poem with more unbounded and sustained enthusiasm than that of women's liberation. In the character and actions of Cythna, and in the wonderful poetry which surrounds her, the poem becomes, more than anything else, a hymn to free love, to women's liberation, and to the essential role which women must play in any revolution.

The story gets going in the second canto when the narrator and hero, Laon, like Shelley, quickly becomes aware of the horrors of the society he lives in. But this awareness is not fully expressed until it is shared with Laon's sister, Cythna.

> Thus, Cythna mourned with me the servitude
> In which the half of humankind were mewed . . .[45]

But mourning alone was not enough, and there follows a conversation in which Laon argues for more:

> Cythna sweet,
> Well with the world art thou unreconciled;
> Never will peace and human nature meet
> Till free and equal man and woman greet
> Domestic peace; and ere this power can make
> In human hearts its calm and holy seat,
> This slavery must be broken.[46]

To this Cythna responds so enthusiastically as to cause Laon some embarrassment:

> It shall be mine,
> This task, mine, Laon![47]

This is not quite what Laon, masculine teacher and inspirer, has in mind.

> I smiled and spake not.[48]

This annoys Cythna who suspects, rightly, that she is being patronized.

> Wherefore dost thou smile
> At what I say? Laon, I am not weak . . .[49]

She then pledges herself to revolutionary agitation – agitation which starts with women, and with the oppression of women:

> Yes, I will tread Pride's golden palaces,
>   Through Penury's roofless huts and squalid cells
> Will I descend, where'er in abjectness
>   Woman with some vile slave her tyrant dwells,
>   There with the music of thine own sweet spells

Will disenchant the captives, and will pour
  For the despairing, from the crystal wells
Of thy deep spirit, reason's mighty lore,
And power shall then abound, and hope arise once more.[50]

There follows an eloquent expression of woman's oppression – and its indissoluble links with the oppression of
humanity:

Can man be free if woman be a slave?
  Chain one who lives, and breathes this boundless air,
To the corruption of a closèd grave!
  Can they whose mates are beasts, condemned to bear
  Scorn, heavier far than toil or anguish, dare
To trample their oppressors? in their home
  Among their babes, thou knowest a curse would wear
The shape of woman—hoary Crime would come
Behind, and Fraud rebuild Religion's tottering dome.[51]

News gets abroad of the subversive thoughts of Laon and
Cythna, and their house is raided by the special branch.
Cythna is captured. Laon kills three of his assailants before
he too is overcome, chained to a rock in the middle of the
desert, and left to starve. He is saved by an old man, whose
former commitment to radical ideas is revived by the new,
revolutionary mood which is sweeping the country. News
of Laon's resistance to his capture spreads, and Laon, believed dead, is lionized by revolutionaries meeting in secret
'when their tyrants sleep'. For seven years, the old man
nurses Laon through sickness and madness. When Laon
recovers the old man recounts some astonishing political
events in the 'Golden City'.

                    —for lately did a maiden fair,
  Who from her childhood has been taught to bear
The tyrant's heaviest yoke, arise, and make
  Her sex the law of truth and freedom hear, . . .[52]

Women had flocked to this strange agitator:

The wild-eyed women throng around her path:
  From their luxurious dungeons, from the dust

Of meaner thralls, from the oppressor's wrath,
    Or the caresses of his sated lust
They congregate:—[53]

And again:

Thousands thus dwell beside her, virgins bright,
    And matrons with their babes, a stately throng![54]

These crowds of women had succeeded in isolating and humiliating the source of their own isolation and humiliation.

In squalid huts, and in its palaces
Sits Lust alone, . . .[55]

Inspired by the old man's story, Laon joins the revolutionary armies as they successfully storm the city and overthrow the tyrant. On the day after the revolution, he hears the mysterious woman who led it speak to the masses:

My brethren, we are free! The plains and mountains,
The gray sea-shore, the forests and the fountains,
    Are haunts of happiest dwellers;—man and woman,
    Their common bondage burst, may freely borrow
From lawless love a solace for their sorrow; . . .[56]

And then Shelley adds a line which shows that he realized (as he is so often accused of not realizing) that revolution does *not* usher in utopia; 'For oft we still must weep, since we are human.'[57]

Cythna's speech goes on for two more magnificent verses. The language reaches the peak of Shelley's 'unbounded enthusiasm':

'Victory, Victory to the prostrate nations!
Bear witness Night, and ye mute Constellations
Who gaze on us from your crystalline cars!
    Thoughts have gone forth whose powers can sleep no
                                                    more!

Victory! Victory! Earth's remotest shore,

Regions which groan beneath the Antarctic stars,
  The green lands cradled in the roar
Of western waves, and wildernesses
  Peopled and vast, which skirt the oceans
Where morning dyes her golden tresses,
  Shall soon partake our high emotions:
  Kings shall turn pale! Almighty Fear
The Fiend-God, when our charmèd name he hear,
Shall fade like shadow from his thousand fanes,
While Truth with Joy enthroned o'er his lost empire reigns!'[58]

For a few days and nights the revolutionary armies are left alone to build a new future. But suddenly, from some other country, the tyrant (who was spared by the revolutionaries) re-arms and leads new armies on to the Golden City. There follows a long and bloody war, won by the counter-revolution.

In the middle of the fighting, Cythna, mounted rather absurdly on a huge horse, bears down on Laon and sweeps him away out of the fighting into the countryside. There the two revolutionaries make love together. Three triumphantly erotic verses ask the simple questions about sexual passion which no one has ever answered.

The Meteor to its far morass returned:
  The beating of our veins one interval
Made still; and then I felt the blood that burned
  Within her frame, mingle with mine, and fall
  Around my heart like fire; and over all
A mist was spread, the sickness of a deep
  And speechless swoon of joy, as might befall
Two disunited spirits when they leap
In union from this earth's obscure and fading sleep.

Was it one moment that confounded thus
  All thought, all sense, all feeling, into one
Unutterable power, which shielded us
  Even from our own cold looks, when we had gone
  Into a wild and wide oblivion
Of tumult and of tenderness? or now
  Had ages, such as make the moon and sun,
The seasons, and mankind their changes know,
Left fear and time unfelt by us alone below?

I know not. What are kisses whose fire clasps
    The failing heart in languishment, or limb
Twined within limb? or the quick dying gasps
    Of the life meeting, when the faint eyes swim
    Through tears of a wide mist boundless and dim,
In one caress? What is the strong control
    Which leads the heart that dizzy steep to climb
Where far over the world those vapours roll,
Which blend two restless frames in one reposing soul?[59]

The morning after, she tells him of her adventures.

    And we sate linked in the inwoven charm
Of converse and caresses sweet and deep,—
    Speechless caresses, talk that might disarm
Time, . . .[60]

She was carried away in a slave ship, she says, and attached
to the tyrant's slave harem. In a verse which captures all
Shelley's disgust for enforced sex, she describes how she
was raped by the tyrant:

    She told me what a loathsome agony
        Is that when selfishness mocks love's delight,
    Foul as in dream's most fearful imagery
        To dally with the mowing dead—that night
        All torture, fear, or horror made seem light
    Which the soul dreams or knows, and when the day
        Shone on her awful frenzy, from the sight
    Where like a Spirit in fleshly chains she lay
Struggling, aghast and pale, the Tyrant fled away.[61]

As if to punish her for showing her displeasure at being
raped, the tyrant banishes her to prison in an underwater
cave. There she gives birth to his child, which is taken from
her. Eventually, an earthquake destroys the cave and she is
rescued by a passing ship.

She then speaks to the sailors, urging them to mutiny. Her
speech starts by attacking established religion, faith and God.
She warms to the theme which first inspired her to her
revolutionary mission: the tyranny of property in the hands
of a few – and the resulting tyranny of man over woman.

The two most powerful verses in the speech follow one another and are connected to one another:

> Man seeks for gold in mines, that he may weave
>   A lasting chain for his own slavery;—
> In fear and restless care that he may live
>   He toils for others, who must ever be
>   The joyless thralls of like captivity;
> He murders, for his chiefs delight in ruin;
>   He builds the altar, that its idol's fee
> May be his very blood; he is pursuing—
> O, blind and willing wretch!— his own obscure undoing.
>
> Woman!—she is his slave, she has become
>   A thing I weep to speak—the child of scorn,
> The outcast of a desolated home;
>   Falsehood, and fear, and toil, like waves have worn
>   Channels upon her cheek, which smiles adorn,
> As calm decks the false Ocean;—well ye know
>   What Woman is, for none of Woman born
> Can choose but drain the bitter dregs of woe,
> Which ever from the oppressed to the oppressors flow.[62]

And at the end of another verse:

>   Woman as the bond-slave dwells
> Of man, a slave; and life is poisoned in its wells.[63]

The argument wins, and the sailors take over the ship and forswear their rulers. The ship acts as a beacon to other ships, which join it, until a great revolutionary fleet arrives at the Golden City. Cythna continues with her agitation through the city streets, directing herself to all the poor and the oppressed, but, again, mainly to her own sex:

> But chiefly women, whom my voice did waken
>   From their cold, careless, willing slavery,
> Sought me: one truth their dreary prison has shaken,—
>   They looked around, and lo! they became free!
>   Their many tyrants sitting desolately
> In slave-deserted halls, could none restrain;
>   For wrath's red fire had withered in the eye,
> Whose lightning once was death,—nor fear, nor gain
> Could tempt one captive now to lock another's chain.[64]

Women can free themselves from being the 'bond slaves of slaves', and that act of liberation acts as a spur to the liberation of all oppressed humanity. Small wonder, as Cythna's story continues, that among the most hysterical advocates of the old order are those who cry down the women's campaign, saying:

> that the rule of men was over now,
> And hence, the subject world to woman's will must
>   bow; . . .[65]

This argument is easily countered. Cythna is not interested in a society where women dominate men. She wants a society of free and equal men and women, where relationships can be formed, developed or dissolved without being corrupted by the bullying or the insecurity of male (or female) power.

So the story of the revolution, told for the third time in the poem, comes to an end. Laon leaves again for the Golden City, there, in disguise, to plead before the tyrant's 'senate'. He offers to find and deliver Laon to the tyrant, in exchange for a pledge to allow Cythna to seek asylum in free America. This request is granted. Laon removes his disguise, gives himself up and is tied to a stake ready for execution.

But the poem is primarily about women in revolution, and could not end with a conventional sacrifice of a man for a woman. Cythna appears on her horse. The kings and priests promptly break their promise to give her asylum, and she is executed too.

All Shelley's ideas about women and love can be found in *The Revolt of Islam*: his horror of legally enforced sexual morality; his belief in free love not as a passport for lust but so that men and women can decide their love-making free of legal or religious constraint; his hatred of forced sex; his desire for openness about sex; and finally his belief in the indispensable role of women in every aspect of revolutionary politics.

How did all these grand ideas match with Shelley's own life and relationships?

IN PRACTICE

At Oxford in 1811, Shelley recovered very quickly from the snub of his cousin Harriet Grove with whom he had fallen in love, but who spurned him because of his atheism. Soon after leaving Oxford he started to take an interest in another Harriet – Harriet Westbrook – a sixteen-year-old friend and schoolmate of his sister Elizabeth. Harriet's father was an up-and-coming coffee house owner, who tolerated no nonsense from his children, especially as they were both girls. Harriet, the younger sister, was thrilled by Shelley's florid talk of love and freedom. Partly under his influence, she came to hate school. Girls' schools were devoted to deportment, a smattering of foreign languages and anything else which would make the pupils into adequate wives. 'Women,' the educationalist, Lord Kames, had written in 1781, 'destined to be obedient, ought to be disciplined early to bear wrongs without murmuring.'[66] Mr Westbrook agreed with that, and told his daughter that if she didn't go to school she would be punished. Harriet, with some assistance from her elder sister Eliza (who quickly saw what an excellent match the son of a wealthy Sussex baronet would make for Harriet), threw herself on Shelley's protection. The couple eloped from London, and married in Edinburgh.

The best account of Harriet Shelley comes from Thomas Love Peacock, who befriended the Shelleys in 1812. 'Her complexion was beautifully transparent; the tint of the blush rose shining through the lily. The tone of her voice was pleasant; her speech the essence of frankness and cordiality; her spirits always cheerful; her laugh spontaneous, hearty, and joyous. She was well educated . . . her whole aspect and demeanour such manifest emanations of pure and truthful nature, that to be once in her company was to know her thoroughly.'[67] She was kind, gentle and honest. And she was by no means the 'dumb blonde' which Shelley worshippers have made her out to be. She was won by Shelley from the inanities and cruelties of her parents' society. She took an alert interest in the world about her, and was outraged by what she saw.

From Dublin she wrote to Shelley's friend Elizabeth Hitchener in 1812:

Poor Irish people how much I feel for them . . . People talk of the fiery spirit of these distressed creatures, but that spirit is very much broken and ground down by the oppressors of this poor country . . .

How often do we hear people say that poverty is no evil. I think that if they had experienced it they would soon alter their tone. To my idea it is the worst of all evils, as the miseries that flow from it are certainly very great; the many crimes we hear of daily are the consequences of poverty, and that to a very great degree . . .[68]

Very few fashionable young women of the time would have held such views, let alone dared to write about them. When the Luddites were hanged at York, it was Harriet, not Shelley, who wrote asking for a subscription to be raised for the hanged men's families – and sending money.

Harriet lived with Shelley for just under three years, the first two of which were a happy time for both of them. They were marked by Shelley's incurable restlessness. The couple were always on the move, from Edinburgh to York, to Cumberland, to Dublin, to Nangtwillt in North Wales, to Lynmouth in North Devon, to Tremadoc in North Wales, back to Ireland, to London, to Bracknell, back to Cumberland, back to Edinburgh, to Bath. They never spent more than six months in the same house. For much of 1812 and 1813 Shelley was writing his first major poem, *Queen Mab*. Harriet encouraged him in writing it, and praised it when it was written. It is dedicated to her:

> Beneath whose looks did my reviving soul
> Riper in truth and virtuous daring grow?
>   Whose eyes have I gazed fondly on,
>   And loved mankind the more?
>
> Harriet! on thine:—thou wert my purer mind;
> Thou wert the inspiration of my song; . . .[69]

There are several other Shelley poems to Harriet written in
the same mould.

Harriet called those two years 'the happiest and the longest
years of my life'. She was content to be Shelley's companion
and disciple. He was flattered by her passive adoration, and
even promoted it. But, increasingly, he was frustrated by
it.

There are early signs of this frustration. One poem, written probably at Lynmouth in 1812, seems to be an effort to
make up some marital dispute. It begs for '*One* soul-reviving
kiss'[70] and then goes on to argue, as though this point were
at the centre of the debate, that the poet's love is bound
inexorably to action:

> The thirst for action, and the impassioned thought
> Prolong my being; if I wake no more,
> My life more actual living will contain
> Than some grey veteran's of the world's cold school,
> Whose listless hours unprofitably roll
> By one enthusiast feeling unredeemed, . . .[71]

His 'thirst for action' at Lynmouth had landed him in
trouble. His servant had gone to prison for six months for
pasting up Shelley's Declaration of Rights, and Shelley's
home was being watched by Home Office agents. Perhaps
Harriet was worried about what lay in store.

The dispute passed away quickly, and the couple moved
on once again to Tremadoc in Wales, where they spent a
happy winter on the hill over an embankment where Shelley
worked as an agent. This interlude was broken by an assas-
sination attempt on Shelley organized by the local gentry.
The sudden danger re-awakened the dispute. Harriet lived
her life through Shelley; her thoughts came from Shelley.
Yet what if this life and these thoughts led to danger for
Shelley? This dilemma tormented her, and led to further
upsets in the household.

In April 1813 the couple returned to London, and in June
their daughter Ianthe was born. Peacock writes that Shelley
was 'extremely fond' of the baby. 'He would walk up and

down a room with it in his arms for a long time singing to
it in a monotonous melody of his own making, which ran
on the repetition of a word of his own making. His song
was "Yahmani, Yahmani, Yahmani, Yahmani". It did not
please me, but, what was important, it pleased the child,
and lulled it when it was fretful.'[72]

But Peacock also noticed that there were 'accompaniments' to the birth of the child which led to further arguments between Shelley and Harriet. Shelley thought he
knew best about how the child should be fed and reared.
Harriet differed. He wanted her to feed it; she insisted on a
wet nurse. Harriet's side was taken by her more assertive
sister, Eliza, who came to live with them, and whom Shelley
grew to loathe.

Such disagreements are common anywhere. But they disguised a more serious anguish which was racking both Shelley and Harriet. How, Harriet wondered, would the family
ever settle down?

Shelley's father still refused to allow him more than £200
a year, and would certainly continue to do so as long as he
continued on his radical path. Harriet's own allowance from
her father was also in jeopardy as long as the couple lived
as wandering agitators. Shelley, for his part, could not decide what to do. He could not settle down, since that meant
making peace with his father and ripping up everything he
believed in. On the other hand, he could not see any way
ahead as an agitator. The birth of his child heightened his
sense of insecurity.

To make matters worse, he had fallen in with a radical
chic set at Bracknell, centred around the house of a Mrs
Boinville. For the first time, Shelley found himself in the
daily company of well-read radicals, one of whom was Mrs
Boinville's attractive daughter, Cornelia. They flattered him,
and he flattered them. Harriet detested the whole set, and
cowered at home during Shelley's visits to the Boinvilles,
comforted only occasionally by Peacock, with his sharp
satire against people who expressed 'with fervour opinions
utterly unconducive to any practical result'.

The gap between the couple was growing wider – but it was by no means unbridgeable. Shelley still wrote handsome love poems to Harriet. In March 1814, partly, no doubt, to please both sets of parents, they married again, more formally, at Hanover Square in London. They still lived and made love together, proof of which is the birth of Charles Shelley, a month premature, in November. Yet the early months of 1814, about which there is little or no record from any source, were a time of increasing unhappiness for both of them. Her passivity and his tempestuousness, which had seemed to blend so perfectly two years previously, now grated on one another. To Harriet's distress Shelley spent more and more time away from her. In the summer of 1814, Shelley broke the relationship to pieces by eloping with Mary Godwin.

Harriet has been terribly wronged by the Shelley-worshippers. It was in their interests to blame *her* for the collapse of the relationship and the end of the marriage. Various extravagant attempts have been made to fix her up with another lover, or to pretend that she abandoned an ever-loyal husband.

Louise Boas has written a book to restore Harriet's reputation. It shows how Harriet's life was inextricably bound to Shelley's; how she saw no other life as possible; and how Shelley, knowing all this, abandoned her. Yet even Louise Boas cannot escape from Harriet's role as passive observer and supplier: 'It is a tribute to Harriet,' she writes, 'and to the housekeeping of Eliza that Shelley had time to read so many books, to compose so many thousand lines, arrange and write so many notes . . . '[73]

Although Harriet read aloud a great deal (Hogg wrote in his *Life of Shelley* that her reading was intolerably long and dull), there is little evidence of Shelley and Harriet reading together, let alone arguing or challenging one another over what they read.

This was not all Shelley's fault, but it was certainly not Harriet's either. Shelley's half-hearted attempt to blame Harriet for the break-up of the marriage is indefensible. He told

Peacock (or at any rate so Peacock records): 'Everyone who knows me must know that the partner of my life should be one who can feel poetry and understand philosophy. Harriet is a noble animal but she can do neither.'[74]

The description of someone who had lovingly shared his life for two years (and was pregnant by him) as a 'noble animal' was bad enough, but it was nothing like as bad as the letters which Shelley wrote to Harriet after eloping with Mary. Luckily for the Shelley worshippers of the late nineteenth century, these were not found until 1930. They make it difficult to uphold the image of Shelley as the wounded angel, wronged by the dull and hard-hearted Harriet.

In the first letter after he had broken the news to Harriet that he was leaving her, Shelley wrote (as part of the argument that his 'attachment' to Harriet was 'unimpaired'): 'Our connection was not one of passion & impulse . . . It is no reproach to me that you have never filled my heart with an all-sufficing passion—perhaps, you are even yourself a stranger to these impulses, . . .'[75]

Two months later, still determined not to admit to any mistake, he wrote: 'You think that I have injured you. Since I first beheld you almost, my chief study has been to overwhelm you with benefits. Even now when a violent and lasting passion for another leads me to prefer her society to yours, I am perpetually employed in devising how I can be permanently & truly useful to you, in what manner my time and my fortune may be most securely expended for your real interests . . .'[76]

'And it would be generous, nay even just', he went on, twisting the knife in the wound, 'to consider with kindness that woman whom my judgment and my heart have selected as the noblest and the most excellent of human beings.'[77]

When Harriet went to a lawyer to see what money she could get out of him, Shelley exploded in rage: 'I was an idiot to expect greatness or generosity from you, that when an occasion of the sublimest virtue occurred, you would fail to play a part of mean & despicable selfishness.'[78]

Then, as Shelley became poorer, his letters to Harriet

changed from abuse and patronage to begging. Harriet's gloom deepened. Her position was hopeless. She had been convinced that her parents' way of life was pernicious and trivial. Yet now there was nothing for it but to submit to perniciousness and trivia. Her fury with Shelley ('The man I once loved is dead. This is a vampire,'[79] she wrote) was no compensation for her loneliness. In November, alone and poor, she gave birth to Shelley's son, Charles. Two miserable years later she flung herself into the Serpentine, and drowned.

This grim story reflects little credit on Shelley. His plea that he was acting according to the principles of free love has a hollow ring. For, as he wrote to Elizabeth Hitchener from York on 8 October 1811 when first he married Harriet, idealists, like everyone else, have to live in the real world, and their behaviour affects real people. Harriet was hardly in a position to change her partner, even if she had wanted to. He may not have wanted to live with her, but she plainly wanted to live with him. This dilemma could not be solved by the slogans of free love. The letters to Harriet which demean the love which she and Shelley had shared and then seek to win her friendship for Mary are insulting and offensive.

In contrast to the breezy, self-justifying tone of these letters was the lifelong anguish which Shelley suffered over Harriet, to which Mary testified long after his death. And the letters to Harriet are accurate at least in this: that he had left Harriet not out of any dislike for her. He left because he had fallen irreversibly in love with the daughter of Mary Wollstonecraft.

Mary Wollstonecraft Godwin was, in almost every particular, the opposite of Harriet Westbrook. She had been brought up in a household in which the children, including the girls, had been taught to read for themselves, think for themselves and speak for themselves. William Godwin had a pulpit built in his front room from which he required his children, from a very young age, to read lectures. Mary found herself writing these, even when her half-brother had to deliver them. She was sixteen when Shelley met her. She had read almost as much as he had, and had her own opinions about nearly everything. They corresponded closely to Shelley's. In particular the couple shared a heroine-worship of Mary Wollstonecraft. Their first, secret meetings were held at the side of Mary Wollstonecraft's grave in St Pancras churchyard. There they would whisper quotations from her, talk, and start, falteringly, to make love.

Thomas Love Peacock met Shelley in those first weeks, and wrote: 'Between his old feelings towards Harriet, *from whom he was not then separated*, and his new passion for Mary, he showed in his looks, in his gestures, in his speech, the state of a mind "suffering, like a little kingdom, the nature of an insurrection". His eyes were bloodshot, his hair and dress disordered.'[80]

There was no alternative to elopement. Harriet would not consider a legal separation. Divorce was impossible. And so, on 28 July 1814, at the crack of dawn, Mary slipped away from her house with her half-sister Claire and a small suitcase. Shelley met them, and they fled to France.

There followed a weird honeymoon – weird because their time was spent, with very little money, wandering through the desolation of post-war France; weird, too, because they were accompanied throughout by Claire. After six weeks they were back in England again, shunned by Shelley's family, Harriet's family, Mary's family and most of their friends. Their elopement was the gossip of high society, and few from such society dared associate with the young atheists and libertines.

They were almost without any income, and Shelley spent many miserable hours with property lawyers and money-lenders begging and borrowing at high interest on what he might inherit when his father died. Mary had become pregnant in France; she was sick and uncomfortable. Yet the passion and intelligence of their relationship survived and even increased. Between them, amid much ribald argument, they worked out stern programmes for reading and discussion. Mary's journal for most of that time (indeed right up to Shelley's death) was taken up mainly with a record of what she read, and (more briefly) what she thought of it. But from time to time she wandered into a description of the life she was leading:

> October 30, 1814: Rise late. Talk with Shelley all day . . . in the evening Shelley and I go to an inn at John Street to sleep. Those that love cannot separate: Shelley could not have gone away without me again.
> November 6. Talk to Shelley. He writes a great heap of letters. Talk with him all evening. This is a day devoted to love in idleness.
> November 18. A great deal of talk as usual.[81]

The talk wandered across every conceivable subject. It leapt from the intellectual to the trivial. It hovered around politics – not so much day-to-day politics (which always interested Shelley), but deeper political ideas.

Mary's journal in France tells of a plague of expatriate bores who would drone on about 'the way the old country is going down the drain'. These they would frighten off by proclaiming their republicanism or their anti-slavery fanatacism, for republican and anti-slavery fanatics they both were, and the ideas of both were enriched by the other's instinctive agreement as well as by their different patterns of thought, expression and reading.

In March 1815 fell the first of the many blows which were eventually to crush Mary's spirit. Her baby was born prematurely and died a few days later. Suddenly the tone of her journal changes – from reading lists and 'love in idleness' to grief.

> Monday March 6. Find my baby dead. A miserable day.
> March 9. Read and talk. Still think about my baby. 'Tis hard indeed for a mother to lose a child.
> March 13. Shelley and Clara go to town. Stay at home; net, and think of my little dead baby. This is foolish, I suppose. Yet whenever I am left alone to my own thoughts, and do not read to divert them, they always come back to the same point: that I was a mother, and am no longer.
> March 19. Dream that my little baby came to life again; and

that it had only been cold, and that we rubbed it before the fire, and it lived. Awake and find no baby. I think about the thing all day.

March 20. Dream again about my baby.[82]

Her recovery was very slow. She was pregnant again, almost at once. Shelley's annuity rose to a handsome £1,000 a year when his grandfather died. They moved to Bishop-gate near Windsor for the summer, and Shelley wrote his first major poem since leaving Harriet. It was *Alastor*, the epitaph to a young man who imagines that ideals alone are enough to sustain him through life; who deliberately for-sakes the joys and griefs of human love; and who perishes without his ideals being realised.

In January 1816, a healthy son, William, was born, and in the spring the whole family left for Geneva for a summer by the lakes, with Byron. One lonely, misty morning Byron challenged the Shelleys to a competition. 'We will each write a ghost story,' he suggested. The two accomplished authors dashed off trivial pieces. Mary, who had never written any-thing substantial before, won the competition outright with a story which was to become better known than anything ever written by Byron or Shelley. It was called *Frankenstein*. In a preface written fifteen years later, after Shelley's death, Mary explained how vital her relationship with Shelley had been to the writing of *Frankenstein*, indeed to the writing of anything: 'My husband was from the first very anxious that I should prove myself worthy of my parentage and enrol myself on the page of fame . . . He desired that I should write . . . that he might judge how far I possessed the promise of better things hereafter.'[83]

She had listened attentively to Shelley and Byron talking about the famous scientist and doctor Erasmus Darwin and his weird experiments with the human body. Her monstrous idea thus took shape. 'At first I thought of but a few pages – of a short tale, but Shelley urged me to develop the idea at greater length . . . but for his incitement it would never have taken the form in which it was presented to the outside world.'[84]

This picture emerges from all the records of Mary's relationship with Shelley over those years. He believed even more than she did in her ability and in her judgement. *Frankenstein* is the first, and perhaps the most marvellous, result. As her introduction points out, it was written at a time of great composure and content. How many more such stories might have come from Mary Shelley if that content had lasted.

It is the story of a brilliant young scientist who creates a ready-made, adult human being. The being's form is so vast and grotesque that he cannot find any place in human society. Despite his natural intelligence, kindness and sensitivity he is spurned by everyone, and he eventually takes revenge by slaughtering the loved ones of his creator. Reactionaries have pounced on the book as evidence of Mary's views about the hideous consequences of the revolution which her husband urged. Here, they cry, is Mary's belief that a Shelleyan revolution would lead to more violence and distress than existed before it. But that interpretation in no way describes how Mary felt about the world. At the time her political views were close to Shelley's. *Frankenstein*'s monster represents the potential in mankind – of co-operation and brotherhood on the one hand; of isolation, violence and ruin on the other. As the monster watches human beings from his hiding place, he is appalled: 'I learned that the possessions most esteemed by your fellow creatures were high and unsullied descent united with riches. A man might be respected with only one of these advantages, but without either he was considered, except in very rare instances, as a vagabond and a slave, doomed to waste his powers for the profits of a chosen few!'[85]

It is the *spurning* of the revolutionary image, rather than the image itself, which leads to catastrophe. If Mary did intend a political message in *Frankenstein* (and it is worth remembering that she wrote it for a ghost story competition; and that *Frankenstein*, as millions of people have since testified, is a very good story, regardless of its alleged message) she was warning of what can happen when people react with automatic horror to something strange.

The keynote of the story is not pessimism, though there is perhaps a caution, which Shelley could well have heeded, that behind every idealist there lurks a fanatic, that behind every revolutionary who cannot tolerate disobedience or dissent there lurks a dictator.

At any rate, Shelley was delighted with *Frankenstein*. Back in England for the winter, he spent many hours with publishers urging them to publish it, and eventually succeeded. He rejoiced in this proof of Mary's ability, which he had so consistently diagnosed. He urged her on with her reading, and her writing.

By the end of the year (1816), the Shelleys had moved into a house by the Thames at Marlow, where they spent the whole of 1817. This was perhaps the most settled period of Shelley's life. Little Willmouse, as their son came to be called, prospered. In September a daughter, Clara, was born. Both Shelley and Mary spent a great deal of time visiting lacemaker's cottages, where they discovered the awful effects of the post-war slump. Friends came and went from the cottage, especially Peacock and Hogg. The Shelleys made friends with Leigh and Marianne Hunt and were welcome guests at Hunt's house in Hampstead (where Shelley met Keats and Hazlitt).

In the spring Shelley promised Mary a poem by the end of the summer. It stretched him to the limit of his patience and his powers; when it was finished it was the longest of all his poems, *The Revolt of Islam*. It was dedicated in fourteen majestic verses to Mary, to her love, her comradeship and her contribution to the poem.

> Its doubtful promise thus I would unite
> With thy belovèd name, thou Child of love and light.[86]

The dedication traces the brief history of Shelley's and Mary's life together. Through poverty and through calumny,

> There is the wisdom of a stern content
> When Poverty can blight the just and good,
> When Infamy dares mock the innocent,
> And cherished friends turn with the multitude
> To trample: this was ours, and we unshaken stood![87]

There is a rapturous verse about Mary.

> Yet in the paleness of thy thoughtful cheek,
> And in the light thine ample forehead wears,
> And in thy sweetest smiles, and in thy tears,
> And in thy gentle speech, a prophecy
> Is whispered, to subdue my fondest fears:
> And through thine eyes, even in thy soul I see
> A lamp of vestal fire burning internally.[88]

After a reflection on Mary Wollstonecraft and on the French Revolution, the dedication ends where it began, with joy in the love which lightened the prevailing gloom:

> Truth's deathless voice pauses among mankind!
> If there must be no response to my cry—
> If men must rise and stamp with fury blind
> On his pure name who loves them,—thou and I,
> Sweet friend! can look from our tranquillity
> Like lamps into the world's tempestuous night—
> Two tranquil stars, while clouds are passing by
> Which wrap them from the foundering seaman's sight,
> That burn from year to year with unextinguished light.[89]

While the dedication of *Queen Mab* to Harriet four years previously had read uneasily, almost as if it were expected of the author, this one throbs with devotion. *Queen Mab* is an angry, sparkling denunciation of society and the principles upon which it is founded. *The Revolt of Islam* declares that man *and* woman, brother *and* sister, Thou *and* I, acting together can change the world, and can sustain even the pain and humiliation of counter-revolution. There is throughout the poem a confidence and ease of mind which is missing from almost all his other work. For that brief year at Marlow, Shelley and Mary started to realize in practice something of the principles of love which both had drawn up for themselves long before they met each other.

It was not to last. In March 1818 they were on the move again, this time to Italy. But in Venice, in September, the baby Clara died of a fever. Mary was swallowed up by grief. She kept up her reading, but was for many months impervious even to Shelley's soothing. The little group (Shelley, Mary, Claire and William) left Venice, spent a miserable winter in Naples, and then travelled on to Rome. There, in June 1819, little William, three and a half years old, fell ill and died in his father's arms.

Mary started her journal again a month later – on 4 August: 'I begin my journal on Shelley's birthday. We have now lived five years together; and if all the events of the five years were blotted out, I might be happy. But to have won, and then cruelly to have lost, the associations of four years, is not an accident to which the human mind can bend without much suffering.'[90]

The suffering was intense. She withdrew from everything, even the books which had comforted her through previous disasters. She described her withdrawal from Shelley in a short poem written soon after Shelley's death:

> My heart was all thine own – but yet a shell
> Closed in its core, which seemed impenetrable.[91]

And Shelley himself wrote in a notebook, which he kept hidden from her:

> My dearest Mary, wherefore has thou gone,
> And left me in this dreary world alone?
> Thy form is here indeed – a lovely one –
> But thou art fled, gone down the dreary road,
> That leads to Sorrow's most obscure abode;
> Thou sittest on the hearth of pale despair,
> > Where
> For thine own sake I cannot follow thee.[92]

The couple never again recovered what they had discovered together before their children's deaths.

He, meanwhile, mourned her loss, and lost no opportunity to cheer her up or soothe her distress. There were fleeting moments of the old content. In August 1820 they were at San Guiliano, during a fair. Mary wrote later: 'Shelley read to us his *Ode to Liberty*; and was riotously accompanied by the grunting of a quantity of pigs brought for sale to the fair. He compared it to the "chorus of frogs", in the satiric drama of Aristophanes; and, it being an hour of merriment, and one ludicrous association suggesting another, he imagined a political-satirical drama on the circumstances of the day, to which the pigs would serve as chorus.'[93] From that hilarious moment, the hilarious *Swellfoot the Tyrant* was conceived and written.

At Pisa, in 1821, Mary reported: 'Shelley's birthday. Seven years are now gone; what changes! What a life! We now appear tranquil. . .'[94] Evidence of this tranquility is a beautiful little poem which Shelley wrote at San Guiliano in the spring of 1821:

> 'Do you not hear the Aziola cry?
>   Methinks she must be nigh,'
>   Said Mary, as we sate
> In dusk, ere stars were lit, or candles brought;
>   And I, who thought
>   This Aziola was some tedious woman,
>   Asked, 'Who is Aziola?' How elate
> I felt to know that it was nothing human,
>   No mockery of myself to fear or hate;
>   And Mary saw my soul,
> And laughed, and said, 'Disquiet yourself not;
>   'Tis nothing but a little downy owl.'[95]

This poem reveals a source of some conflict between Mary and Shelley during those last sad years. In her grief and loneliness Mary yearned for company – any company, but particularly 'society' company, English or Italian. She was not at all content in the company in which Shelley revelled – that of a few friends, including always Claire, living on top of one another in the same house. She especially hated the house at Lerici, on the Bay of Spezia, in which another

child, Percy Florence, was born, and in which she was living
when Shelley was drowned.

Shelley hated 'society'. He was, all his life, terrified by
bores of every description. He implored Mary and implored
the others in the house to implore her, not to force him to
go to parties – or indeed anywhere where he might be
waylaid by bores.

Yet the relationship survived. There was never any question of Shelley deserting Mary as he had deserted Harriet.
He had lost Mary's passion and her political comradeship,
but their love ran deep, and could well have come to the
surface again.

Proof of that is the terrible effect on Mary of Shelley's
drowning in the summer of 1822. It was two and a half
months before she could lift a pen again to write, and what
she wrote then was so racked by grief that it is almost
impossible to read: 'I have no friend. For eight years I
communicated, with unlimited freedom, with one whose
genius, far transcending mine, awakened and guided my
thoughts. I conversed with him; rectified my errors of
judgement; obtained new lights from him; and my mind
was satisfied. Now I am alone, oh how alone!'[96] The journal
is entirely different to the succint record it was before. Again
and again she breaks out in cries of agony:

October 7, 1822. His voice can no longer be heard; the earth
no longer receives the shadow of his form; annihilation has come
over the appearance of the most gentle creature that ever breathed
the air. . .

October 19, 1822. When in company with Albe [Byron] I can
never cease for a second to have Shelley in my heart and brain
with a clearness that mocks reality – interfering even by its force
with the functions of life – until, if tears do not relieve me, the
hysterical feeling analagous to that which the murmur of the sea
gives me, presses painfully upon me.[97]

Nineteen months later she is writing:

May 15, 1824: Can I forget his attentions and consolations to
me during my deepest misery? Never.

May 17, 1826: Great God! If there be any pity for human suffering, tell me what I am to do. I strive to study, I strive to write, but I cannot live without loving and being loved, without sympathy; if this is denied to me I must die. Would that the hour was come.[98]

The agony of grief persecuted her relentlessly for nearly twenty years. Had it not been for little Percy Florence, she would certainly have killed herself.

Instead, she set herself assiduously to editing Shelley's poems. She had to negotiate and wheedle with the old brute Sir Timothy Shelley, who continued to treat her as the slut with whom his atheist son had run away. From time to time, to keep the little bit of money which Sir Timothy allowed to his grandson and heir, she acceded, in doubt and distress, to his mean censorship of his son's poems (though in almost every case she quickly put the deleted passage back again). Her notes and commentary to the first complete edition of Shelley's poems (1839) are handsomely written, and an honest, intimate account of the man she loved.

If Shelley's abandonment of Harriet was an ugly caricature of his attitudes to women in society, his life with Mary came much closer to them. That life with Mary, from first to last, was shared with another woman, Claire Clairmont.

Claire was the daughter by an earlier marriage of William Godwin's second wife. She was slightly younger than Mary, and grew up in the Godwin household alongside her. When Claire was eighteen, most young London women of decent birth had fantasies about Lord Byron. Byron's poems – many of them mockeries of the adoration and hysteria they provoked – were read aloud at balls and tea parties where women swooned, or pretended to swoon, at every verse. Claire, never much of a swooner, decided to do something about it. She got herself an introduction to Byron and coolly proposed that they become lovers. She believed in free love, she explained, and she intended to act by it. Byron, amused and attracted, responded. There followed a short love affair, in which Claire became pregnant. But Byron expected women,' whether or not they believed in free love, to respect his genius, satisfy his lust and keep quiet. He soon grew testy at Claire's fractious independence, and threw her over. Soon after their daughter Allegra was born, he took responsibility for his daughter and banned Claire even from seeing her. Eventually, on Byron's orders, Allegra was sent to a convent, where she died, ill and neglected, at the age of five.

Claire was in close contact with Shelley for the last eight years of his life. She accompanied him and Mary when they eloped to France in 1814. She lived with Shelley and Mary for much of their remaining time in England. She travelled with them to Switzerland in 1816, where she briefly continued her affair with Byron. When the Shelleys left for Italy in 1818, Claire went with them. For most of the four years in Italy, Claire lived in the same house as Shelley and Mary.

Almost from the beginning, Shelley enjoyed Claire's company. Her temperament, with its sudden, darting enthusiasms and dejections, matched his. Like him, and unlike Mary, she was quickly bored and irritated by formal social occasions, especially parties.

One example of the difference between the two women was their attitudes to William Cobbett. When she started to read Cobbett, at Marlow in 1817, Mary was shocked. In a letter to Shelley in London she wrote: 'Have you seen Cobbett's 23 No. to the Borough mongers. Why he appears to be making out a list for a proscription – I actually shudder to read it – a revolution in this country would not be *bloodless* if that man has any power in it. He is I fear somewhat of a Marius perhaps of a Marat – I like him not – I fear he is a bad man. He encourages in the multitude the worst possible human passion *revenge* . . .'[99]

This attitude to Cobbett can be found in some of Shelley's writings at the time and soon afterwards. Claire did not agree with it. She enjoyed Cobbett's *Registers*. She went on reading them in Italy in 1819. On 13 March 1819, for instance, Claire's journal records: 'Read Cobbett, which is a strange book to read with one's head full of the ruins of Rome.'[100] Whenever books arrived from England, they always included some of Cobbett's *Registers* and his other books, which Claire leapt upon and read avidly. During this time, Shelley began to change his mind about Cobbett, and grew to enjoy him more and more.

Claire read Tom Paine and other radical writers of the time with equal enthusiasm. Her journals in Italy are full of political asides. She quoted with approval an extract from Paine's 'Crisis' papers about the savagery of the British army in India under General Clive. She inveighed against the 'putrefaction, creeping, crawling worms'[101] of Italian feudal society. She commented more and more frequently on the exploitation of the poor by the rich. She refers, no doubt repeating Cobbett, to the 'great robbery' – the interest on the national debt.[102] In Pisa, in September 1920, she wrote a long attack on what she called 'the language of bankers'. In particular she attacked the Austrian empire's habit of burning currency and therefore devaluing it. 'Judge,' she writes to herself in her journal, 'of the enormous sum thus stolen out of the people's pocket.'[103]

She followed with interest and excitement the risings in Naples and Sicily against the Austrian empire. She and Shelley would go out each day to find out news of the rebellions. She encouraged Shelley in his more revolutionary ideas, and was always arguing with Mary not just about domestic matters but also about politics. Her sharp, if flimsy, radicalism contrasted with Mary's more cautious reformism.

Claire understood, as of course Mary did, that Shelley's political ideas were crucial to his poetry and to his genius. In 1878, when Claire was eighty, she was interviewed in Florence by William Graham, a young fop of the English literary establishment. Graham mouthed the conventional view that Shelley's only fault was his politics. 'A pity Shelley wasted so much of his short life over matters that did not relate to his art at all,' he volunteered.

'Ah, but you are wrong there!' Claire replied. 'Had it not been for his intense love of mankind, that fervid zeal of his which could not content itself with poetry alone, he would never have been the great poet you admire!'[104]

She was defiant in defence of her independence and contemptuous of any suggestion that she was there to adorn the 'great men' among whom she had lived. When the drivelling William Graham begged her to talk to him of the 'golden days of passion and all the glamour of romance':

'A pretty background,' she replied dreamily, as though her thoughts were far away in some other world, 'but life has been so long, so wearisome, after all,' she said; and then, as if suddenly wakening from a reverie, 'a woman's life is not intended merely to serve as part of a *mise en scène* for the tableaux of a poet's career, however great he may be; my life was worth as much as his.'[105]

Shelley's interest in Claire was by no means confined to admiration for her sharp tongue or to political agreement with her. At Marlowe in 1817, Claire used to sing to the company in the evenings. One evening, Shelley wrote the singer a poem. It was called 'To Constantia, Singing'. Its meaning is beyond doubt.

> Her voice is hovering o'er my soul—it lingers
>   O'ershadowing it with soft and lulling wings,
> The blood and life within those snowy fingers
>   Teach witchcraft to the instrumental strings.
> My brain is wild, my breath comes quick—
>   The blood is listening in my frame,
> And thronging shadows, fast and thick,
>   Fall on my overflowing eyes;
> My heart is quivering like a flame;
>   As morning dew, that in the sunbeam dies,
>   I am dissolved in these consuming ecstasies.[106]

No wonder that Shelley would not let Mary see the poem before he dispatched it, anonymously, to an Oxford newspaper, where it was published.

In the upper right-hand corner of the last page of the manuscript, Shelley wrote eight more lines to his lovesickness:

> To thirst and find no fill – to wail and wander
> With short unsteady steps – to pause and ponder—

To feel the blood run through the veins and tingle
Where busy thought and blind sensation mingle;
To nurse the image of unfelt caresses
Till dim imagination just possesses
The half-created shadow, and, clasping air,
To find the form, then all the night
Sick . . .[107]

The lines, in a shortened and less vivid form, were eventually stuffed into the mouth of the lascivious priest, Orsino, in Shelley's play *The Cenci*. From Orsino they sound listless, almost nauseating. But in the context of Shelley's feelings for Claire they take on a new meaning. Shelley was not just fond of Claire. He did not just enjoy her company or his political conversations with her. He *wanted* her. He was sick with wanting her.

Mountains of posthumous speculation have been written as to whether or not Claire and Shelley ever had sex with one another. They were accused of this by their maid Elise, who was with them for three weeks in the late summer of 1818 at Byron's villa at Este. Richard Holmes's view[108] is that Elise's accusation was justified, and that a child was conceived which Claire miscarried in Naples four months later.

One piece of evidence that the couple did make love at Este is a letter written to Claire only a week after leaving Este – telling her of the death of his baby daughter. 'All this is miserable enough—is it not? but must be borne,' he writes, in conclusion.[109] Then there is a line crossed out, which reads: 'Meanwhile forget me and relive not the other thing.'[110]

No one will ever know for certain about this, and it does not really matter. What does matter is that the relationship between Claire and Shelley was certainly no cheap affair. From the outset, during those honeymoon wanderings in Europe, Shelley developed a deep affection for Claire, which was warmly reciprocated. He went to the most extravagant lengths to persuade his friend Byron to behave with some generosity over his daughter by Claire, Allegra (Byron responded instead with consistent brutishness). He wrote countless letters to Byron on the subject, and even arranged all his family's movements around Claire's desire to see Allegra.

During the worst period of Mary's depression, Shelley's affection for and dependence on Claire grew stronger. When Claire was forced out by Mary's jealousy and bad temper, Shelley wrote to her again and again:

29 October 1820: You know, . . . whatever you shall determine on, where to find one ever affectionate Friend, to whom your absence is too painful for your return ever to be unwelcome.[111]

15 November 1820: How I long to see you again, and take what care I can of you—but do not imagine that if I did not most seriously think it best for you that I would advise you to return. . . . May it [my life] be prolonged that I may be the source of whatever consolation or happiness you are capable of receiving! . . .

Adieu, dearest—be careful to tear this letter to pieces as I have written [confidentially?].[112]

11 December 1821: I should be very glad to receive a confidential letter from you—one totally the reverse of those I write to you; detailing all your present occupation & intimacies, & giving me some insight into your future plans. Do not think that my affection & anxiety for you ever cease, or that I ever love you less although that love has been & still must be a source of disquietude to me.[113]

The 'source of disquietude' had just appeared in the loveliest passage Shelley wrote about Claire – in the *Epipsychidion*:

Thou too, O Comet beautiful and fierce,
Who drew the heart of this frail Universe
Towards thine own; till, wrecked in that convulsion,
Alternating attraction and repulsion,
Thine went astray, and that was rent in twain;
Oh, float into our azure heaven again![114]

Was Claire, then, a rival to Mary? Mary certainly thought so sometimes. Her understandable irritation at the constant presence of Claire bursts out again and again. Typical of her diary entries is one on 8 June 1820: 'A better day than most days, and good reason for it . . . Claire away at Pugnano.'[115] Claire herself in her journals wrote more poetically:

> Heigh Ho The Claire and the Ma
> Find something to fight about every day.[116]

Shelley was confused and irritated by the hostility between the two women. His love for Mary was of a different texture and went deeper than his affection and attraction for Claire, yet he looked on neither woman (nor on any other woman in his life) as a rival to anyone. If he did make love to Claire at Este or afterwards it was not because his love for Mary had dimmed. He wrote Mary love letters and love poems from Este, for he was openly and sincerely disturbed by her absence. He believed and acted quite consistently by the 'love principle' he laid down in *Epipsychidion*: 'That to divide is not to take away.'[117]

He spent a lot of his life searching for a commune in which he and his friends of both sexes could live and share their passions and their thoughts. He was always happiest when the house he lived in was full of his friends, as at Lerici shortly before he died when his house was shared by his friends Edward and Jane Williams, both of whom he loved.

He did not suffer from jealousy, and did not understand it. Much sport has been made of a passage in one of his letters to Elizabeth Hitchener, dated 8 November 1811, in which he complained bitterly that his friend Hogg had tried to 'seduce my wife'.[118] This is often taken as proof that Shelley was jealous of his wife's chastity, jealous even of his closest friend. But the passage means something quite different. Shelley was not in the least upset that his best friend should make love to his wife. On the contrary, as Geoffrey Matthews has shown, he wrote a poem to Harriet in 1814 begging her to be a little less frosty to Hogg's advances:

> For pale with anguish in his cheek,
>   His breath comes fast, his eyes are dim;
>   Thy name is struggling ere he speak;

> Weak is each trembling limb.
> In mercy let him not endure
> The misery of a fatal cure.[119]

His horror was that Hogg should try to *seduce* his wife; to lure her to bed as though she were some society hanger-on, rather than a friend and an equal.

A common criticism of Shelley's attitude towards women is that he *idealized* them. He was, it is said, constantly on the search for the 'perfect woman' and the 'perfect love', and when his search was frustrated, he reacted bitterly and rudely. There are signs of this in his letters to Elizabeth Hitchener, to whom he wrote long, argumentative and passionate letters during 1811 and 1812. When Miss Hitchener finally came to stay with Shelley and Harriet, Shelley quickly became disillusioned and sent her packing.

In 1820, he met a young girl in a convent in Pisa and instantly fell in love with her. He wrote her the glorious love poem, *Epipsychidion*:

> Soft as an Incarnation of the Sun,
> When light is changed to love, this glorious One
> Floated into the cavern where I lay,
> And called my Spirit, and the dreaming clay
> Was lifted by the thing that dreamed below
> As smoke by fire, and in her beauty's glow
> I stood, and felt the dawn of my long night
> Was penetrating me with living light.
> I knew it was the Vision veiled from me
> So many years—that it was Emily.[120]

The vision didn't last long. A year later, and only a few weeks before his death, Shelley wrote to John Gisborne 'The "Epipsychidion" I cannot look at; the person whom it celebrates was a cloud instead of a Juno; . . . I think one is always in love with something or other; the error, and I confess it is not easy for spirits cased in flesh and blood to avoid it, consists in seeking in a mortal image the likeness of what is perhaps eternal.'[121]

It is, indeed, *not* easy for 'spirits cased in flesh and blood' to avoid such searching. No doubt Shelley was always searching for his perfect love. But this did not mean that he treated the women he knew and liked with disrespect or with other-worldly adoration. He was constantly attentive to the cares and worries of these women, often in strikingly practical ways. When Mary suffered her last, terrible mis-carriage at Lerici, while the rest of the household stood by in panic, and when it was clear that a doctor could not be fetched in time, Shelley prepared a bath of ice and plunged Mary into it, unquestionably saving her life. Again, his letters to Byron over Allegra are full of practical advice about what was the best course for the child. In contrast to the many ethereal dreams (as at the end of *Epipsychidion*) of sailing away in boats with a loved one and making love eternally under the stars, we can get some glimpses of what he really liked doing, and could do, in the real world with real people. In a wonderful poem to Maria Gisborne, who, with her husband, befriended the Shelleys in Italy, he wrote of his utopia:

> Though we eat little flesh and drink no wine,
> Yet let's be merry: we'll have tea and toast;
> Custards for supper, and an endless host
> Of syllabubs and jellies and mince-pies,
> And other such lady-like luxuries,—
> Feasting on which we will philosophize![122]

Similarly, although some of his descriptions of sex are idealized, he was not above very ordinary flirtations with some of the young women who came to stay.

To Sophie Stacey, a young cousin, who attracted him, he wrote a poem with such simple imagery that she could not have misunderstood it. It was called 'Love's Philosophy' (1819).

> The fountains mingle with the river
>   And the rivers with the Ocean,
> The winds of Heaven mix for ever
>   With a sweet emotion;

> Nothing in the world is single;
>   All things by a law divine
> In one spirit meet and mingle
>   Why not I with thine?—
>
> See the mountains kiss high Heaven
>   And the waves clasp one another;
> No sister-flower would be forgiven
>   If it disdained its brother;
> And the sunlight clasps the earth
>   And the moonbeams kiss the sea:
> What is all this sweet work worth
>   If thou kiss not me?[123]

After Sophie had bidden him 'Good Night', Shelley wrote
a poem the following day with an even more straightfor-
ward proposition:

> Good-night? ah! no; the hour is ill
>   Which severs those it should unite;
> Let us remain together still,
>   Then it will be *good* night. . . .
>
> To hearts which near each other move
>   From evening close to morning light,
> The night is good; because, my love,
>   They never *say* good-night.[124]

Whether Sophie Stacey responded to this cheerful humbug
is not known. Nor does it matter very much. Shelley himself
wrote to Leigh Hunt (?20 December 1818): 'I never will be
a party in making my private affairs or those of others topics
of general discussion; who can know them but the actors?
And if they have erred, or often when they have not erred,
is there not pain enough to punish them?'[125]

There is an element of prurience in any close examination
of Shelley's personal relations, even though so much of what
he thought and felt about them are laid bare in his poetry.
But people's personal behaviour can never be entirely disas-
sociated from their ideas. Few socialists are stockbrokers,
and a wife-beater makes a poor feminist. On almost any
test, including the testimony of everyone who knew him,

including Peacock, his most severe and honest critic, Shelley in his relationships with women strove to live up to his own high ideals.

Byron wrote to his friend Moore after Shelley's death: 'As to poor Shelley, who is another bugbear to you and the world, he is to my knowledge the *least* selfish and the mildest of men – a man who has made more sacrifices of his fortune and feelings for others than any I have ever heard of.'[126]

Byron must have been thinking, at least partly, of Shelley's interest in and respect for women. Byron himself had written:

> Women are but the margin of our lives:
> The course flows on unheeded.[127]

That was not Shelley's view, nor did it guide Shelley's behaviour. He enjoyed and respected the company of women. He detested puritans *and* pornographers. He was never ashamed or embarrassed by sexual attraction, nor was he dominated by it. He noticed to his horror that the conventions of society demanded that women be both glamorized and patronized. He did neither. He was willing to learn from his women friends and lovers, and in the process all his ideas were enriched and strengthened. It was not just Shelley's own abilities, but the intelligence and the emotions of Harriet Shelley, Mary Shelley, Claire Clairmont, Elizabeth Hitchener, Jane Williams, Cornelia Boinville, Marianne Hunt, Maria Gisborne, Sophie Stacey and even Emilia Viviani which enabled Shelley so eloquently to express the ideas of the Marquis de Condorcet and the other feminist writers of the French Revolution and so confidently to fling them forward into a century of Victorian prudery, masculine supremacy and make-believe love.

IN HISTORY

The discussion of women's equality in the French Revolution had been dominated almost exclusively by the Revolution's right wing, by the middle classes. Condorcet, Madame Roland, Brissot and the other writers about women's equality associated themselves with the Gironde, the party of the businessmen and the merchants. The Montagne, the party of Marat, Robespierre and the Paris masses, is associated, not altogether fairly, with an almost opposite view.

This curious polarization between Left and Right has persevered. It can be dimly detected in the history of the British Labour movement. The Left has often inclined to the view that 'working class struggle' is far too serious a matter for 'women's issues'; that 'women's issues' arise from 'personal politics' which have nothing to do with the 'real struggle' to change society in a socialist direction. Symbolically, one of the few British biographers of Marat, the 'left-wing' Belfort Bax, a leader of the Social Democratic Federation, is also one of the most disgusting male chauvinists in the history of British socialism. Challengers for that title include many other leaders of the allegedly 'Marxist' Left in the early British socialist movement, in particular H. M. Hyndman and Harry Quelch, also leaders of the Social Democratic Federation. This tradition of 'tough', masculine socialists who put 'personal politics' on one side for the 'nitty-gritty' of the class struggle perseveres, though in a less aggressive form, in the Left today.

The absurdity of this hardly requires explanation. The oppression of women, in Shelley's day as now, eats away at the unity of working people. Among working men it promotes the bully; among working women obsequiousness and subservience. Among both men and women it militates against political involvement and in favour of the status quo. If society is to be transformed from below – a view normally associated with the Left – the fight against the values and priorities of male domination is inescapable. Vague theses on equality, even Equal Pay Acts or Sex Discrimination Acts which emerge from the goodwill of reformers, are no substitute whatever for agitation for feminist ideas among the masses.

That is Shelley's great contribution on this subject. He took the feminist ideas out of the drawing rooms of the Gironde and applied them to the mass movement. That is, I suspect, why *The Revolt of Islam*, the poem in which his revolutionary feminism is most apparent, has been perhaps the most systematically downgraded of all his major poems. Downgraded, that is, by respectable opinion, which adopted Shelley and separated him from his ideas. But not by all his readers. The posthumous influence of Shelley among working people has been buried both by his idolaters and by his detractors. His influence among women has been buried deeper still. But it is there all right, wherever and whenever women have fought for their rights.

Only three years after Shelley died, a powerful statement of the case for women's equality was published. It was called, rather cumbersomely, *Appeal on Behalf of One Half of the Human Race, Women, Against the Pretensions of the Other Half, Men, to Retain Them in Political and Thence in Civil and Domestic Slavery*. It was written by the Irish socialist William Thompson, whose economic theories earned him a glowing tribute in James Connolly's *Labour in Irish History*.[128] The *Appeal* is perhaps the most important and substantial published work setting out the case for women's equality and women's suffrage in the eighty years between Mary Wollstonecraft and John Stuart Mill. It would never have been written without the influence of a pioneer fighter for women's rights, Anna Wheeler.

Anna Wheeler had been married at the age of fifteen to a lout from the Irish aristocracy. She gave birth to and tended six children, four of whom died in infancy, while her husband lounged drunkenly in the stables, and at night demanded his 'rights'. During all those years, Anna Wheeler educated herself with whatever books she could get hold of from London. In particular she read Mary Wollstonecraft, some of whose pamphlets she learned to recite by heart.

In 1812 – ironically the year in which Shelley went to Ireland to start the revolution – she escaped to England, where she immediately fell in with radicals and 'utopian socialists' such as the Frenchmen Fourier and St Simon, and Robert Owen, who became a close friend. She and William Thompson became close friends. She opened his eyes to the women's cause. Thompson's passionate introduction to the *Appeal* makes it clear that many of his ideas – and not only his ideas about women – came directly from Anna.

Anna Wheeler almost certainly never met Shelley, but she read and proclaimed his more revolutionary poetry long before it was fashionable to do so. She ended one letter to Robert Owen: ' "Shall man be free and woman a slave" – and idiot? says Shelley. "Never, say I." '[129]

Another early admirer of Shelley was Caroline Norton, who started her married life as a celebrated society hostess, but was soon engaged in a prolonged battle with a vindictive husband whom she loathed. Norton made use of the law to take Caroline's children away from her. She fought back with a pamphlet, 'The Natural Claim of a Mother to the Custody of her Children as Affected by the Common Law Right of the Father'. Her agitation won from a grudging Parliament the Infants Custody Act, which allowed women custody over their children until the age of seven. Before that Act, men had an absolute right to do with their children as they pleased.

When Mary Shelley returned to England after Shelley's death, Caroline Norton sought her out, and the two women became friends and correspondents. Although Caroline was not in general a public advocate for women's rights, her letters to Mary Shelley are full of indignation about the treatment of her sex. The references to Shelley in the letters are few, but the influence of his ideas shines through them all.

At the same time, the poems and ideas of Shelley were having an effect in a way which was to prove even more substantial in the long struggle for women's rights.

Harriet Taylor was an almost exact contemporary of Caroline Norton. She was married at the age of eighteen to a radical city druggist called John Taylor. With her husband she frequented the circle around W. J. Fox, who edited the *Monthly Repository*. Of all the radical themes of the *Repository* the most pronounced was equal rights for women. One of the inspirers of this was Shelley.

It was at a meeting organized by Fox's circle that Harriet Taylor met John Stuart Mill, the brilliant son of the old politician and philosopher James Mill, who had detested the notion of women's equality. John was already moving towards a different opinion when he met Harriet, and fell in love with her. The love affair between the two grew in passion and intensity over a period of some twenty-five years. John Taylor, loved, respected and cared for by his wife, died of cancer in 1849, and soon afterwards Mill and Harriet were married.

All through her life, Harriet Taylor learned from Shelley. She passed on this enthusiasm to John Stuart Mill. In a draft of his *Autobiography*, Mill wrote: 'The first years of my friendship with her were in respect of my own development mainly years of poetic culture. I did cultivate this taste as well as a taste for paintings and sculpture and did read with enthusiasm her favourite poets, especially the one whom she placed far above all the others, Shelley.'[130] In the *Autobiography* itself he wrote: 'In general spiritual characteristics, as well as in temperament and organisation, I have often compared her, as she was at this time, to Shelley.'[131]

Shelley's ideas and Harriet's advocacy made a profound impact on the straight-laced and liberal John Stuart Mill. In 1848, he published the first edition of his *Political Economy*, one of whose original purposes was to denounce the ideas of socialism and communism. This part of the essay was not approved by Harriet, who remonstrated sharply with her friend and lover. As one writer on Mill put it: 'She told Mill to abolish, in the second edition, all his objections against Socialism and Communism. She demanded a complete reversal of his economic treatise in its most essential feature.'[132]

She won the argument. In his second edition, Mill wrote: 'On the Communistic scheme, supposing it to be successful, there would be an end to all anxiety concerning the means of subsistence: and this would be much gained for human happiness.'[133]

In another respect, Harriet's views were just as influential. Mill had absorbed the formal arguments in the Fox circle about equality of women. Harriet Taylor brought the arguments to life. The equality of his relationship with Harriet, perhaps more than anything else, convinced Mill that the issue of equality for women was perhaps the most important of his age, if not of any age. Only a few years after meeting, Mill and Harriet wrote essays which formed the basis of the essay 'On the Subjection of Woman', published in 1869, ten years after Harriet's death.

This majestic essay – perhaps the clearest statement of the case against women's banishment to 'hot house and stove cultivation' – is one of the very few pamphlets in our political history which heralded real social change. It gave birth to the long fight for the woman's vote. Mill himself was the founder of the first woman's suffrage society. He stood for Parliament on the issue of votes for women, won one election and lost the next. The influence of Shelley never left him. Years after Harriet Taylor died, Mill went to dine with Bertrand Russell's mother. She remembered: 'He read us Shelley's "Ode to Liberty", and he got quite excited and moved over it, rocking backwards and forwards and nearly choking with emotion. He said to himself: "It is almost too much for one." '[134]

The same influence can be found throughout the long battle for the woman's vote after Mill's death, which lasted sixty years. In her short summary of that battle, written in 1912 and called *Woman's Suffrage: A Short History of a Great Movement*; Millicent Fawcett, who had led the 'constitutional' movement for the woman's vote for three decades, wrote: 'The torch which was lighted by Mary Wollstonecraft was never afterwards extinguished. There are glimpses of its light in the poems of her son-in-law, Shelley. The frequent references to the principle of equality between men and women in the *Revolt of Islam* will occur to every reader.'[135]

Shelley was also popular during the suffragette agitation from 1906 to 1914. He was an early favourite of the Pankhurst family, of Emmeline and her daughter Christobel who led the Women's Social and Political Union in the heyday of suffragette militancy, and especially of Christobel's sister Sylvia who was not only a fighter for women's rights but also an active socialist. When her father Richard Pankhurst died, the Independent Labour Party built a hall in his memory in Salford. Sylvia, a young art student, undertook the interior design. The large hall walls were decorated with a series of panels, above which was flung in huge letters these lines from *The Revolt of Islam*:

> But Hope will make thee young, for Hope and Youth
> Are children of one mother, even Love—[136]

In 1909, the Women's Freedom League was formed as a breakaway from, though never in competition with, the W.S.P.U. Its president was Mrs Charlotte Despard, who had been a member of the Independent Labour Party. Unlike the Pankhursts, Mrs Despard refused to support the First World War when it was declared in 1914, and went to prison for her opposition to it. She also went to prison many times after demonstrations and disturbances during her fight for the woman's vote.

In a pamphlet produced by the Women's Freedom League about their president, the second paragraph was headed 'Influence of Shelley'. It ran:

Our President attributes her passion for social equality and justice of every kind to the poet Shelley. In this, however, I think she does the poet too great honour. Poets cannot create, though they may influence, minds. If Mrs Despard, who was but a young girl when she first made acquaintance with the beauty and mystery, the power and truth of Shelley's works, had not been born with a passion for righteousness, not even the greatness of a Shelley could have bestowed it. What the poet did was to show the need for reform. His teaching fired the faggot that was already there – and was lately to blaze forth with a mighty warmth of passionate indignation at the wrongs of humanity, and, beacon-like, illumine others with its own radiance.

Mrs Despard did not keep Shelley to herself. On 5 January 1908 she spoke in Cardiff on 'Shelley: the Poet of Revolution'. And two years later the *Vote*, the Women's Freedom Movement's weekly paper, reported a packed meeting held in the Freedom Hall, Bournemouth: 'Mrs Despard followed with an inspiring account of the New Woman, taking as her text Shelley's ideal in *Prometheus Unbound*. This address evoked such enthusiasm that it was proposed to hold a Shelley Commemoration in Bournemouth, in which Mrs Despard promised to take part, provided that a Women's Freedom League branch were formed in the town, through which a lot of the work could be done.'

A branch was formed, and a commemoration was held. Mrs Despard was called upon to speak again and again on Shelley and women's freedom. Her address at the Queen's Hall, London, on 6 November 1910, for instance, was one of the W.F.L.'s most successful and enthusiastic occasions. All the tickets were sold three weeks before the meeting.

Shelley influenced the women's movement all through the long sixty-year struggle for woman's suffrage all over the world. Olive Schreiner, for instance, the great South African feminist and socialist, loved Shelley. In one of her letters to Havelock Ellis, she asked: 'Did you ever read the passage in Shelley's letters where he talks about genius? *Genius does not invent, it perceives.* I think that is so wonderfully true, and more true the more one looks at it.'[137]

Even more intimately, to Mrs Francis Smith she wrote: 'If anyone showed me a lock of hair and said: "This is Wordsworth's", I should look at it and pass on; if they said it is Shakespeare's or Shelley's, I should stroke it, and if it was Shelley's, I should kiss it.'[138]

The influence of Shelley among women suffragists and

feminists is almost completely neglected today. It conflicts
with the Shelley cult, which grew up among the self-indul-
gent literary circles of high society in the 1880s and 1890s,
and which worshipped Shelley for his lovely lyrics about
women. These 'lovely lyrics' were written, so the cult pretended, so that men could more lyrically *adore* their women,
and more successfully seduce them.

Olive Schreiner's feelings were passed on to her admirers
among the feminist writers of the 1920s and 1930s. When
Vera Brittain's doomed fiancée asks her, in the televised
version of her first autobiographical account of the horrors
of the First World War, *Testament of Youth*, who is her
favourite author, she replies, 'Shelley, of course'. And the
influence of Shelley shines generously through all Vera
Brittain's long and prolific literary life. So it does too in that
of her friend, the novelist Winifred Holtby. And in a beautiful review in 1927 of Professor Walter Peck's huge biography of Shelley, Virginia Woolf singles out not so much
Shelley's literary qualities, of which she was not an uncon-
ditional admirer, but his effect upon the behaviour towards
each other of the men and women who read him: 'Shelley,
both as son and as husband, fought for reason and freedom
in private life, and his experiments, disastrous as they were
in many ways, have helped us to greater sincerity and happiness in our own conflicts.'[139] I doubt whether there has
been an epitaph which he would have treasured more.

Shelley's belief in free love was exploited to excuse chiv-
alry and seduction. Many young women in and around the
Shelley-worshipping cult found to their surprise and chagrin
that 'free love' was expected to mean 'free sex'. Shelley was
taken over by young men of radical mood who fancied
themselves as wonderful lovers. The political passion and
agitation which is so vital a part of Shelley's writing about
women was squeezed out of him.

The effect was devastating, not so much during the wom-
en's movement of the time, but later – and now. The cult
of Shelley worship was taken over and adapted by formal
education. Soppy love poems and lyrical idolizing were

selected by the textbook anthologies. Cythna of *The Revolt of Islam* vanished altogether. *Rosalind and Helen* were buried. Even Asia in *Prometheus Unbound* was relegated.

The Shelley cults which have grown up over the last hundred years have been dominated by men. The annals of the Shelley Society show very few women as members, let alone lecturers or contributors to discussion. Shelley's formal celebration has been left to men, young and old, who have fancied themselves as misty lovers; to male idolizers of women; to male literary lyricists; to vicars and parsons (all necessarily male); and to a few male socialists.

Yet the real Shelley, the red Shelley, the revolutionary Shelley, is not even primarily a man's poet. He was writing for women as few other male poets have written in the English language. If radical or revolutionary women can forget any Shelley which may have been quoted to them by lovers on the make, if they start to read where those lovers left off, then and only then can he set fire to some of the imaginations and agitations to which so much of his writing was directed.

6

Reform or Revolution?

'THIS NEED NOT BE'

'Don't worry yourself so much, old chap. It's only human nature. God put sin into people when they were born. He marked them with a badge of greed. So people are naturally selfish, naturally hostile to their fellow beings. It follows just as night follows day that the human race divides itself into kings and subjects, into rich and poor. That's the way it always has been, and the way it always will be. For well-bred and intelligent people like you to try to alter the pattern is a dangerous waste of time and talent.'

The argument came at Shelley from all sides: from school-masters, family and friends; from people like Byron and Peacock whom he admired and respected as much as from people whom he despised. Yet from the beginning he categorically rejected it.

Queen Mab, the most forceful of Shelley's propagandists, anticipated the 'human nature' argument, and turned it on its head. Tyranny or monarchy, she suggested, were the opposite of anything which could be called natural. They upset the equilibrium of humanity, and cramped all human potential:

> Nature rejects the monarch, not the man;
> The subject, not the citizen: for kings
> And subjects, mutual foes, forever play
> A losing game into each other's hands
> Whose stakes are vice and misery.[1]

According to the 'human nature' school, the 'vice and misery' could never be changed. They were part of a natural pattern, and there was nothing ordinary human beings could do about them. There was, then, no connection between the plight of human beings and their powers. In the face of famine and war, human beings were impotent, and therefore terrified. As Queen Mab and her charge, Ianthe, gazed down on the horrors of the world of 1812, Ianthe shivered. Queen Mab quickly resassured her:

> I see thee shrink
> Surpassing Spirit!—wert thou human else?
> I see a shade of doubt and horror fleet
> Across thy stainless features; yet fear not;
> This is no unconnected misery,
> Nor stands uncaused, and irretrievable.
> Man's evil nature, that apology
> Which kings who rule, and cowards who crouch, set up
> For their unnumbered crimes, sheds not the blood
> Which desolates the discord-wasted land.
> From kings, and priests, and statesmen, war arose, . . .[2]

And later on, more fiercely:

> Nature!—no!
> Kings, priests, and statesmen, blast the human flower.[3]

The idea that the 'human flower' was 'blasted' by some divine or natural force was *promoted* by 'kings, priests and statesmen' so that their power and wealth would be seen as part of an unalterable pattern, and therefore left alone. Those who submissively accepted this humbug were, according to Queen Mab, also flouting everything that was natural:

> When Nero
> High over flaming Rome, with savage joy
> Lowered like a fiend, drank with enraptured ear
> The shrieks of agonizing death, beheld
> The frightful desolation spread, . . .
> Think'st thou his grandeur had not overcome
> The force of human kindness? And, when Rome,

With one stern blow, hurled not the tyrant down,
Crushed not the arm red with her dearest blood,
Had not submissive abjectiveness destroyed
Nature's suggestions?[4]

But Shelley did not base his arguments for change on 'nature's suggestions'. Just as human nature could not be blamed for selfishness and greed, so it could not be called on to change it. People's behaviour to one another, Shelley noticed, was shaped not by natural instinct but by the political and economic circumstances in which they lived. When those circumstances changed, so did people.

This was not just inspired belief. It was founded on observation. When the Greek people rose against the Turkish empire in 1820, Shelley observed how people started to behave in the most unlikely way. In a footnote to his poem on the Greek rising, *Hellas*, he remarked: 'A Greek who had been Lord Byron's servant commands the insurgents in Attica. This Greek, Lord Byron informs me, though a poet and an enthusiastic patriot, gave him rather the idea of a timid and unenterprising person. It appears that circumstances make men what they are, and that we all contain the germ of a degree of degradation or of greatness whose connection with our character is determined by events.'[5]

A society like that in England in the second decade of the nineteenth century promoted 'the germ of degradation' until it grew into a plague. But, equally, human society could promote the 'germ of greatness', of co-operation and unselfishness, and reap a rich reward. The obstacles in the path of such a society were not natural or divine. They were human beings themselves – 'kings, priests and statesmen' for a start. The power of these people had to be removed. Monarchy, superstition, exploitation and masculine domination were all human; they could all be changed by human effort and endeavour. Queen Mab advised:

Let the axe
Strike at the root, the poison-tree will fall; . . .[6]

But *how*? What sort of axe, and what sort of blow? What sort of effort and endeavour? How could and should change be brought about?

REFORM

For most Shelley commentators, there are simple answers to these questions. Shelley, they tell us, was a 'radical', but he was a decent, respectable radical. He wanted to see reform carried out in the 'proper' way. He was a reformer in the same way that all the other great writers of the age – Byron, Keats, Southey, Coleridge, even Wordsworth and Leigh Hunt – were reformers. Like them, he hated injustice, but he was at the same time strongly opposed to removing injustice through the ferocious activity of a stirred-up mob.

And so Shelley is usually portrayed as a sort of Felix Holt before his time. Felix Holt, the hero of George Eliot's novel of the same name, was a thoroughly decent, respectable and disarming fellow who liked the people but was frightened of them when they were stirred up. He wanted reform, but slowly. He didn't even want to see the people trusted with the vote. In the end, he got caught up in a working class demonstration. He tried to head it off, but was shot. His has been the prototype nightmare of middle class radicals ever since.

This is the Shelley handed down to us by his worshippers. They have plenty of his writings to draw upon.

Shelley had little enough to say about the two great risings of his time – of the Luddites in 1812 and at Pentridge in 1817. But a lot of what he did write reeked of suspicion and doubt about 'the mob'. In the middle of the Luddite uprisings in May 1812, he wrote to Catherine Nugent in Ireland: 'I fear that hunger is the only excitement of our English riotings; any change which they may produce appears to me likely to be devoid of principle & method.'[7]

In January 1813, fourteen Luddite leaders were hanged at York Castle. Shelley was outraged. With her husband's agreement, Harriet Shelley wrote a letter on 31 January to the publisher, Hookham: 'I see by the Papers that those poor men who were executed at York have left a great many children. Do you think a subscription would be attended to for their relief? If you think it would, pray put down our names and advertise it in the Papers. Put down my Sister's name, Mr. Shelley's and mine for two guineas each . . ."[8]

Five days later, Leigh and John Hunt, the editors of the *Examiner*, were sentenced to two years' imprisonment and a fine of £500 each for publishing an attack on the Prince Regent. Shelley wrote to Hookham: 'Altho I do not retract in the slightest degree my wish for a subscription for the widows & children of those poor men hung at York yet this 1000£ which the Hunts are sentenced to pay is an affair of more consequence."[9]

This classic liberal formula – that the freedom to write is more important than the freedom to eat – was underwritten by Shelley even while he was writing his most revolutionary poem, *Queen Mab*.

His famous pamphlet on the second working class uprising of his time – the Pentridge rising of 1817 – compared the mourning for Princess Charlotte with the lack of mourning for the three Pentridge leaders executed at Nottingham. It is a powerful expression of fury at the hard-heartedness of wealthy society. It is also an exposé of the government's spy system. Yet the brunt of Shelley's attack on the spies was that 'they betrayed some innocent and unsuspecting rustics into a crime whose penalty is hideous death'.[10]

This is the standard liberal view of the Pentridge uprising: that good-hearted but rather dull working fellows were trapped by government spies into a pathetic attempt at a rebellion. The view has been laid to rest by Edward Thompson, who shows that the uprising was part of a widespread, planned revolt among the new working class. 'We may see the Pentridge rising,' Edward Thompson concludes, 'as one of the first attempts in history to mount a wholly proletarian insurrection, without any middle class support.'[11] With the carefully organized plans for that insurrection, and with the depth of feeling, solidarity and sacrifice which inspired it, Shelley had no contact whatever.

'You know what is meant by a mob,' he wrote in the
'Address to the Irish People'. 'It is an assembly of people
who without foresight or thought, collect themselves to
disapprove of by force any measure which they dislike. An
assembly like this can never do any thing but harm, tu-
multuous proceedings must retard the period when thought
and coolness will produce freedom and happiness, and that
to the very people who make the mob, . . .'[12]

By force. That was the point. Violence for political ends
shocked and horrified Shelley. And violence seemed to be
inextricably bound up with revolutions. 'The French Revolution,' he wrote (also in the 'Address'), 'although under-
taken with the best intentions, ended ill for the people;
because violence was employed, . . .'[13]

This view stayed with him to the end of his life. So
terrified was he of violence that much of his writing for the
masses was patronizing to the point of offensiveness. Here
is the 'Address to the Irish People' again: 'Temperance,
sobriety, charity, and independence will give you virtue;
and reading, talking, thinking and searching will give you
wisdom; when you have those things you may defy the
tyrant . . . Do your work regularly and quickly, when you
have done, think, read, and talk; do not spend your money
in idleness and drinking, which so far from doing good to
your cause, will do it harm.'[14]

'Thank you very much indeed, Sir,' the 'mob' might have
been expected to reply. Indeed, there is a lot in Shelley's
writing which suggests that reform was the job of the few
who had the time and the money to be cultured. He wrote
to Byron in November 1816: 'The whole fabric of society
presents a most threatening aspect. What is most ominous
of an approaching change is the strength which the popular
party have suddenly acquired, and the importance which the
violence of demagogues has assumed. But the people appear
calm, and steady even under situations of great excitement;
and reform may come without revolution.'[15]

Such change from above had to be, as he wrote in the
preface to *The Revolt of Islam*, 'slow and gradual'.[16] It could

not come all at once. Wise, cultured men would pass wise, cultured laws which would gradually transform war and chaos into peace and order. He wrote to Peacock in 1819: 'The change should commence among the higher orders, or anarchy will only be the last flash before despotism.'[17] And to Leigh Hunt, two months later: 'In the name of all we hope for in human nature what are the people of England about? Or rather how long will they, & *those whose hereditary duty it is to lead them*, endure . . .'[18] (Author's italics.)

In 1817, he wrote the 'Proposal for Putting Reform to the Vote' in which he *opposed* the vote for all adults in language which borders on snobbery:

With respect to Universal Suffrage, I confess I consider its adoption, in the present unprepared state of public knowledge and feeling, a measure fraught with peril. I think that none but those who register their names as paying a certain small sum in *direct taxes* ought, at present, to send Members to Parliament. The consequence of the immediate extension of the elective franchise to every male adult, would be to place power in the hands of men who have been rendered brutal and torpid and ferocious by ages of slavery.'[19]

These were the arguments of the liberals of the day. Reform, they agreed, was all very well, but politics had to be kept in the hands of the 'higher orders'. People like Shelley, for instance.

Shelley stood to inherit one of the biggest estates in southern England. From time to time, consideration for his property affected his political thinking. In July 1820 he wrote from Pisa to his wife:

Tatty is planning a journey to England to secure his property in the event of a Revolution, which he is persuaded is on the eve of exploding. I neither believe that, nor do I fear that the consequences will be so immediately destructive to the existing forms of social order. Money will be delayed, & the exchange reduced very low, & my annuity & Mrs. Masons on account of their being *money* will be in some danger, but land is quite safe— Besides, it will not be so rapid. Let us hope we shall have a Reform.[20]

And here ends the familiar, popular presentation of Shelley's politics – of the gentle, pacifist reformer, who liked to keep politics carefully sealed in the cultured élite to which he belonged; who loved liberty in the abstract, and the fight for liberty only when it took place in a land far distant from his own; who feared the violence of the rabble; whose politics fitted perfectly into the world of Leigh Hunt and Lord Byron, with whom, significantly enough, he was planning on the day of his death to· establish a monthly magazine called *The Liberal*.

This was the Shelley of whom his most devoted British biographer, Professor Edward Dowden, could write, without apparently a qualm of conscience: 'Shelley's *chief desire* was that the liberal movement in English politics should be kept within constitutional lines, and should be unstained by blood-letting or violence.'[21] (Author's italics.)

But there is another Shelley, a Shelley who emerges just as strongly from his writings as the cautious, reforming Shelley. This other Shelley contradicts the Dowden image in every particular.

REVOLUTION

For every quotation or reference in Shelley which proves his suspicions of the mob, his hatred of violence or his belief that political reform can only be accomplished gradually by constitutional means, there is another which proves the opposite.

'Shelley loved the people,' Mary Shelley wrote in a note to one of his poems. 'He believed that a clash between the two classes of society was inevitable and he eagerly ranged himself on the people's side'.[22] But this support for the people was not always cautious, and certainly not always demagogic. Again and again, Shelley wrote of the poverty-stricken masses of Britain and Ireland not just with affection but in the belief that they, not he and his class, held the key to human change and progress. There is a passage in *Queen Mab* which is very rarely quoted but which shows how, at

any rate at that time, Shelley found himself at loggerheads
with the liberal reformers:

> The man of ease, who, by his warm fireside,
> To deeds of charitable intercourse,
> And bare fulfilment of the common laws
> Of decency and prejudice, confines
> The struggling nature of his human heart,
> Is duped by their cold sophistry; he sheds
> A passing tear perchance upon the wreck
> Of earthly peace, when near his dwelling's door
> The frightful waves are driven,—when his son
> Is murdered by the tyrant, or religion
> Drives his wife raving mad. But the poor man,
> Whose life is misery, and fear, and care;
> Whom the morn wakens but to fruitless toil;
> Who ever hears his famished offspring's scream,
> Whom their pale mother's uncomplaining gaze
> For ever meets, and the proud rich man's eye
> Flashing command, and the heart-breaking scene
> Of thousands like himself;—he little heeds
> The rhetoric of tyranny; his hate
> Is quenchless as his wrongs; he laughs to scorn
> The vain and bitter mockery of words,
> Feeling the horror of the tyrant's deeds,
> And unrestrained but by the arm of power,
> That knows and dreads his enmity.[23]

This is the exact opposite of all his talk about the danger of
the mob. In this amazing passage it is not the mob which
will hold back advance and progress; it is the fireside reformers who like the idea of reform, but dread the idea of
the people taking it for themselves.

This is the inspiration which drags Shelley again and again
away from his liberal circle towards the masses. The prospect of mass action filled him with far more excitement –
and his poetry with far greater resonance and power – than
did the prospect of 'slow, gradual reform'.

In *The Revolt of Islam* he wrote:

> And earth's immense and trampled multitude
> In hope on their own powers began to look.[24]

And in *Hellas*:

> The Spirit that lifts the slave before his lord
> Stalks through the capitals of armèd kings,
> And spreads his ensign in the wilderness.[25]

When he was angered by specific acts of oppression in England, he stopped patronizing the mob and turned his scorn instead on the leaders who tried to hold them back. In November 1819, only a few months after writing to Peacock (as quoted on p. 166) that change had to come from the 'higher orders', he wrote to John and Maria Gisborne implying the precise opposite: 'But the people are nearly in a state of insurrection, & the least unpopular noblemen perceive the necessity of conducting [*sic*] a spirit which it is no longer possible to oppose. For submitting to this necessity—which be assured the haughty aristocrats unwillingly did—Lord Fitzwilliam has been degraded from his situation as Lord Lieutenant . . .'[26]

When he wrote to Peacock about the 'higher orders' he was musing in general on the state of English politics. When he wrote to the Gisbornes in contempt for Fitzwilliam and his noblemen, he was boiling with fury at the news of the massacre of Peterloo. A long string of shorter poems written at the same time bear testimony to that fury. Most of these were 'hate songs' directed against the Castlereaghs, the Eldons, the Sidmouths and the royal family. Often they ended with vaporous appeals, so common among political demagogues who duck the real issues. At the end of 'England in 1819', for instance, Shelley hopes for 'a glorious phantom' which will 'burst to illumine our tempestuous day'.

But other, lesser quoted, poems are direct and deliberate appeals to the masses to rise up and trample their oppressors. 'An Ode' (1819) starts with the lines:

> Arise, arise, arise!
> There is blood on the earth that denies ye bread![27]

One verse, not recommended for those who hold that Shelley was a pacifist, reads:

> Awaken, awaken, awaken!
> The slave and the tyrant are twin-born foes;
> Be the cold chains shaken
> To the dust where your kindred repose, repose:
> Their bones in the grave will start and move,
> When they hear the voices of those they love,
> Most loud in the holy combat above.[28]

But the most specific of the shorter poems, also written
in 1819, goes even further. It is addressed, clearly and simply, to the 'Men of England'. The instructions in it leave no
room for doubt – and no time to hang about waiting for the
Lord Fitzwilliams to get on with reforming legislation. First
the question:

> Men of England, wherefore plough
> For the lords who lay ye low?
> Wherefore weave with toil and care
> The rich robes your tyrants wear?[29]

Then the explanation:

> The seed ye sow, another reaps;
> The wealth ye find, another keeps;
> The robes ye weave, another wears;
> The arms ye forge, another bears.[30]

And then the appeal, the agitation:

> Sow seed,—but let no tyrant reap;
> Find wealth,—let no imposter heap;
> Weave robes,—let not the idle wear;
> Forge arms,—in your defence to bear.[31]

'*Forge arms in your defence to bear*!' And this from the Shelley
who pleaded again and again in his 'Address to the Irish
People' that the people should not resort to violence!
   Shelley's attitude to political violence was equivocal. In
theory and by instinct he was against it. He often imagined
himself, in the heat of revolutionary turmoil, pleading for
mercy for captive tyrants who had been overthrown. When,
in *The Revolt of Islam*, the revolutionary armies seize power

they are confronted by the tyrant emperor Othman, sitting alone in his palace accompanied only by his child. The mob, needless to say, clamours for blood:

> Then was heard—'He who judged let him be brought
> To judgement! blood for blood cries from the soil
> On which his crimes have deep pollution wrought! . . .'[32]

But Laon, the hero (Shelley in disguise), begs for mercy for the old king. Othman, he points out, is alone, powerless, and a human being with every bit as much right to life as any of his accusers. The 'mob' are persuaded, and Othman goes free.

The result is terrible. Using his freedom to regather his forces, 'the tyrant' soon returns with cavalry and artillery to hew down the revolutionary masses. In the massacre that follows, no one, least of all Laon, stops to question the wisdom of having allowed Othman to go free.

In the abstract, it seemed, Shelley was absolutely opposed to violence in such circumstances, however violent the consequences for the people he supported. This principle was put to the test in real life three years later in circumstances uncannily similar to those of *The Revolt of Islam*.

In July 1820, the noblemen and middle classes of Naples, outraged by the taxation without representation imposed by their Austrian imperial rulers, rose in revolt. As so often, the revolt sparked off a deeper revolutionary movement, in Naples' sister state, Sicily. The peasants and workers of Sicily found themselves fighting – quite without hope of victory – against Neapolitan troops, who in turn were in revolt against the Austrians. Unlike most liberals of the day, Shelley unconditionally supported the doomed Silician revolt agains the Neapolitan forces.

Encouraged by the split between Naples and Sicily, the Austrian generals launched an attack on Naples. The Neapolitans promptly seized Austria's puppet king of Naples, Ferdinand IV, and held him and his family as hostages. The Austrian government were informed that if war was declared on Naples, the King and all his family would be put to death. Shelley wrote of this action to Mary on 1 September 1820: 'A necessary, & most just measure when the forces of the combatants as well as the merits of their respective causes are so unequal. *That kings should be every where hostages for liberty were admirable.*'[33] (Author's italics).

No doubt Ferdinand, like Othman, was alone, pitiable and powerless. Around him in his death cell were his defenceless wife and charming children. Yet Shelley supported their incarceration, and would also have supported their execution as hostages. His non-violence in the abstract vanished in reality, not because Shelley hated violence any the less – he was horrified and disgusted by it all his life – but because he saw that there were occasions when the violence of the oppressor could only be countered by the violence of the oppressed.

In his gruesome play, *The Cenci*, Beatrice, the raped, wronged daughter of the ogre-nobleman Cenci, arranges the killing of her father by hired assassins. When they temporize about the killing, she urges them on. The play is written in unequivocal sympathy for Beatrice, even though the preface to the play moralizes against her and declares: 'the fit return to make to the most enormous injuries is kindness and forbearance'. In *The Assassins*, an allegory about a tribe of people who came out of Israel at the time of Christ and set up an ideal society, Shelley identifies himself unequivocally with the violence which counters the violence of tyranny:

Who hesitates to destroy a venomous serpent that has crept near his sleeping friend, except the man who selfishly dreads lest the malignant reptile should turn his fury on himself? And if the poisoner has assumed a human shape, if the bane be distinguished only from the viper's venom by the excess and extent of its devastation, will the saviour and avenger here retract and pause entrenched behind the superstition of the indefeasible divinity of man? Is the human form, then, the mere badge of a prerogative for unlicensed wickedness and mischief? Can the power derived from the weakness of the oppressed, or the ignorance of the deceived, confer the right in security to tyrannise and defraud? . . .

No Assassin would submissively temporize with vice, . . . His path through the wilderness of civilised society would be marked with the blood of the oppressor and the ruiner. The wretch, whom nations tremblingly adore, would expiate in his throttling grasp a thousand licensed and venerable crimes.

How many holy liars and parasites, in solemn guise, would his saviour arm drag from their luxurious couches, and plunge in the cold charnel, that the green and many-legged monsters of the slimy grave might eat off at their leisure the lineaments of rooted malignity and detested cunning. The respectable man—the smooth, smiling, polished villain, whom all the city honours; whose very trade is lies and murder; who buys his daily bread with the blood and tears of men, would feed the ravens with his limbs.[34]

One of Shelley's most familiar images is that of the volcano, representing the sudden upheaval of matter which has lain dormant for long periods. When he heard of the Spanish revolution of 1820, Shelley did not simply join in the general, liberal joy at the end of an old tyranny. He linked the Spanish revolution with the need for an English revolution, and a volcanic one at that:

> England yet sleeps: was she not called of old?
>   Spain calls her now, as with its thrilling thunder
> Vesuvius wakes Aetna, . . .[35]

When Laon, in *The Revolt of Islam*, decides to tread the path of reform, he does not seek to obtain a place in Parliament, nor to write a series of articles in the *Examiner*, nor to meet a Cobbett or join a Hampden Club. His resolve is of a different order:

>   —I will arise and waken
>   The multitude, and like a sulphurous hill,
> Which on a sudden from its snows has shaken
>   The swoon of ages, it shall burst and fill
>   The world with cleansing fire: . . .[36]

As Geoffrey Matthews shows in his wonderful essay 'A Volcano's Voice in Shelley',[37] these volcanoes are symbols of human revolution, of unused, dormant human capacity suddenly erupting and changing the face of society.

The 'thrilling thunder' of all those volcanoes continually drowns the more placid whine of Shelley's liberal reformism. The two noises, like the political theories they represent, are quite different, quite irreconcilable. Yet very often they occur in the same poem or pamphlet.

THE CONTRADICTION EXPOSED

Swellfoot the Tyrant

Swellfoot the Tyrant, written in 1820, is a satire on the Castlereagh ministry and its overthrow by a combination of Queen Iona (representing Queen Caroline) and the Pigs (the people). Shortly before the Pigs rise in revolution, the Spirit of Liberty appears to remind the Queen of the principles of non-violence so firmly adhered to by Shelley, the reformer.

> I charge thee! when thou wake the multitude,
> Thou lead them not upon the paths of blood.
> The earth did never mean her foison
> For those who crown life's cup with poison
> Of fanatic rage and meaningless revenge—[38]

This advice, however, is *not* accepted. At the instant of revolution the Pigs are turned into Bulls; the King and all his ministers into 'a number of filthy and ugly animals'. The Bulls line up for battle. A Minotaur arrives and asks the Queen to mount him and lead the charge. Iona, according to Shelley's stage directions, 'has been putting on boots and spurs, and a hunting cap buckishly cocked on one side'; tucking up her hair, she leaps nimbly on his back, yelling:

> Hoa! hoa! tallyho! tallyho! ho! ho!
> Come, let us hunt these ugly badgers down,
> These stinking foxes, these devouring otters,
> These hares, these wolves, these anything but men.

> Hey, for a whipper-in! My loyal Pigs,
> Now let your noses be as keen as beagles',
> Your steps as swift as greyhounds', and your cries
> More dulcet and symphonious than the bells
> Of village-towers, on sunshine holiday;
> Wake all the dewy woods with jangling music.
> Give them no law (are they not beasts of blood?)
> But such as they gave you . . .[39]

And so the play ends, in vengeful violence without a trace
of the forgiveness and forgetting which the Spirit of Liberty
had so eloquently invoked.

The Mask of Anarchy

There is a certain playfulness about *Swellfoot the Tyrant*, but
none at all about what Richard Holmes rightly describes as
'the greatest poem of political protest ever written in English':[40] *The Mask of Anarchy*. The ninety-two verses of *The
Mask* were written in hot indignation in September 1819,
immediately after Shelley heard the news of the massacre at
Peterloo. It is the most concise, the most popularly written
and the most explicit statement of his political ideas in
poetry.

It starts with a devastating attack on the Tory ministry.
In the seven verses quoted at the beginning of this book,
Shelley imagines, as if in a dream, the three English despots,
Castlereagh, Eldon and Sidmouth, gliding past him in
masks, disguised as Murder, Fraud and Hypocrisy. Castlereagh is feeding seven bloodhounds with human hearts.[41]
These are Britain's seven allies, whom Castlereagh appeased
at the Congress of Vienna after Waterloo by agreeing not
to press for the abolition of slavery.

At the back of the procession, leading his regiment from
behind, is Anarchy, who represents 'GOD, AND KING AND
LAW',[42] A 'mighty troop around', who take their orders
from Anarchy, ride through England tearing everything to
pieces and terrifying the people. They are met on the out-

skirts of London by a host of army officers, lawyers and priests, who fling themselves down in obeisance, muttering.

> . . .Our purses are empty, our swords are cold,
> Give us glory, and blood, and gold.[43]

Anarchy 'bowed and grinned' to them all, and sends his spies to launch a provocative assault on the Bank of England and the Tower of London (as Sidmouth's spies had provoked a handful of conspirators in 1816),

> And was proceeding with intent
> To meet his pensioned Parliament.[44]

The forces of God and King and Law represented by this grotesque parade seem omnipotent. They drown with their clamour every syllable of generosity or peace. But suddenly, just at the moment of their highest triumph, there rushes into their path 'a maniac maid'.

> And her name was Hope, she said:
> But she looked more like Despair, . . .[45]

The maid is at her wits' end. She yells out that her Father, Time, had watched all his children die in gloom and poverty, and was himself driven mad with disease and despair. She is the only child left. There is nothing for it but the most desperate direct action.

> Then she lay down in the street,
> Right before the horses' feet,
> Expecting, with a patient eye,
> Murder, Fraud, and Anarchy.[46]

But she is not run down. For suddenly in between her and the advancing horde, 'A mist, a light, an image rose.' It is 'small at first', but then 'it grew' into a great shape in armour, with luminous wings and a helmet which glistens like the sun. The image cannot really be seen by human beings, but they know it is there. It is the spirit of Hope,

mingled with the spirit of direct action. And it has the most
astonishing effect:

> As flowers beneath May's footstep waken,
> As stars from Night's loose hair are shaken,
> As waves arise when loud winds call,
> Thoughts sprung where'er that step did fall.[47]

'*Thoughts sprung.*' People start to think about their condition, and the way out of it. Nothing, in Shelley's view, is
more powerful.

> And the prostrate multitude
> Looked—and ankle-deep in blood,
> Hope, that maiden most serene,
> Was walking with a quiet mien:[48]

Before this, Hope was a 'maniac maid', who looked more
like despair. But now she becomes confident and serene.

> And Anarchy, the ghastly birth,
> Lay dead earth upon the earth;
> The Horse of Death tameless as wind
> Fled and with his hoofs did grind
> To dust the murderers thronged behind him.[49]

If Shelley had been a mere dreamer, the poem might have
ended there. The death of all that is horrible on earth, he
might have concluded, can be put to flight by mists and
images, or by abstract concepts such as Hope. But the poem
does not end there. It is only a third of the way through.
The bulk of the poem is a speech. Who makes the speech
is not quite clear, though the speaker is certainly female.

The words, the poem tells us, 'arose' as if the very earth
had uttered them in an 'accent unwithstood', forced out by
the blood of English people that had fallen on it. But its
message, in contrast to the imagery which has given birth
to it, is practical. There are no more images – just plain,
blunt language which any working man or woman could
understand.

The speech has three sections, directed to the three questions all agitators must ask and answer. What is wrong? What would you put in its place? And what are you going to *do* to replace the former with the latter?

What is wrong? Or, as the speech puts it, what is slavery? That is easily answered. Slavery, she replies, is exploitation. It is, as we have seen, the consequence of one set of men having command over the labour of others, without any responsibility to them.

> So that ye for them are made
> Loom, and plough, and sword, and spade,
> With or without your own will bent
> To their defence and nourishment.[50]

Exploitation brings poverty and homelessness:

> 'Tis to see your children weak
> With their mothers pine and peak,
> When the winter winds are bleak,—
> They are dying whilst I speak.[51]

Exploitation means robbed labour, far more valuable than anything stolen from the poor in the 'tyrannies of old'. But above all, it means the crushing of the human spirit in the interests of a few purses:

> 'Tis to be a slave in soul
> And to hold no strong control
> Over your own wills, but be
> All that others make of ye.[52]

What would you put in its place? Freedom, of course. And what is freedom? It is bread and clothes and warmth. It is 'a check' on the rich. It is a system of law which favours no one above another and 'shieldst alike the high and low'. It is a secular society, where people are free to believe what they like about religion. It is peace. It is based on 'science, poetry and thought . . .'

> Spirit, Patience, Gentleness,
> All that can adorn and bless
> Art thou—[53]

But stop! Shelley stops himself in mid-verse, for he knows that as soon as an agitator gets carried away with verbal descriptions of his ideal, he will lose his audience and his key to success. The verse goes on:

> Let *deeds, not words*, express
> Thine exceeding loveliness.[54] [Author's italics.]

The last twenty-six verses of the poem are about these 'deeds, not words'. They begin with a call for a demonstration:

> Let a great Assembly be
> Of the fearless and the free[55]

Who would come to this demonstration?

> From the workhouse and the prison
> Where pale as corpses newly risen,
> Women, children, young and old,
> Groan for pain, and weep for cold—[56]

Mingled with these people who have 'common wants and common cares' are a few 'from the palaces' who feel compassion for the exploited.

Inevitably, the poem continues, such a demonstration would provoke a reaction. The yeomanry would fall upon it firing their guns, flashing their bayonets and scything at the crowd with their scimitars. What should the crowd do then? Shelley gives two different answers. The first comes early on in the speech as he relives the horror of Peterloo and feels the fury rising.

> . . . the Tyrants' crew
> Ride over your wives and you—
> Blood is on the grass like dew.
>
> Then it is to feel revenge,
> Fiercely thirsting to exchange
> Blood for blood—and wrong for wrong—[57]

Blood for blood! The old cry of the Luddites suddenly seemed appropriate in revenge for Peterloo. Revenge at such times is natural, if not necessary. But, as Shelley reminds himself in the last line of the verse, revenge should only be *sought* by the weak, never *exacted* by the strong: 'Do not thus when ye are strong'.

The idea of the poor and the weak uniting and organizing around the cry for revenge did not upset Shelley. The exaction of such revenge by successful – (and therefore powerful) – revolutionaries revolted him. Had he stuck to that formula, his practical advice to the masses might have been better than it was. But in his advice to the demonstrators, incitement to revenge is replaced by something rather different:

> Stand ye calm and resolute,
> Like a forest close and mute. . . . [58]

When the yeomanry charge,

> What they like, that let them do.

> With folded arms and steady eyes,
> And little fear, and less surprise,
> Look upon them as they slay
> Till their rage has died away. [59]

Such a tactic, Shelley suggests, would conquer the yeomanry. They would be *shamed* out of further repression. Women would point them out, and ridicule them. Acquaintances in the street would embarrass them by reminding them that they were among the monsters who had attacked an innocent crowd.

More practically, Shelley suggests, the passive resistance of the masses would split the yeomanry from the soldiers.

> And the bold, true warriors
> Who have hugged Danger in wars
> Will turn to those who would be free,
> Ashamed of such base company. [60]

There was some prospect of this. The soldiers at Peterloo had not joined in the slaughter. One or two senior officers had even intervened with the yeomanry to try to stop the charges. 'For shame, gentlemen,' one army officer had yelled at the magistrates, 'What are you about? The people cannot get away.' The soldiers, what is more, did not have the same quarrel with the masses as did the yeomanry. They were continuously bullied by the same sort of people as those who charged down the meeting at St Peter's Fields. Many soldiers were tired of discipline and susceptible to agitation. The splitting of the soldiers from the class who gave them orders was possible and potentially explosive.

This has since become an aim of revolutionaries all over the world, but at that time it was almost unheard of. That Shelley should have tried to engineer such a split shows how sharp was his tactical sense of action. He was not just for the idea of protest. He applied himself rigorously to the details of protest in action.

Yet, for all that, Shelley's was bad advice. Only rarely does passive disobedience change the course of governments and dictatorships, and then only when it is so widely used that it stretches beyond endurance the armed forces against whom it is ranged.

Such resistance would have had little effect on the British Tory government of 1819, for two reasons. First, the weapons used by the armed upper classes were far too savage to be resisted simply by courage and 'folded arms'. Swords and scythes kill people. Crowds do not stand 'calm and resolute' while some of their number are being killed. At Peterloo the only speaker who ever got to the platform, Henry Hunt, begged the crowd to stay still and resist passively, but his words were lost in the pandemonium. Shelley's exhortation,

> And let Panic, who outspeeds
> The career of armèd steeds
> Pass, a disregarded shade . . .[61]

was whistling in the dark. Panic inevitably sets in in such

circumstances, and the crowd is lost.

The second reason is even more powerful. The yeomanry had not been shamed by Peterloo. In towns and cities all over England the yeomanry gathered in uniform to pay tribute to their 'brave brothers of Manchester'. The violence of the yeomanry was fanned, not shamed, by their murderous successes at Peterloo. The class solidarity of the rich stiffened. Upper class women did not desert their menfolk. They praised them, and urged them on. And in spite of the few protests from officers at St Peter's Fields, there was no evidence afterwards of any disobedience in the army.

'Shame' only stops or alters a course of action where that course of action is susceptible to shame. Where people act in incidental or unexpected anger or distress, they can be shamed into changing their course. But the action of the yeomanry at Peterloo was not taken in panic or in sudden rage. It was planned in cold blood. In Edward Thompson's words, it was 'class war':[62] people with property lashing out in order to protect it. Such actions are not susceptible to shame. They have no morality save the 'morality' of holding on to property. They respond to no discipline except the discipline of force.

The only way the masses could have stopped the yeomanry at Peterloo was by pulling them off their horses, disarming them with as much violence as was necessary, and organizing an insurrection. Part of Shelley shrank from such a course, and sought a substitute, a 'practical solution', a campaign of passive resistance which he hoped would lead to reform. This solution drove him into appeals which he himself knew were hopeless:

> Let the laws of your own land,
> Good or ill, between ye stand,
> Hand to hand, and foot to foot,
> Arbiters of the dispute,
>
> The old laws of England—they
> Whose reverend heads with age are gray,
> Children of a wiser day;

> And whose solemn voice must be
> Thine own echo—Liberty![63]

This was preposterous – and Shelley knew it. He was an ardent reader of the work of 'down-to-earth' reformers like Francis Place, and other ancestors of what became the right wing of the trade union movement. The most powerful contribution these people made to the politics of the time was to dispel sentimental notions about the 'good old days' when 'the old laws of England' looked after the common folk. There had never been such laws, nor such a 'wiser day'. The law had always been an instrument in the hands of the people with property who controlled the government. The 'old laws' had been just as cruel and unfair as the new ones.

The idea that the 'laws of your own land' should stand between oppressors and oppressed as 'arbiters of the dispute' directly contradicted what Shelley had written earlier in the poem about justice:

> ne'er for gold
> May thy righteous laws be sold
> As laws are in England . . .[64]

How could laws which were 'sold for gold' be 'arbiters of the dispute' between the armies of the rich and the demonstrations of the poor? The gentle Shelley now found himself contradicting his own analysis.

At the same time, the tough Shelley could not restrain himself. Immediately after the verse suggesting that the 'bold true warriors' would be split from the yeomanry by the masses' passive resistance he launches into his peroration, three clarion verses which have inspired revolutionaries all over the world for 150 years:

> And that slaughter to the Nation
> Shall steam up like inspiration,
> Eloquent, oracular;
> A volcano heard afar.

> And these words shall then become
> Like Oppression's thundered doom
> Ringing through each heart and brain,
> Heard again—again—again—
>
> Rise like Lions after slumber
> In unvanquishable number—
> Shake your chains to earth like dew
> Which in sleep had fallen on you—
> Ye are many—they are few.[65]

The tone of these verses is quite different to that of their predecessors. There is nothing passive about them; and the images are of fierce and sudden action. The reference to unvanquishable numbers implies that the people will win *in a fight* – for if there is no fight, and if they cannot vote, of what use are their superior numbers? These verses are not accidental, nor an exaggeration of what Shelley felt. The same insurrectionary theme is struck at the very beginning of the poem's revolutionary speech.

> Men of England, heirs of Glory,
> Heroes of unwritten story,
> Nurslings of one mighty Mother,
> Hopes of her, and one another;
>
> Rise like Lions after slumber
> In unvanquishable number,
> Shake your chains to earth like dew
> Which in sleep had fallen on you—
> Ye are many—they are few.[66]

For all the caution of his practical proposals, Shelley's chief anxiety was that the masses were apathetic, and that their apathy was the government's central prop. That was why the people had to *rise like lions* – even if the only action they should take, having risen, was to stand together waiting for slaughter like sheep.

The contradiction racks this, his most persuasive and agitational poem, as it racked Shelley himself. Was there not some way of ending the dictatorship's violence and atrocities without committing or provoking more violence and more atrocities, he continued to ask himself. Patiently, practically, he searched for such a course, straying occasionally into empty rhetoric in the process. But he never allowed this search to deflect him from his agitation of the masses out of their quietism and their acceptance of their fate. This clash – between the search for the 'patient course' and the demand for immediate, insurrectionary, action – was to occur again, three months after *The Mask* was finished, when he began to write down his ideas in detail for a political pamphlet.

A Philosophical View of Reform

'A Philosophical View of Reform' was written in a notebook in November and December 1819. It was never copied out or properly revised. The pamphlet, as we have already seen, develops Shelley's view of property, and of the emerging struggle between the 'new aristocracy', the capitalists, and the 'unrepresented multitude'. But the pamphlet was written as a manifesto. Its chief interest is in Shelley's proposals for reform.

The proposals are listed clearly: establishment of democratic government (abolition of monarchy and House of Lords, all power to an elected House of Commons); abolition of the standing army; abolition of sinecures; abolition of tithes and disestablishment of the Church; access to the courts for all, and trial by jury in all cases; and, finally, the most important in Shelley's eyes, the writing off of the national debt, to be paid for exclusively by the rich.[67]

This was a powerful programme, but how was it to be put into effect? Here the old 'reform or revolution' dilemma rises up again to dog Shelley. The first great issue was the reform of Parliament.

Immediately recollecting the sober purpose of his pamphlet, Shelley goes on to consider the 'first step to reform'. Should the vote be granted to everyone? Repeating the view expressed in his 'Proposal to Put Reform to the Vote' three years earlier, he declares that an 'immediate attempt' at universal suffrage appears to him 'immature'. In the next paragraph, he goes on to recommend what in practice *is* universal suffrage: a plan for 500 constituencies each with a population of about 40,000 and a male adult electorate of about 13,000.[68]

Should women get the vote? Shelley starts off, 'mature' and pompous as before: 'Mr. Bentham and other writers have urged the admission of females to the right of suffrage; this attempt seems somewhat immature.'[69]

The words stuck in his throat. Perhaps he recalled Cythna in *The Revolt of Islam*: 'Can man be free if woman be a slave?'[70] Can men vote for freedom, if women can't even vote? In the next sentence he apologizes, and almost withdraws: 'Should my opinion be the result of despondency, the writer of these pages would be the last to withhold his vote from any system which might tend to an equal and full development of the capacities of all living beings.'

How was it possible for the Shelley who wrote *The Revolt of Islam* and *Queen Mab* to find himself advocating a 'limited beginning' on the simple issues of universal and female suffrage? How could this rabid egalitarian advocate the vote only for people with 'a certain small property'?[71] Because he was determined to discipline himself to the argument for *practical* reform. If an extension of the franchise and the abolition of rotten boroughs could be conceded by the existing government, it was better, he argued, to settle for that than to run the risk of revolutionary violence.

So he takes the argument forward:

If the Houses of Parliament obstinately and perpetually refuse to concede any reform to the people, my vote is for universal suffrage and equal representation. My vote is—but, it is asked, *how shall this be accomplished*, in defiance of and in opposition to the constituted authorities of the Nation, they who possess whether with or without its consent the command of a standing army, and of a legion of spies and police officers, and hold the strings of that complicated mechanism with which the hopes and fears of men are moved like puppets? They would disperse any assembly really chosen by the people, they would shoot and hew down any multitude, . . . they would calumniate, imprison, starve, ruin and expatriate every person who wrote or acted, or thought, or might be suspected to think against them . . .'[72] [Authors italics.]

How indeed? Here Shelley accepts that under the existing government, indeed under any system where 'the minority' assumes power against the interests of the majority, 'a struggle must ensue'.

What forms will that struggle take? Shelley ticks off the possibilities. First, 'If the majority are enlightened, united, impelled by a uniform enthusiasm', then 'the struggle is merely nominal'. The powerful and the wealthy will see the forces united against them and 'divest themselves of their usurped distinctions'. The dream of every idealistic revolutionary will be fulfilled: 'the public tranquillity is not disturbed by the revolution.'[73] It all happens without trouble and without violence. Everyone lives happily ever after.

Shelley knew this was fantasy. He knew that long before any such 'divesting' of power took place the people would be 'panic-stricken and disunited' by their oppressors. 'The position of the conspirators, . . .' he concludes, 'may be tenable until the siege can be vigorously urged.'[74]

More had to be done than demanding reform and waiting for the government to concede. But what? Open parties declaring for reform needed to be formed; reform meetings needed to be held; demonstrations needed to be called. For one and a half pages Shelley repeats the fantasy of *The Mask of Anarchy* – that people who take part in demonstrations which are attacked should wait 'with folded arms the fire of the artillery'.

All this, he admits, 'might however be ineffectual to produce so uniform an impulse of the national will as to preclude a further struggle'. And here he dwells, in an extraordinary passage, on what he calls the danger of 'quietism'. Unless those who want change get together and agitate for it, the masses will sink into abjectness and despair.[75]

It is in vain to exhort us to wait until all men shall desire Freedom . . . It is in vain to hope to enlighten them whilst their tyrants employ the utmost artifices of all their complicated engine to perpetuate the infection of every species of fanatacism and error from generation to generation. The advocates of Reform ought indeed to leave no effort unexerted, and they ought to be indefatigable in exciting all men to examine.—

But if they wait until those neutral politicians, a class whose opinions represent the actions of this class, are persuaded that so soon [as] effectual reform is necessary, *the occasion will have passed or will never arrive,* and the people will have exhausted their strength in ineffectual expectation and will have sunk into incurable supineness.[76] [Author's italics.]

So Shelley constructs another list of agitations, even sharper than the last. They include publication in open defiance of the libel laws; refusal to pay taxes; the collection of monster reform petitions, written by the great writers of the age – Hazlitt, Godwin, Hunt, Bentham (perhaps even Shelley himself, though he was modest enough not to suggest it). All these forms of agitation, incidentally, were used by reformers and socialists later in the century, often to great effect. But still, as Shelley's argument forces him to admit, they might not work. Tyranny and oppression could well contain them all.

'Let us hope,' he writes, 'that at this stage of the progress of Reform, the oppressors would feel their impotence and reluctantly and imperfectly concede some limited portion of the rights of the people, and disgorge some morsels of their undigested prey.'[77] If such hopes were fulfilled, of course, it would be better to accept small reforms and wait for bigger ones than to take arms.

But if, as Shelley suspected, these hopes were not fulfilled, if the rulers considered 'the infamy of figuring on the page of history as the promoters of civil war preferable to resigning any portion . . . of their usurped authority', *then* there was only one alternative. The last section starts: 'The last resort of resistance is undoubtedly insurrection.'[78] He then wrote, and crossed out, the following sentence:

'Insurrection is, in certain emergencies, . . . not only an inalienable right, but is a duty from which no . . . temporary consequences can dispense us.'[79]

After the crossing out, Shelley breaks off to warn his readers again of the horrors of violence, and civil war. He concludes that 'the true friend of mankind . . . would hesitate before he recommended measures which tend to bring down so heavy a calamity as war'.[80]

But, and this is his final conclusion, there is *nothing for it*. 'I imagine however that before the English Nation shall arrive at that point of moral and political degradation now occupied by the Chinese, it will be necessary to appeal to an exertion of physical strength . . . If the madness of parties admits no other mode of determining the question at issue, . . .'[81]

Suddenly the manuscript breaks off. The words 'determining the question at issue' appear on the top of the left-hand page of Shelley's notebook. The whole of the rest of that page is left blank. So is the page opposite. The top quarter of the left-hand page overleaf is blank too. Then Shelley starts again: 'When the people shall have obtained, by whatever means, the victory over their oppressors . . .'[82] and the pamphlet dribbles away in yet more cautions against violence and revenge.

Shelley set out to write a moderate appeal to the masses to unite around demands for minimal reforms. He intended to curb his revolutionary passions and instincts. The pamphlet, he wrote to Hunt, is 'temperately written'.[83] The volcanoes were camouflaged under gentle, green hills. But the argument, almost to his surprise, led him not away from his passions and instincts but towards them.

We must, Shelley the reformer argued, ask only for minimal reforms, even less than universal suffrage, because something would be better than nothing.

But, came his own reply, the government will concede nothing, nothing at all. It will only give up what is wrung from it.

Very well, said the reformer, we must write and argue and persuade the government to concede reform.

But, came the reply, that will achieve nothing. Our writings and arguments can easily be contained and repressed by the government. And in the meantime they will use all their propaganda and their church to keep the masses in error and in lethargy.

Very well, said the reformer, we must agitate among the masses. We must form parties, hold mass meetings and demonstrations, organize monster petitions . . .

But all these things are banned, came the reply. We can't have parties and petitions, we can't circulate newspapers and pamphlets. The government stamps on demonstrations by force, using their army, their police, their spies . . .

Well, perhaps we can resist that passively, stutters the reformer – only to be swept aside by the reply that 'passive disobedience' was of little effect at Peterloo, and would be even more useless if the government used the army.

In the way of all the appeals for reform, all the demands for caution, there remained one insurmountable obstacle: the refusal of the people with power and property to give them up – and their willingness, if necessary, to defend them by force. Shelley describes this obstacle in one graphic sentence: 'for so dear is power that the tyrants themselves neither then, nor now, nor ever, left or leave a path to freedom but through their own blood.'[84] Or, from the other point of view: 'the labouring classes, when they cannot get food for their labour, are impelled to take it by force.'[85]

The paths to all the reforms which Shelley wanted were blocked by the realities of power. The national debt would not be written off by the people who profited from the interest on it; the standing army would not be disbanded by the people whose power and property it protected; the judges and the wealthy lawyers would not be displaced by the people whose property was enshrined in the 'rule of law'; and Parliament, while it remained the seat of political power, would not be transferred to people without property by the people who controlled it. There was no escaping the struggle for reform, and no escaping the likelihood of an insurrection arising from such a struggle. The agitations which he proposed could only be confidently carried out as part of a revolutionary strategy.

But in the end, as the argument drove him inexorably to the revolutionary conclusions which he had reached over and over again in his poems, Shelley suddenly and tantalizingly broke off. Perhaps he meant to return to his blank pages after more thought or discussion. In the event, the blank pages remained blank, and the central 'reform or revolution' contradiction in the pamphlet remained unresolved.

THE CONTRADICTION RESOLVED

Prometheus Unbound

Did he ever resolve it? Yes, he did – though not in any of his political pamphlets, nor in any of the openly political poems which he wrote after Peterloo. The work in which he grappled with and solved the problem was written before Peterloo. It is at once his greatest and most difficult poem: *Prometheus Unbound* (1818–19).

The Greek legend of Prometheus has provided inspiration for poets, composers and writers throughout the ages. Prometheus was a rebel god who dared to invent fire, and to challenge the authority of the king of the gods, Jupiter, or Jove. His punishment was brutal, a model for torturers for all time. He was chained to a rock in the Caucasus. Every day a vulture came to eat his liver. By the following day the liver had grown again, and could be chewed out again. And so an endless orgy of pain for the rebel brought comfort to Jupiter and his courtiers.

The legend is open to whatever interpretation suits the reader. In the tradition of 'the classics' taught in English public schools over the last 400 years, Prometheus has been held up as an example to anyone who dares defy authority: the headmaster, the monitor, or, in later life, the company director, the police chief, the colonial governor. Defiance, in this tradition, is a dreadful sin, and torture a suitable means of dealing with it.

More commonly, Prometheus figures as a rebel hero who

challenges the dark forces of tyranny. This is how Shelley saw him, but in Shelley's poem Prometheus is more than just a rebel. He represents cultured, intellectual man; scientific man who has made discoveries which can change the world. He represents, in short, Shelley as he imagined himself. He is wise, kind, brave. But he is also a god, a Titan, born, bred and educated as Jupiter himself. Though his spirit is unbroken by the torture, he cannot do anything to free himself. There is a sort of stalemate between Prometheus on his rock, representing the idea of progress but unable to put it into effect, and Jupiter in heaven, able to contain Prometheus but unable to break his spirit or destroy his knowledge.

Shelley's Prometheus is no abstraction. He is going through his agonies in the second decade of the nineteenth century. When, in the first act, the 'Furies' come to torture him, the worst torture of all comes not from the one which inflicts physical pain, but from the one which reminds him of the failure of the French Revolution, and suggests that such failure is inevitable because it is rooted deep in the human condition. All revolutions, warns this Fury, are hopeless, as was the French Revolution. Any attempt to improve the human condition only assists the tyrants.

> In each human heart terror survives
> The ravin it has gorged: the loftiest fear
> All that they would disdain to think were true:
> Hypocrisy and custom make their minds
> The fanes of many a worship, now outworn.
> They dare not devise good for man's estate
> And yet they know not that they do not dare.[86]

By contrast, the Spirits of the Mind swarm round to remind Prometheus of the power of the revolution, and how the essential ideas of the revolution continue in people's minds. They rally his powers of resistance, but cannot solve his agonizing dilemma: he still has the will to resist, but not the power to break his chains.

Hope is represented at Prometheus's feet by Panthea. After watching the tortures, she travels to meet her sister,

Asia, Prometheus's lover, who has been banished by Jupiter
to the Indian Caucasus. Asia is Love. She is full of hope and
confidence that things will change. Panthea tells her that
while she watched Prometheus's tortures she had two
dreams. The first is a familiar Shelleyan love dream. The
second she cannot remember.

As the two sisters talk, Asia sees a vision. It is Prometheus,
but between him and her is a 'shape'. It is not so lovely as
Prometheus is.

> Its rude hair
> Roughens the wind that lifts it, its regard
> Is wild and quick, yet 'tis a thing of air,
> For through its gray robe gleams the golden dew
> Whose stars the noon has quenched not.[87]

The shape calls out: 'Follow, Follow.' Panthea sees the shape
and suddenly recognizes it as the second dream she had
during Prometheus's tortures. The dream then calls, and
echoes the call. It calls again and again for the two women
to 'Follow, follow'.

To Hope (Panthea) and Love (Asia) is added the *determination* of both women, especially Asia, to free Prometheus.
Prometheus himself is resigned to his fate, but the women
want to *do* something about it. Their coming together, their
dreams, visions and aspirations, lead them relentlessly in
one direction: to the cave of Demogorgon.

Demorgorgon is the pivot of the poem. Who is he?
Hundreds of thousands of words have been written by
Shelleyans and anti-Shelleyans in answer to this question.
Scholars have delved back into the mythology of Boccacio
and of Hesiod to find other Demogorgons and to hammer
their discoveries into Shelley's poems.

The most popular view of Demogorgon is that he
represents an idea: the idea of necessity. Shelley himself,
especially in his youth, had flirted with this doctrine. It
comes straight from William Godwin. It is founded on the
belief that the 'perfectibility' of man will eventually triumph
over tyranny and destruction.

This theory, in various disguises, has appealed to radicals and revolutionaries throughout history. It is comforting. However bad things may be, there is always the certainty that good will triumph over bad. There is another advantage to it. It requires no action. The triumph is coming anyway, so there is no need to hurry it along. The doctrine sometimes comforted Shelley in his impotence, and allowed him to fudge the difference between reform and revolution. In an unfinished fragment, he wrote: 'Call it reform or revolution, as you will, a change must take place; one of the consequences of which will be, the wresting of political power from those who are at present the depositories of it.'[88]

But there is also plenty of evidence that Shelley could see the flaw in the doctrine of necessity – or perfectibility. Unless people who wanted change got together and did something about it, there was the danger of 'quietism'.[89] The minds of men and women would become hunting grounds for ignorance, fear, superstition and lies. Barbarism, in short, was just as possible as progress.

An idea could not change society, he concluded. Prometheus, the chained idealistic intellectual, couldn't change it. Hope couldn't change it. Even love couldn't change it. So who could? Who had the power to overthrow Jupiter?

Who *was* Demogorgon? One answer, a very obvious one which is often overlooked, is that he was who his name said he was. Shelley was always making up names from Greek words. Demos in Greek means the people; gorgon, the monster. Demogorgon is the 'people-monster'.

The habit of introducing figures from Greek mythology was common in reform literature at the time. One example was a radical working class paper, started in April 1818, called the *Gorgon*. John Wade, its editor, was a wool-sorter. He started the *Gorgon* as an attempt to involve working people in 'practical politics'. Wade was not a revolutionary, but he did believe that the condition and behaviour of the working masses was crucial to the politics of reform. In one of the first issues – 23 May 1818 – Wade wrote: 'The people have nothing to expect from any exertions but their own.'

The paper, unhappily, does not say why it was called the *Gorgon*. The Gorgons, in Greek legend, were three women whom Perseus was sent to slay. Only one of them, Medusa, could see – with one eye; but anyone who gazed on the face of any of the monsters perished instantly. The idea of such a 'monster' as the working class terrifying their employers was popular among the more radical reformers of the time. Wade's *Gorgon* was not the only example. Another popular radical sheet was called *Medusa*. The *Gorgon* itself announced, in January 1819, the first attempt at a general union in Britain, which called for penny-a-week subscriptions from workers in all trades in order to assist agitation against the anti-union Combination Acts. It was called, again after Greek legend, the Philanthropic Hercules.

We can only speculate as to whether there was any association in Shelley's mind between the *Gorgon* and his Demogorgon. There is no reference in Shelley – or none that I can find – to the *Gorgon*. But the fact that Shelley doesn't mention the *Gorgon* doesn't mean that he never saw it. He left England for Italy in March 1818, before the first issue of the *Gorgon*, so he could not have bought it himself. From then on, he relied on his friends Thomas Love Peacock and Leigh Hunt, and to a lesser extent the publisher Ollier, to send him papers from England.

The first box of papers – from Peacock – reached Shelley in September, just as he first conceived the idea of *Prometheus Unbound*. Other boxes and parcels arrived during the long period in which the poem was written – though the bulk of the best part of it, the first two acts, were written in four weeks in Rome in the spring of 1819.

Of all the radical political papers, apart from the *Examiner* and the *Political Register*, which Peacock might have sent to Shelley, the *Gorgon* seems the most likely. It caused a considerable stir at all levels of the reform movement in England. Peacock was a Tory by inclination, though by no means a bigot. But he was a close friend of Shelley's, and understood his friend's passion for radical politics and sympathy for the working people. Francis Place, the cautious reformer, was a collaborator with Wade on the *Gorgon* and he would have represented to Peacock, as he parked his friend's box, a much more respectable strain of politics than, say, the *Black Dwarf* or the *Medusa*.

It is, at any rate, probable that at least one copy of the *Gorgon* found its way to Shelley while he was writing the *Prometheus* and while he was composing its strangest and most crucial figure, Demogorgon. The idea of the people as a monster may have come from there.

All his life, Shelley was fascinated by monsters, ghouls and spectres. The image of the people-monster came quite naturally to him. It fitted exactly his indentification with the people together with his ignorance of them. In 'A Philosophical View of Reform' he described the English working class as 'the unrepresented multitude'.[90] This 'unrepresented multitude' – the Luddites and the Derbyshire insurrectionists, the starved stockingers, the iron workers from Staffordshire marching for the right to work, the striking spinners from Manchester, the miners of Somerset facing down the armed yeomanry with sticks and stones – this was Demogorgon.

Demogorgon was, for Shelley, dim and shapeless – a strange, dark, brooding mass. When Asia and Panthea arrive at the people-monster's cave, they stand there peering and blinking in the gloom:

> *Panthea*: What veilèd form sits on that ebon throne?
> *Asia*: The veil has fallen.
> *Panthea*:   I see a mighty darkness
> Filling the seat of power, and rays of gloom
> Dart round, as light from the meridian sun.
> —Ungazed upon and shapeless; neither limb,
> Nor form, nor outline; yet we feel it is
> A living Spirit.[91]

Suddenly, the 'mighty darkness' speaks:

> *Demogorgon*: Ask what thou wouldst know.
> *Asia*: What canst thou tell?
> *Demogorgon*: All things thou dar'st demand.[92]

From now on, Asia takes the lead. In the famous and furious dialogue which follows, Panthea says nothing at all. Asia knows she has found 'the seat of power', but sees that there remains a problem. She knows from her own experience in exile that ideas alone, or those few people who have time to develop ideas – isolated revolutionary intellectuals like Shelley and Prometheus – cannot overthrow governments and ruling classes. But just as ideas are impotent without the masses, so the masses are impotent without ideas. They can be stultified by their poverty; doped by religion; duped by the trickery of royalty and its scribblers. In fear and superstitition they can become arrogant and reactionary. So Asia, inspired by her desire to liberate Prometheus, devotes herself to provoking Demogorgon into action. She introduces him to the ideas which can make him confident of his own power, and of his rulers' weakness.

She becomes an agitator – not a didactic, hectoring, intellectual bully, but an agitator who respects the people she is addressing and starts from what they think, and how they think. Her first question is a simple one. She expects, and gets, a simple answer:

> *Asia*: Who made the living world?
> *Demogorgon*: God.[93]

Immediately, she confirms him in his error by mentioning the five things which Shelley regarded as the most important in that living world. The answer is even more pat:

> *Asia*:   Who made all
> That it contains? thought, passion, reason, will
> Imagination?
> *Demogorgon*: God; Almighty God.[94]

And again she lulls him into this expected answer:

> *Asia*: Who made that sense which, when the winds of
>   Spring
> In rarest visitation, or the voice
> Of one belovèd heard in youth alone,
> Fills the faint eyes with falling tears which dim

The radiant looks of unbewailing flowers,
And leaves this peopled earth a solitude
When it returns no more?
  Demogorgon: Merciful God.[95]

Then, suddenly and lethally, she turns on him:

  Asia: And who made terror, madness, crime, remorse,
Which from the links of the great chain of things,
To every thought within the mind of men
Sway and drag heavily, and each one reels
Under the load toward the pit of death;
Abandoned hope, and love that turns to hate;
And self-contempt, bitterer to drink than blood;
Pain, whose unheeded and familiar speech
Is howling, and keen shrieks, day after day;
And Hell, or the sharp fear of Hell?[96]

Demogorgon can only stammer: 'He reigns.' But she is not finished with him yet.

  Asia: Utter his name! a world pining in pain
Asks but his name: curses shall drag him down.
  Demogorgon: He reigns.
  Asia: I feel, I know it: who?
  Demogorgon: He reigns.[97]

She has him listening now, whipped by the argument, and stunned into meaningless repetition. She speaks then at length, asking 'who reigns?' Prometheus, she reminds him, has given humanity many wonderful gifts; science; the power to beat the elements; love; speech; music; the ability to build cities; the possibility of cooperation between people of different races ('and the Celt knew the Indian'). For all this, Prometheus 'hangs withering in destined pain'. Her magnificent speech ends where it started by demanding to know 'who rains down evil'.[98] She refuses to accept another answer of 'God' or 'Jupiter':

  Not Jove: while yet his frown shook Heaven, ay when
  His adversary from adamantine chains

Cursed him, he trembled like a slave. Declare
Who is his master? Is he too a slave?[99]

She knows that there *is* something more powerful than
tyranny: a united and risen people. Her problem is to breathe
a spirit of confidence and unity into the shapeless Demogorgon in his cave. So she continues to lash him with the
questions to which he has only half-replies.

> *Demogorgon*: All spirits are enslaved which serve
> things evil:
> Thou knowest if Jupiter be such or no.
> *Asia*: Whom calledst thou God?
> *Demogorgon*: I spoke but as ye speak,
> For Jove is the supreme of living things.
> *Asia*: Who is the master of the slave?
> *Demogorgon*: If the abysm
> Could vomit forth its secrets. . . . But a voice
> Is wanting, the deep truth is imageless;
> For what would it avail to bid thee gaze
> On the revolving world? What to bid speak
> Fate, Time, Occasion, Chance, and Change? To
> these
> All things are subject but eternal Love.[100]

This is prevarication, by way of a half compliment. Asia
accepts the compliment, and soothes him once again:

> *Asia*: So much I asked before, and my heart gave
> The response thou hast given; aid of such truths
> Each to itself must be the oracle.[101]

But then, with one final supreme effort, she returns to the
business in hand:

> *Asia*: One more demand; and do thou answer me
> As my own soul would answer, did it know
> That which I ask. Prometheus shall arise
> Henceforth the sun of this rejoicing world:
> When shall the destined hour arrive?[102]

And then, in one glorious, mighty explosion, Demogorgon moves. His cave, deep in the mountain, erupts in a

volcano. From the 'cloven' rocks, there emerge two cars, each driven by charioteers. The first, described by Asia, is driven by 'A spirit with a dreadful countenance.' It soars upwards into the night, terrifying everything in its path. Asia murmurs to herself, stunned by what she has done: 'Thus I am answered: strange!'[103] But then another chariot appears, whose driver has 'dove-like eyes of hope' and 'soft smiles'. Asia and Panthea get into this one and ascend out of the cave.

What do these two entirely different chariots signify? All through Shelley's writing, especially in his metaphorical and legendary writing, there is a conflict of opposites. Where there is darkness, there is the prospect of light. Where there is winter, there is the prospect of spring. Where (as in one lovely passage in *Prometheus*) there is desolation, there are 'visions of aerial joy'. The opposites always show up the subject, and lead the argument for progress forward. As he once wrote about Michaelangelo's painting, 'The Last Judgement': 'What is terror without a contrast with and a connection with loveliness?'

So with revolution. One side of it is dark and terrifying: violence, civil war, a new bureaucracy or tyranny in the place of the old. On the other, there is light, hope, peace, democracy and security. The revolution holds out both prospects. How much of which occurs can depend partly on circumstances, partly on the decisions and actions of the revolutionaries. Yet 'in either case', as Richard Holmes concludes, 'it is to be celebrated'.[104] Either way, what follows will be better than what went before.

Realistically, perhaps, Demogorgon gets into the dark, violent chariot. He arrives at the throne of Jupiter in the next scene. Jupiter is waiting for him, confident that he has, as on so many occasions in the past, the power to crush any popular force. His 'secret weapon' on this occasion is his 'fatal child', who represents the doctrines of Malthus. By persuading the people that there 'simply wasn't enough to go round', Jupiter imagines that he can easily quell their revolt.

Not so, however. As soon as Jupiter sees Demogorgon he senses that this is not the people as he knew them, ignorant, gullible and divided. This is the people inspired by the vision of a new society, armed with their own confidence, and, above all, unscrupulous in their determination to destroy him. Any doubt that Demogorgon represents the common people is dispelled by Jupiter's reaction on his overthrow:

> *Jupiter*:   Detested prodigy!
> Even thus beneath the deep Titanian prisons
> I trample thee! thou lingerest?
>   Mercy! mercy!
> No pity, no release, no respite! Oh,
> That thou wouldst make mine enemy my judge,
> Even where he hangs, seared by my long revenge,
> On Caucasus! He would not doom me thus.
> Gentle, and just, and dreadless, is he not
> The monarch of the world? What then art thou?
> No refuge! no appeal![105]

The tyrant begs to be judged and dealt with by the idealistic intellectual of his own class, rather than by the people. He knows that from the rebels of his own class he can expect mercy, and, with mercy, probably a breathing space in which to regather his forces, redouble his propaganda, and start the counter-revolution. The tyrant Othman in *The Revolt of Islam* was saved from the fury of the people by the Shelleyan superman Laon. He was then able to strike back and regain his power. Jupiter is not so lucky. His last wish is that he might be judged by an unchained Prometheus – as kings, employers and imperialists thoughout history have released, honoured and promoted middle class leaders at times of mass unrest, in return for a 'breathing space' in the struggle. From the masses, however, there is no pity, no release, no respite, no refuge, no appeal. Jupiter sinks at once without trace, taking Demogorgon and the ugly spirit of the revolution with him.

In this the most wonderful of all his poems, Shelley worked out the contradiction which dogs so much of his straight political writing. Reform, the poem concludes, is impossible without revolution. The forces of wealth and power in England in 1819 would not, in the foreseeable future, concede that wealth and power. They could easily contain the movement for reform for as long as that movement confined itself to the 'enlightened few'. The only power which could not be contained was the power of the people, organized, united and confident in revolutionary action.

This did not mean that there was no place for Shelley, or people like him born into upper or middle class families who saw the need for reform. There was a role for them but not in the pages of the *Examiner*, still less as hereditary Members of Parliament for rotten boroughs. Reformers who took that road ended up assisting their opponents in holding back the masses. The role of Shelley and those like him was to act as agitators in the cause of revolution. They had to place their skills and talents at the disposal of the revolutionary forces, the more quickly to excite them to action. That side of Shelley which held him back from such agitation for fear of the consequences has vanished from *Prometheus Unbound*. The gap which he left a year later in 'A Philosophical View of Reform' is filled by the poem. The revolution had to be made by the masses. Poets, writers and intellectuals could use their talents to hurry it along.

THE CONTRADICTION EXPLAINED

Shelley's life, contemporaries, and friends

Shelley was one of the great intellectuals of his time. Everyone who knew him testified to his prodigious learning. He would read sometimes thirteen hours a day, at school he learned Latin and Greek, and he read voraciously in both subjects all his life. He learned French while he was young, and read eagerly through French literature. He taught himself German and Spanish and read deeply in both. In the

literature of his native country there was hardly an established author in print whom Shelley did not read in full.
Everything interested him – not just poetry, and certainly
not just politics. He was fascinated by science, natural history, philosophy. The depth and breadth of the knowledge
he acquired from reading was astonishing.

Many of Shelley's political ideas came from books. But
ideas, especially political ideas, cannot all come from books.
They depend at least to some extent on experience and on
people. Shelley the reformer can only be reconciled with
Shelley the revolutionary if one appreciates the kind of life
he led and the people who met and influenced him during
it.

His sheltered youth and education limited his friendships
and his experience. His politics at Oxford, though vehemently radical, veered between conspiratorial terrorism and
Parliamentarianism. In March 1811, the editor of the *Examiner*, Leigh Hunt, was surprised to get a letter from an
undergraduate at Oxford called P. B. Shelley which con-
gratulated him on his acquittal on charges of seditious libel,
and continued with some amazing suggestions:

The ultimate intention of my aim is to induce a *meeting* of such
enlightened unprejudiced members of the community, whose
independent principles expose them to evils which might thus
become alleviated, and to form a methodical society which should
be organized so as to resist the coalition of the enemies of liberty
which at present renders any expression of opinion on matters of
policy dangerous to individuals. It has been for want of societies
of this nature that corruption has attained the height at which we
now behold it, nor can any of us bear in mind the very great
influence, which some years since was gained by *Illuminism* without considering that a society of equal extent might establish
rational liberty on as firm a basis as that which would have
supported the visionary schemes of a completely-equalized
community.[106]

The Illuminists were a secret, anarchist, revolutionary sect
which had grown up alongside the Jacobin movement in
France. Their aim was the destruction or abolition of private

property, religion and sexual taboos. Poor Leigh Hunt must have been scared out of his gentle wits when he read that passage. But perhaps he was cheered by the last paragraph of the same letter, which started: 'My father is in Parliament, and, on attaining 21, I shall in all probability fill his vacant seat.'

There is a saying – though it does not date back to Shelley's time – that an anarchist is a liberal with a bomb in his hand. It suits Shelley's Oxford politics perfectly. He dreamed of wild terrorist conspiracies while at the same time confidently looking forward to his seat in Parliament.

Shelley's expulsion from Oxford cut him off from his Parliamentary lifeline. He suddenly found himself without even the prospect of a decent income. His father refused to see him. His old masters and many of his family turned aside from him. All this affected his political attitude. He fled north with Harriet, and stayed at Cumberland, Edinburgh and York. In Cumberland he saw at first hand the full extent of the 1811 depression. The experience added to his personal bitterness and hardened his political arteries. His letters to Elizabeth Hitchener betray a new radicalism, tougher than the anarcho–liberalism of his undergraduate days. On 17 November 1811 he wrote: 'My soul is bursting, ideas millions of ideas are crowding into it.'[107] And on 26 December: 'I have been led into reasons which make me *hate* more & more the existing establishment of every kind.'[108]

He was thinking through those hectic months of what he could do to end the wretchedness around him. It was, he discovered, still possible for him to crawl back to Parliament and the Whigs. The Duke of Norfolk was making advances to him. But he had been 'led into reasonings' which made the path back into Parliament impassable. Instead, he decided to become a full-time political agitator. He realized that the idea of forming an Illuminist gang was absurd. He had to organize openly among the people who were most oppressed. And so, in February 1812, he went to Dublin to work as an agitator among the Irish poor.

His Illuminist anarchism vanished with his liberalism. He

wrote the 'Address to the Irish People', which, for all its patronizing tone, is, in contrast to the angry poems of his early youth, a pamphlet directed to the masses, with the purpose of involving them in political action.

He had nothing but his pamphlet and his enthusiasm, and he used the latter to distribute the former. He and Harriet would stand on Dublin balconies, dropping the 'Address' into the streets. When no one picked it up, he would run behind people dropping copies into the hoods of their coats. A day or two of this was enough to prove its inadequacy. Hardly had he set foot in Dublin than he realized that what was needed was an association, a party, a *group* of people who could pool their resources in the interests of Catholic emancipation and reform.

He wrote, almost at once, 'Proposals for an Association'. Partly to appease the censor, partly because he was frightened by the brutality and drunkenness in the Dublin streets, the little pamphlet is full of patronizing rhetoric about the need to keep calm. But there are also passages which show clearly that he intended to act not as a representative of a reforming élite, but as part of an association working with the people. Here for the first time he lashes out at the 'fireside politician' whom he later savaged in *Queen Mab*: 'Benevolent feeling has gone out in this country in favor of the happiness of its inhabitants . . . But it will not be kept alive by each citizen sitting quietly by his own fireside, and saying that things are going on well, because the rain does not beat on *him,* and *he* has books and leisure to read them, because *he* has money and is at liberty to accumulate luxuries to *himself.*'[109]

'Individuals acting singly,' he went on, 'with whatever energy can never effect so much as a society.' So a society has to be formed, first for discussion and, second, 'for carrying, by united or individual exertion, such measures into effect when determined on.'[110]

This seems obvious enough, 170 years later, but at the time it was highly inflammatory. The government would not tolerate books encouraging reform even if they were available to only a handful of intellectuals. Pamphlets which called for the formation of reform societies or emancipation associations were palpable treason. In London William Godwin, the fireside philosopher, grew alarmed. Shelley had written to him from Cumberland, flattering his *Political Justice* and begging for advice. At first Godwin was not greatly interested. But as it emerged that Shelley was heir to a great fortune, his attitude changed. The young man, Godwin decided, must be cultivated, patronized, and as soon as possible, milked. When Shelley sent him the 'Address to the Irish People' he was horrified. He wrote at once: 'Discussion, reading, inquiry, perpetual communication, these are my favourite methods for the improvement of mankind; but associations, organised societies, I firmly condemn; you may as well tell the adder not to sting . . .'[111]

Shelley replied, almost as sharply:

Political Justice was first published in 1793; nearly twenty years have elapsed since the general diffusion of its doctrines. What has followed? have men ceased to fight, has vice and misery vanished from the earth.—Have the fireside communications which it recommends taken place? . . . The state of society appears to me to be retrogressive,—if there be any truth in the hopes which I so fondly cherish, then this cannot be. Yet even if it be stationary the eager activity of Philanthropists is demanded.—I think of the last twenty years with impatient scepticism . . . I will own that I am eager that something should be done.[112]

Godwin wrote back, hysterically: 'Shelley, you are preparing a scene of blood!'[113]

The philosopher used every trick in his book – from petulance to flattery – to win his young admirer away from this 'scene of blood'. And he succeeded. Shelley capitulated. In a letter dated 18 March 1812, only four weeks after his arrival in Dublin, Shelley replied: 'I acquiesce in your decisions . . . I have withdrawn from circulation the publications wherein I erred, & am preparing to quit Dublin: . . .'

The letter went on to insist that he had not been wrong in principle: 'It *is* possible to festinate [hasten] or retard the

progress of human perfectibility, such associations as I
would have recommended would be calculated to produce
the former effect, . . . My schemes of organizing the ignorant I confess to be [dangerous and *cancelled*] ill-timed: I
cannot conceive that they were dangerous.' And so declaring, almost in a huff, 'I shall address myself no more to the
illiterate',[114] Shelley packed his bags and set sail again for
England.

Why did he go? Certainly not only because of Godwin's
arguments and anger. Shelley admired Godwin, but, as even
his last letter on the subject proves, he felt he was right to
try to form an association. But the attempt was a failure.
'As to an Association,' he had written to Elizabeth Hitchener
only two days beforehand, 'my hopes daily grow fainter on
the subject, as my perceptions of its necessity gain
strength.'[115]

No one would join his party. The Catholic aristocracy,
of course, would have nothing to do with it. Shelley was
snubbed not only by Lord Fingal, the leader of the upper
class movement for Catholic emancipation, but by all the
leading Catholics whom he met. He spoke at a meeting
called to put the case for votes for Catholics, he was cheered
when he called for Catholic emancipation, but booed just as
loudly when he called for a secular association to promote
it. His attempt to interest formerly liberal lawyers in his
ideas came to nothing. Above all, he found that being a
political agitator among the masses was hard, undignified
work. Much as he saw the necessity for it, such work didn't
suit him.

When Shelley left Dublin, he left all practical agitation
behind him. He never tried again to work among the common people. 'I will look,' he wrote, full of self-pity, to
Godwin, 'to events in which it will be impossible that I can
share.'[116]

Despite the lure of London and what he castigated as the
'fireside' set, Shelley did not go there. In September 1812,
he came across the dam projects at Tremadoc in North
Wales. Two thousand workers had been engaged by the

M.P. William Madocks on a huge scheme to reclaim the land from the sea. Shelley saw here the possibility of a perfect, idealistic society, and settled down as an agent to raise money for the dam.

His work at Tremadoc brought him once again in close contact with working people. He spent many hours, often at night, visiting the dam workers, talking and arguing with them. All his aspirations and hopes for a new society blossomed once again. The writing of *Queen Mab* proceeded with vigour and speed.

To patriots and people with property in that part of Wales, Shelley appeared as a terrorist monster. He had no love for the county set, whom he continually insulted. He was forever pleading the cause of the workers, even when there was no money to pay them. He was, they all assumed, probably associated with the Luddites who were rioting close by. They decided to get rid of him. On 26 February 1813, an assassin was sent, twice, to his house. Both times a pistol was fired at Shelley. He escaped with his life, but not his dressing gown, which was shot through. Frightened and disillusioned, Shelley left again, this time for the radical chic set in London and Berkshire, among whom he spent an amusing, titillating but unproductive year.

His pilgrimage through France in the summer of 1814 brought him close to the victims of poverty and famine and inspired Shelley's most violent writing against authority, 'The Assassins'.

In 1815 and 1816 Shelley wrote little. Those years were spent in and around London, out of all contact with the working people. His only major work has *Alastor*.

In Marlow in 1817, at the height of the post-war economic depression, Shelley had many acquaintances among the laceworkers of the area, almost all of whom were unemployed and hungry. There is very little record of his conversations and experiences with them, but they had the effect of awakening his political consciousness.

He wrote, in that single year at Marlow, his longest and perhaps his most revolutionary poem, *The Revolt of Islam*, and two political pamphlets: 'Proposal to Put Reform to the Vote' and the 'Address to the People on the Death of Princess Charlotte'. These pamphlets were not addressed to the 'literate few' but to the masses. They herald the return of Shelley's political confidence, and, with it, his faith in the common people.

Yet in March 1818 he decided to leave England, never to return. This was the third retreat of his life, after the retreat from Ireland and the retreat from Tremadoc, and the most tragic. For although he was to write his best-known work in Italy during his last four years, he was completely cut off there from the experience of the English working people, for whom so many of his works were written. His confidence in them, upon which so much of his political writing depended, rose and fell according to what he could glean from newspapers or from unsympathetic accounts from friends or tourists.

During that time, Shelley showed little or no interest in Italian politics. He rhapsodized on the scenery; he appreciated the architecture and the painting; he enjoyed the weather. But he never identified with the Italian poor as he did with the English poor 1,000 miles away. Like so many political exiles, his interest in politics was rooted in his own country. But for the last four years of his life he had no Dublin masses, no Welsh dam workers, no unemployed lace workers, to talk to. He was politically isolated and his isolation ran through his writing like an open wound.

Yet in spite of that isolation he managed to keep his political position well to the left of all his friends and famous contemporaries.

The Apostates: Coleridge, Southey, Wordsworth

What shocked Shelley perhaps most of all about Coleridge, Southey and Wordsworth was their attitude to the French Revolution. Like them, Shelley was appalled by the course of the revolution under Napoleon. But Shelley noticed that the other poets – all of them were more closely identified with the revolution than he was – used the shortcomings of the revolution as excuses for ignoring the gains it had made.

One by one, he noticed, they started to deplore the fact that the revolution had ever happened, and to side with the reaction against which it had been directed. In the preface to *The Revolt of Islam*, he wrote:

But, on the first reverses of hope in the progress of French liberty, the sanguine eagerness for good overleaped the solution of these questions, and for a time extinguished itself in the unexpectedness of their result. Thus, many of the most ardent and tender-hearted of the worshippers of public good have been morally ruined by what a partial glimpse of the events they deplored appeared to show as the melancholy desolation of all their cherished hopes. Hence gloom and misanthropy have become the characteristics of the age in which we live, the solace of a disappointment that unconsciously finds relief only in the wilful exaggeration of its own despair. This influence has tainted the literature of the age with the hopelessness of the minds from which it flows.[117]

Samuel Taylor Coleridge, one of the great poets of the revolution, had taken refuge in opium and reaction. Shelley wrote of him:

> You will see Coleridge – he who sits obscure
> In the exceeding lustre and the pure
> Intense irradiation of a mind
> Which, with its own internal lightning blind,
> Flags wearily through darkness and despair –
> A cloud-encircled meteor of the air,
> A hooded eagle among blinking owls.[118]

Robert Southey, author of the revolutionary poem 'Wat Tyler', became Poet Laureate in 1814, and sycophant-in-chief to the Castlereagh administration. Shelley met him and sponged off him in the Lake District in 1813. But his contempt for the man soon made the relationship intolerable. 'Southey has changed,' he wrote to Elizabeth Hitchener on 15 December 1811. 'I shall see him soon, and I shall reproach him of [for] his tergiversation.—He to whom Bigotry

Tyranny and Law was hateful has become the votary of these Idols, in a form the most disgusting.—The Church of England it's Hell and all has become the subject of his panegyric.—the war in Spain that prodigal waste of human blood to aggrandise the fame of Statesmen is his delight . . .'[119]

When he did see him, he wrote to Godwin (hardly recognizing perhaps that Godwin was rapidly disappearing down the same hole): 'Southey the Poet whose principles were pure & elevated once, is now the servile champion of every abuse and absurdity.—I have had much conversation with him. He says "You will think as I do when you are as old".'[120]

But the worst apostate was William Wordsworth. Shelley had worshipped Wordsworth's writings around the turn of the century, when he was still inspired by the French Revolution. His deep sympathy for the poor and his hatred of the new rich coincided exactly with Shelley's own feelings. Poems like 'The Cumberland Beggar' were almost certainly models for some of Shelley's fiercest writing.

And yet, partly out of fear, partly out of lack of interest, Wordsworth had drifted with Southey to the extreme right. In the 1818 general election, the liberal lawyer Henry Brougham stood in Westmorland, one of the few seats in the country where there was an electoral contest. The local Tory, who might well have lost his seat, was saved by the enthusiastic support of Wordsworth, who wrote two letters to the electors, arguing that Brougham was too poor to make a good M.P. and that the House of Commons shouldn't be elected by the people but by peers.

For Wordsworth, Shelley wrote one of his best and most biting political poems, *Peter Bell the Third*. A review of Wordsworth's boring *Peter Bell* had reached Shelley in Leghorn, and had, according to Mary 'amused him greatly'. He set to work in the prolific autumn of 1819 to write a satire about another Peter Bell, Wordsworth himself. 'No poem,' wrote Mary, rightly, 'contains more of Shelley's peculiar views with regard to the errors into which many of the wisest have fallen, and the pernicious effects of certain opinions on society.'[121]

The first three parts of the poem introduce the devil, 'like a slop-merchant from Wapping'. He approaches Peter in Westmorland and takes him to hell. Hell 'is a city much like London'. Peter is very swiftly corrupted by praise, fame and money. Before long, he is writing drivel like any former radical in a Sunday newspaper colour supplement:

> For he now raved enormous folly,
>   Of Baptisms, Sunday-schools, and Graves . . .

All of which was flattered in the press:

> Yet the Reviews, who heaped abuse
>   On Peter while he wrote for freedom,
> So soon as in his song they spy
> The folly which soothes tyranny
>   Praise him, for those who feed 'em.[122]

Peter's writing then turned from 'enormous folly' to outright reaction:

> Then Peter wrote odes to the Devil;—
>   In one of which he meekly said:
> 'May Carnage and Slaughter,
> Thy niece and they daughter,
> May Rapine and Famine,
> Thy gorge ever cramming,
>   Glut thee with living and dead!
>
> 'May Death and Damnation,
>   And Consternation,
> Flit up from Hell with pure intent!
>   Slash them at Manchester,
>   Glasgow, Leeds, and Chester;
> Drench all with blood from Avon to Trent.
>
> Let thy body-guard yeomen
>   Hew down babes and women,
> And laugh with bold triumph till Heaven be rent!
>   When Moloch in Jewry
>   Munched children with fury,
> It was thou, Devil, dining with pure intent.'[123]

Wordsworth was now supporting the opposite of what had inspired him during the period of his great poetry, and the change ruined his poetry. His use of language faltered, his vitality and enthusiasm disappeared, and his skill left him. 'A strange and horrid curse hung upon Peter.' It was 'double damnation'.

> Peter was dull—he was at first
>   Dull—oh, so dull—so very dull!
> Whether he talked, wrote, or rehearsed—
> Still with this dulness was he cursed—
>   Dull—beyond all conception—dull. . . .
>
> His sister, wife, and children yawned,
>   With a long, slow, and drear ennui,
> All human patience far beyond;
> Their hopes of Heaven each would have pawned,
>   Anywhere else to be.
>
> His servant-maids and dogs grew dull;
>   His kitten, late a sportive elf;
> The woods and lakes, so beautiful,
> Of dim stupidity were full,
>   All grew dull as Peter's self.[124]

The experience of Wordsworth and the other 'lake poets' haunted Shelley. That was what would happen to him, he reflected, if he suppressed his convictions or allowed them to rot in isolation, idleness, luxury or fame.

Keats

The political inspiration of Shelley's poems came under criticism during his life from an equally brilliant contemporary, John Keats. Keats was a radical in his spare time, and occasionally in his poems (most notably in 'Isabella') there is a flash of anger at the pomp and poverty of the time. But Keats was a 'professional writer'; he disapproved of poets who allowed themselves to be 'swayed' by political ideals. Shortly before he died, Keats wrote a very friendly letter to

Shelley, which included a word of critical advice: 'You, I am sure will forgive me for sincerely remarking that you might curb your magnanimity and be more of an artist, and load every rift of your subject with ore.'[125]

There is no reply to this letter on record – but if there were, Keats' advice would have been, equally politely, rejected. Shelley revered Keats' poetry, but he knew that his own *depended* on its 'magnanimity', its political inspiration. He knew that once that inspiration was doused, his enthusiasm for life – and therefore his poetry – would be doused too. And so, even in his Italian isolation, the ghosts of his former poet-heroes of the revolution, Coleridge, Southey and Wordsworth, haunted him and deterred him from sliding back from his convictions.

Byron

There was, during those Italian years, one friend and companion of Shelley's who was his equal in ability and with whom Shelley could engage in genuine political debate: George Gordon, Lord Byron. Byron's great narrative poems had won him fame and fortune all over Europe, particularly in England where his narrative poem *Childe Harold* was required reading (and swooning) for any successful debutante. Byron loathed pomposity, tyranny and superstition. His two speeches in the House of Lords – one against capital punishment for the Luddites, the other for Catholic emancipation in Ireland – are two of the finest ever made there.

Despite Byron's success and Shelley's failure, the two men liked and respected each other. They first met in 1816 when Claire Clairmont seduced Byron. They spent the summer of 1816 together at Geneva, where Byron wrote one of his finest poems, 'The Prisoner of Chillon'. In Italy they met on several occasions and wrote to each other continually. In the winter of 1821–2, the two men were almost constant companions, in Pisa.

Yet in spite of their common hatred of tyranny, imperi-

alism and Lord Castlereagh, there was a political gulf between them. Both men testified to it – Shelley in one of his
best long poems, *Julian and Maddalo*. The poem starts with
a meeting between the two men in Venice – a real meeting
which took place in 1818. (The poem was written after this
meeting.) The first part of the poem is a political argument:
Julian is Shelley; Maddalo is Byron. This is Julian (Shelley)
speaking:

> It is our will
> That thus enchains us to permitted ill—
> We might be otherwise—we might be all
> We dream of happy, high, majestical.
> Where is the love, beauty and truth we seek,
> But in our mind? and if we were not weak
> Should we be less in deed than in desire?'
> 'Ay, if we *were* not weak—and we aspire
> How vainly to be strong!' said Maddalo:
> 'You talk Utopia.' 'It remains to know,'
> I then rejoined, 'and those who try may find
> How strong the chains are which our spirit bind;
> Brittle perchance as straw . . . We are assured
> Much may be conquered, much may be endured,
> Of what degrades and crushes us. We know
> That we have power over ourselves to do
> And suffer—what, we know not till we try;
> But something nobler than to live and die—. . .'
>   'My dear friend,'
> Said Maddalo, 'my judgement will not bend
> To your opinion, though I think you might
> Make such a system refutation-tight
> As far as words go. . . .'[126]

The argument went on throughout their relationship.
Shelley was a sceptic. He subjected all the shibboleths of
society to ruthless inquiry. But he retained his belief that
'we have power over ourselves', and that people can change
the world. Byron's scepticism toppled into cynicism. He
doubted everything, including the possibility of social
change. He intended no sacrifice of his fame or fortune. For
the sake of both he was prepared to contain his more radical

instincts. Why should he bother, he would argue with Shelley? If there is no real hope of change, why not trim our satire and our assaults on authority and religion? If that was the way the publishers wanted it, perhaps that was the way they should have it.

To Byron 'freedom' was an abstract idea. It meant the 'right' of rich intellectuals to write what they liked and make love to whom they chose. It should, he thought, never interfere with property or rank. Byron was prepared to fight (and, eventually, to die) for the Greeks against the tyranny of feudal Turkey, but, had he lived and returned to England, he would have fought just as hard against the extension of reform, or even the vote, to the common people.

Shelley was always well to the left of Byron. From Ravenna two years after the *Julian and Maddalo* conversation, he wrote of Byron: 'We . . . differed, & I think more than ever.—He affects to patronize a system of criticism fit only for the production of mediocrity.'[127]

Byron was warned against Shelley by friends and publishers in England. If his name was linked to that of Shelley, he was told, the political and religious establishment would hound him. For once, Byron refused to concede. His admiration and respect for Shelley – whom he nicknamed 'the Snake' – knew no bounds. He wrote back to one whiner: 'Today I had another letter warning me against the Snake. He alone in this age of humbug dares to stem the current, as he did today in the flooded Arno in his skiff, although I could not observe that he made any progress. The attempt is better than being swept along as all the rest of us are, with the filthy garbage scoured from its banks.'[128]

Shelley's insistence that he must continue to 'stem the current' drove the two men apart. Shelley grew increasingly irritated by the Byron circle, their ostentatious consumption, their dirty jokes, the men-only camaraderie. Byron in turn was annoyed by Shelley's criticism, if only because he knew it was well-founded. Shelley's writing was strangely muted during his time with Byron, but his political principles remained firm.

Yet Shelley's politics were affected by his isolation in Italy. Apart from Byron, and the extraordinary explorer and traveller Edward Trelawney, Shelley's circle in Italy was limited in the extreme. Most of the people he met or who lived in his house were either devoted admirers who challenged nothing Shelley said – like Edward Williams who was drowned with Shelley when their boat capsized in the Bay of Spezia in July 1822 – or wealthy expatriates, liberal and friendly enough, but awkward and embarrassed by political argument. It was also a time of much personal grief. Shelley's circle became introspective, politically unconcerned. He felt lonely, not because he was alone, but because he was separated from the things and the people who interested and inspired him.

The poet who has been celebrated most for his lyrical descriptions of the countryside was infuriated by a rural solitude. 'Solitude,' he wrote to Hogg on 8 May 1811, 'is most horrible.'[129] To Claire he wrote, in December 1821: 'To write & [in] solitude or put forth thoughts without sympathy is unprofitable vanity.'[130] And to John Gisborne, six months later: 'It is impossible to compose except under the strong excitement of an assurance of finding sympathy in what you write. Imagine Demosthenes reciting a Philippic to the waves of the Atlantic.'[131]

His most remarkable expression of this loneliness was written to Peacock from Livorno in August 1819 – probably on the very day of the Peterloo massacre:

I most devoutedly wish that I were living in London. . . . What are mountains trees heaths, or even the glorious & ever beautiful sky with such sunsets as I have seen at Hampstead to friends? Social enjoyment in some form or other is the alpha & the omega of existence.

All that I see in Italy—and from my tower window I now see the magnificent peaks of the Appenine half enclosing the plain—is nothing—it dwindles into smoke in the mind, when I think of some familiar forms of scenery little perhaps in themselves over which old remembrances have thrown a delightful colour. How we prize what we despised when present! So the ghosts of our dead associations rise & haunt us in revenge for our having let them starve, & abandoned them to perish![132]

Even the Tory Peacock, with his satire and his laughter, would have lifted Shelley from this melancholy. So, more perhaps than he realized, would the Tremadoc dam workers, or the Cumberland farm workers, or the Marlow lace-makers.

Hunt

His isolation stunted his politics in a more obvious way. His only means of expression was to write, but writing only has power and influence if it is published. Shelley in Italy was forced to rely on his liberal friends in London to get his poems and pamphlets published. In part, he was in the hands of Ollier, his publisher. But in the main he depended on his friend and admirer Leigh Hunt. Shelley adored Hunt:

> You will see Hunt – one of those happy souls
> Which are the salt of the earth, and without whom
> This world would smell like what it is – a tomb.[133]

Hunt reciprocated this affection. He always thought highly of Shelley, and was the first newspaper editor to publish him. He welcomed the idea of being joint editor with Byron and Shelley of a new liberal political quarterly.

But politically the two men were poles apart. Hunt was a liberal reformer, though more courageous than many who have followed him. He hated the idea of mass action. He was a deist, not an atheist. He disliked George IV, but he was not a republican. He admired Shelley's lyrical poetry and his reforming spirit, but the revolutionary calls to action of *The Mask of Anarchy* and poems like it terrified him. The more explicit and the more popular the calls, the more Hunt shrank from them.

Shelley's respect and liking for Hunt often blurred the political differences between them. More importantly, they persuaded him to rely on Hunt as a publisher. During his four years in Italy, Shelley never bothered to seek out more radical publishers. When he wrote something, he sent it, automatically, to Ollier and to Hunt. When he wanted advice about publication, he sought it from Hunt.

And so Leigh Hunt, the warm-hearted liberal and supporter of free speech, became, uncomfortably but firmly, the censor of some of the most powerful political writing in the English language. In the great period of Shelley's writing, the autumn and winter of 1819, Shelley's anxious letters to Hunt tell their own story:

From Florence, 14–18 November 1819:
'You do not tell me whether you have received my lines on the Manchester affair.'[134]

From Pisa, 5 April 1820:
'I don't remember if I acknowledged the receipt of "Robin Hood"—no more did you of "Peter Bell". There's tit for tat! . . . Then on my side is the letter to Carlile, in which I must tell you I was considerably interested.'[135]

From Pisa, 1 May 1820:
'I wish to ask you if you know of any bookseller who would like to publish a little volume of *popular songs*, wholly political, . . .'[136]

From Pisa, 26 May 1820:
'One thing I want to ask you—do you know any bookseller who wd. publish for me an octavo volume entitled "A philosophical View of Reform". It is boldly but temperately written— & I think readable—. . . Will you ask & think for me?'[137]

Hunt ignored all these requests and inquiries. The poems he received he didn't publish; with regard to the poems and pamphlets he was asked about, he made no reply. So *The Mask of Anarchy* was not read until ten years after Shelley's death when Hunt himself, assuming correctly that the agitation round the 1832 Reform Bill would save him from censorship, published it at some profit. The Carlile letter, one of the greatest ever defences of free speech, was similarly shelved. So was the satire on Wordsworth, *Peter Bell the*

Third. 'A Philosophical View of Reform' and all the political poems remained in Shelley's notebooks, never to reach the public to which they were so ardently addressed. The reason was political. After a flurry of protest about Peterloo, the liberal publishers began to trim their sails. Shelley protested bitterly in a letter to Hunt in December 1819:

What a state England is in! But you will never write politics. I don't wonder; but I wish then that you would write a paper in the *Examiner* on the actual state of the country, and what, under all the circumstances of the conflicting passions and interests of men, we are to expect,—not what we ought to expect or what if so and so were to happen we might expect—but what, as things are, there is reason to believe will come—and send it me for my information. Every word a man has to say is valuable to the public now, and thus you will at once gratify your friend, nay instruct, and either exhilarate him, or force him to be resigned, and awaken the minds of the people.[138]

It was useless. Hunt's replies were as jolly and as uninformative as ever.

The censorship of all this political writing was the more appalling in that there *were* publishers in England at that time who would have published it. What mighty mischief Richard Carlile would have made with *The Mask of Anarchy*, or 'Men of England' or even the Carlile letter; how delighted he and his young supporters would have been to have been prosecuted for the vicious satire in *Peter Bell*! And there were others, besides Carlile: William Cobbett; Tom Wooler of the *Black Dwarf*; the editors of the *Cap of Liberty* or the *Medusa*; or even Robert Owen of New Lanark, who might have recognized in the 'Philosophical View of Reform' the embryo of the socialism to which he was turning.

But Hunt kept it all firmly locked up. No publisher of his circle would dare to print any of it. The government and its hatchet men in the Society for the Prosecution of Vice were constantly sniffing around the print works for anything remotely subversive. In 1820, Shelley's friend, the stockbroker Horace Smith, financed the publication of *Swellfoot the Tyrant*. No more than seven copies had been sold before the

Society swooped with its threats and its injunctions. Smith, to save his printer and his fortune, obligingly 'made a bon-fire'[139] of all the remaining copies, so no one (save seven prudes and spies) read that either.

All Shelley's 1819 political writing was censored. But Shelley could not reasonably blame Hunt. At least Hunt was in England publishing. Every issue of the *Examiner*, however castrated, was liable to prosecution. Shelley risked nothing. He was basking in the sunshine of Livorno or gazing at pictures in the Florentine galleries or taking part in shooting competitions with Byron at Pisa. Sometimes he looked for excuses. 'I am engaged also in a political work,' he wrote to John and Maria Gisborne on 23 December 1819, '. . . & if the faculties of my mind were not imprisoned within a mind whose bars are daily cares & vulgar difficulties I might yet do something.'[140] Sometimes he blamed his health: 'I consider Poetry very subordinate to moral & political science, & if I were well, certainly I should aspire to the latter.'[141]

But neither his health, nor his 'daily cares and vulgar difficulties', could properly be blamed for his political im-potence. It was his own decision, freely taken, to abandon the seat of politics which interested him for a 'poet's life'. And so, by his own admission in the very first line of *The Mask of Anarchy*, he 'lay asleep in Italy'.

Shelley's anger at the 1819 censorship faded rapidly as Hunt and Ollier did publish his less dangerous material. In 1820, Ollier published *Hellas* ('very prettily', Shelley com-mented) and *The Cenci*. Hunt saw to the publication of *Prometheus Unbound*, and the *Examiner* constantly published his odes to skylarks or selections, safely chosen, from *Prometheus* or *Epipsychidion*. The effects of this censorship, taken together with the publication of his safer, lyrical or meta-physical works, turned Shelley away from openly agitational writing, and, in the process, dimmed his faith in revolution. In the circumstances, this was hardly remarkable.

CONCLUSION: 'THE WEST WIND'

What *is* remarkable is that his revolutionary passion survived everything, even his own retreats and weaknesses, which conspired to quench it. His belief in the spirit of reason and co-operation which had inspired the French Revolution survived the suffocation of that spirit by property and superstition.

His revolutionary enthusiasm rose above his own background, above his self-imposed isolation and the stunted aspirations of his family and friends. It shone through his self-absorbed gloom. It survived the censorship and the patronage of the liberal intelligentsia.

Most remarkable of all, it was linked as though by some invisible thread to the common people from whom, for so much of his life, he was physically separated. As their confidence and activity rose, so did Shelley's revolutionary inspiration. As it fell, so he grasped feebly at the straws of 'gradual reform'.

The three climaxes of working class resistance to the English government during his lifetime were the three periods of Shelley's most prolific political writing. During the Luddite uprising, he composed *Queen Mab*; in its ebb, he composed almost nothing at all. During the Pentridge uprising and the postwar popular agitation which surrounded it, he wrote *The Revolt of Islam*, the 'Proposal for Putting Reform to the Vote' and the 'Address to the People on the Death of Princess Charlotte'. Immediately after Peterloo, the biggest of all the popular risings of his time, his own political volcano erupted and in four fantastic months he wrote '*The Mask of Anarchy*' (92 verses), *Peter Bell the Third* (129 verses), 'A Philosophical View of Reform' (about 20,000 words), the open letter on Carlile (about 10,000 words), at least a dozen shorter political poems, and the last, exquisite act of *Prometheus Unbound*. It is one of the most productive periods in the history of English literature, and its inspiration was the stirring of the English common people. 'These are not times in which one has much spirit for writing Poetry,' he wrote to his cousin. Tom Medwin, 'although there is a keen air in them that sharpens the wits of men and makes them imagine vividly in the midst of despondence.'[142]

As with the Luddite uprising, the ebb of the Peterloo agitation corresponded with an ebb in Shelley's political writing, though each of the three great European risings of the next two years brought a thrilling revolutionary poem. The Naples uprising was heralded by the 'Ode to Naples' (August 1820); the Greek uprising by *Hellas* (autumn 1821); and, most magnificent of all, the Spanish uprising by the 'Ode to Liberty' (1820):

> A glorious people vibrated again
>   The lightning of the nations: Liberty
> From heart to heart, from tower to tower, o'er Spain,
>   Scattering contagious fire into the sky,
> Gleamed.[143]

Shelley's inspiration was the vibration of the 'glorious people'. But the result of that inspiration never reached them. 'I wonder why I write verses,' he wrote sadly to Peacock, 'for no one reads them.'[144] A long time previously, he had written to Elizabeth Hitchener in the course of musing as to whether or not he would be sent to prison for his political agitation: 'I am yet but a viper in the egg, they say. I have all the venon but I cannot sting.'[145]

Shelley's was the agony of the orator who could not reach his audience; of the pamphleteer who could not reach his readership. His was the archetypal voice crying in the wilderness.

These were times when this isolation got the better of him and plunged him into a melancholy from which there seemed no escape. Much of his last and very complicated poem, called *The Triumph of Life*, is so encased in gloom as to deny the meaning of its title. And a lot of his glorious elegy to Keats – *Adonais* – positively welcomes death as a release from the apparently hopeless task of changing the living world. It is as though the death of the brilliant young Keats, hounded to his grave by the Tory clique of critics in

London, symbolized the futility of all radical writing. In a celebrated verse of this poem, he even envies Keats his early death and muses, more eloquently and yet more pessimistically than anywhere else, on his own pointless agitation:

> Peace, peace! He is not dead, he doth not sleep—
> He hath awakened from the dream of life—
> 'Tis we, who lost in stormy visions, keep
> With phantoms an unprofitable strife,
> And in mad trance, strike with our spirit's knife
> Invulnerable nothings.—*We* decay
> Like corpses in a charnel; fear and grief
> Convulse us and consume us day by day,
And cold hopes swarm like worms within our living clay.[146]

This gloom, this fear that he was hitting at nothing, haunted him always. If he had fallen victim to it completely, he would no doubt have taken the road of so many disillusioned revolutionaries, settled for what is 'immediately practicable' and drifted gently to the right.

This he did not do. More often than not he argued himself through his gloom and his isolation and triumphantly redeclared his revolutionary principles. Of this, there is one outstanding example.

One dark autumn afternoon in October 1819, when he was at the very height of his poetic powers, he went for a long walk along the banks of the Arno river, at Florence. He was brooding on a hostile review of *The Revolt of Islam* which he had read in the *Quarterly Review*. As he walked, the wind blew up from the west scattering the autumn leaves in front of him. And Shelley wrote a poem – perhaps his most famous poem.

It was about the wind – but not just about the wind. For as he walked, the wind, and everything associated with it, became a series of shifting symbols each connected with Shelley's ideas, his revolutionary inspiration and his powerlessness to put it into effect. First the wind is a swirling chaos, hurling before it all the different people of the world in a chaos of starvation and plague:

> O wild West Wind, thou breath of Autumn's being,
> Thou, from whose unseen presence the leaves dead
> Are driven, like ghosts from an enchanter fleeing,
>
> Yellow, and black, and pale, and hectic red,
> Pestilence-stricken multitudes: . . .[147]

And then the wind, chaotic as it may seem, becomes a carrier of the seeds of revolution which will bring a brighter day. Like the chariots from Demogorgon's cave, the wind has two qualities – it destroys *and* it preserves:

> O thou,
> Who chariotest to their dark wintry bed
>
> The wingèd seeds, where they lie cold and low,
> Each like a corpse within its grave, until
> Thine azure sister of the Spring shall blow
>
> Her clarion o'er the dreaming earth, and fill
> (Driving sweet buds like flocks to feed in air)
> With living hues and odours plain and hill:
>
> Wild Spirit, which art moving everywhere;
> Destroyer and preserver; hear, oh, hear.[148]

The next section talks of the storm which the wind is brewing up for the world; and the next of the shattering effect which that storm will have on the 'old palaces and towers' lying beneath the sea. Nothing, however deeply ingrained in society, shall escape the wind's revolutionary sweep.

The last two sections switch from the description of the wind to the plight of Shelley, censored and politically impotent, unable to affect the wind's tempestuous course, or even to run with it. This reads, and is often taught, as simple self-pity. Newman Ivey White, the first of the modern American Shelley scholars, who wrote a huge biography of Shelley in 1940, put it differently and very well: '*Ode to the West Wind* . . . loses much of its appearance of sentimental self-pity when seen as a deep realisation of the disparity between the tremendous thing that must somehow be done and the inadequacy of one mind and body to do the task.'[149]

Shelley starts by regretting that the unbounded enthusiasm and energy of his youth, like the ideals which first
inspired him, seem constantly to be on the wane:

> If even
> I were as in my boyhood, and could be
>
> The comrade of thy wanderings over Heaven,
> As then, when to outstrip thy skiey speed
> Scarce seemed a vision; I would ne'er have striven
>
> As thus with thee in prayer in my sore need.[150]

When he was young, the revolution seemed close. It was
possible to run with it, even to 'outstrip it'. Now, things
have changed:

> A heavy weight of hours has chained and bowed
> One too like thee: tameless, and swift, and proud.[151]

And yet the poem ends with a cry to the wind to lift the
poet; to keep his ideas *fierce* and *impetuous* as they had been
in his youth; and to turn his poetry, which seemed dead,
into a mighty agitation which would reach and awaken all
humanity:

> Be thou, Spirit fierce,
> My spirit! Be thou me, impetuous one!
>
> Drive my dead thoughts over the universe
> Like withered leaves to quicken a new birth!
> And, by the incantation of this verse,
>
> Scatter, as from an unextinguished hearth
> Ashes and sparks, my words among mankind!
> Be through my lips to unawakened earth
>
> The trumpet of a prophecy. O, Wind,
> If Winter comes, can Spring be far behind?[152]

Shelley was a revolutionary, through and through. And
in one sense, at least, his call was answered. His poetry,
ignored and censored in his own time, *did* become 'the
trumpet of a prophecy' forever afterwards.

7

The Trumpet of a Prophecy: 1822–1980

You are a funny people, you Shelleyites. You are playing – at a safe distance yourself, maybe – with fire. In spreading Shelley, you are indirectly helping to stir up the great socialist question, the great question of the needs and wants of unhappy men; the one question which bids fair to swamp you for a bit.

Henry M. Stanley, the explorer, 1887[1].

Franz Mehring's life of Karl Marx has the following account of Marx's interest in English literature:

After Marx had become permanently domiciled in London, English literature took first place, and the tremendous figure of Shakespeare dominated the field; in fact the whole family practised what amounted to a Shakesperean cult. Unfortunately, Marx never at any time dealt with Shakespeare's attitude to the great questions of the day. Referring to Byron and Shelley, however, he declared that those who loved and understood these two poets must consider it fortunate that Byron died at the age of thirty-six, for had he lived out his full span he would undoubtedly have become a reactionary bourgeois, whilst regretting on the other hand that Shelley died at the age of twenty-nine, for Shelley was a thorough revolutionary and would have remained in the van of socialism all his life.[2]

This statement, with minor differences, appeared in direct quotations in Edward Aveling's and Eleanor Marx's 1885 lecture, 'Shelley's Socialism'.

Professor Prawer of Oxford University, in his book *Karl Marx and World Literature*, doubts whether Marx ever said this. In all Marx's written work there is, according to Professor Prawer, no reference to Shelley. He concludes that Aveling must have made up the quotation, and presumably would argue that Mehring got it from Aveling.[3]

Eleanor Marx, however, is unlikely to have put her name to a quotation from her father which she knew to be invented. In a letter to Henry Salt, written in 1892, she expanded on Marx's respect for Shelley:

I have heard my father and Engels *again and again* speak of this: and I have heard the same from many Chartists it has been my good fortune to know as a child and young girl – Ernest Jones, Richard Moore, the Watsons, George Julian Harney and others. Only a very few months ago I heard Harney and Engels talking of the Chartist times and of the Byron and especially the Shelley-worship of the Chartists; and on Sunday last, Engels said: 'Oh, we all knew Shelley by heart, then.'[4] [Author's italics.]

Whether Marx said it or not, however, the quotation exactly describes the politics of both poets. Byron, as we have seen, never associated with the English working class in action. Had he returned to England he would have been an enthusiastic supporter of the 1832 Reform Bill, which gave the vote to people with property, and an opponent of the working class agitation for its extension.

Had Shelley returned to England he would have supported all the strikes and demonstrations for extending the Reform Bill. He would have joined enthusiastically in the developing working class Chartist movements of the 1840s. In the freer atmosphere after the downfall of the Tory administration, his poems and pamphlets would have been widely distributed. His isolation, which plagued him all his life, would have ended sooner than he had ever dreamed possible.

All this is speculation. Shelley was drowned in 1822. Yet he *was* 'in the van of socialism' for 100 years and more after his death.

Even while he was alive, the seeds of his later influence were sown. For this he had first to thank the publisher Richard Carlile, who was imprisoned in the autumn of 1819 for publishing the works of Tom Paine. Carlile, a tinsmith from Ashburton in Devon, led the fight for the freedom of the press against Sidmouth's gagging laws. He refused to trim his sails. He believed that the laws would only be changed if they were openly defied.

Before going to prison Carlile came across *Queen Mab*. Copies were scarce. Hookham had printed 250 in 1813, and still had about 180 of them. Many of the remaining seventy had been sent by Shelley to his friends. But the poem continued to circulate. William Polidori, Byron's friend, found a copy independently. The adventurer, Edward Trelawny, bought one in Switzerland— from a priest who was collecting the works of the devil!

Like Polidori and Trelawny, Carlile was thunderstruck by the poem. He did not agree with all of it. Its open delight in sex and its attack on marriage offended his Puritanism. But he loved its defiance and its contempt for authority. He contacted Ollier, who refused him permission to publish it in a pirate edition. Whether he managed to contact Shelley is not clear – but it seems unlikely.

In prison, Carlile continued to publish the *Republican*, and to read *Queen Mab*. In fact, he copied out the whole poem twice, in the hope that he would soon be able to publish it. His hope was fulfilled in a rather curious way.

In 1821, while Carlile was still in prison, a young supporter in his London offices called William Clarke purloined one of the copies of *Queen Mab* and printed it himself. He then put it up for sale in the 'pirate' bookstalls and street barrows around the Charing Cross Road in London. It sold like wildfire – and there were no royalties to pay.

Instead of rejoicing at the distribution of his poem where it would have the greatest effect, Shelley was outraged. He, an author, had been plundered! He mentioned the episode in four letters. To Charles Ollier, on 11 June 1821, he wrote the most angrily: 'I hear that a bookseller of the name of

Clarke has published a poem which I wrote in early youth, called Queen Mab. I have not seen it for some years, but inasmuch as I recollect it is villainous trash; & I dare say much better fitted to injure than to serve the cause which it advocates.'[5] The letter begged Ollier to 'pray give all manner of publicity to all disapprobation of this publication'.

To John Gisborne, five days later, he wrote in different tone:

A droll circumstance has occurred. Queen Mab, a poem written by me when very young, in the most furious style, with long notes against Jesus Christ, & God the Father and the King & the Bishops & marriage & the Devil knows what, is just published by one of the low booksellers in the Strand, against my wish & consent, . . . You may imagine how much I am amused.—For the sake of a dignified appearance however, & really because I wish to protest against all the bad poetry in it, I have given orders to say that it is all done against my desire,—and have directed an attorney to apply to Chancery for an injunction, which he will not get.[6]

To Claire he wrote of his 'annoyance' at the publication,[7] and to the *Examiner* a pompous, formal letter disassociating himself not just from the publication but also from the content of *Queen Mab*.[8] He added that he was, of course, opposed to confiscation of published works; to the imprisonment of authors; and to the 'inculcation of the truth of Christianity or Monarchy' by such methods. But the rider failed to remove the impression that he regarded his own 'reputation' (such as it was – for he was hated in high society) as more important than the defence of his great poem.

It was certainly *not* true that Shelley regarded *Queen Mab* as 'villainous trash'. He had given a copy to his friend Edward Williams, and he revelled in Williams's admiration of it. In November 1817, he had sent a copy to Nicholas-Waller, writing: ' . . . after six years of added experience & reflection, the doctrines of equality & liberty & disinterestedness, & entire unbelief in religion of any sort, to which

this poem is devoted, have gained rather than lost that beauty & that grandeur which first determined him [the author]
to devote his life to the investigation & inculcation of them.'[9]
His disassociation from his own poem can only have been
intended to ingratiate himself with 'respectable' literary
society.

At any rate, as he predicted, he did not get his injunction
to stop Clarke selling *Queen Mab*. The high court ruled that
Queen Mab was blasphemous and seditious, and that therefore its author had no copyright in it. Clarke was stopped,
however, by the Society for the Prosecution of Vice, the
self-appointed and government-supported guardian of the
public morals.

On the Society's instructions, Clarke was arrested for
criminal libel. He was threatened with a turn in Newgate
prison, and immediately capitulated. He agreed, in exchange
for his freedom, to burn all the remaining copies of his
edition of *Queen Mab*. This he did, and departed with a
considerable profit.

Richard Carlile was outraged. He was not, of course, in
the least bit worried that *Queen Mab* had been pirated –
though he did feel that the author's consent should have
been obtained, and that the author should share in the profit.
What infuriated him was that Clarke should have done a
deal with the authorities. '*Queen Mab*,' he bellowed in the
Republican of February 1821, 'was suppressed without going
to a jury, without even a struggle on behalf of its publisher!'

In the same article, Carlile outlined his doctrine of defiance
to the gagging laws: 'Prosecution would only accelerate the
demand.' True to his word, he immediately published his
own edition of *Queen Mab*, with the French, Latin and
German in the notes translated into English, and challenged
the Vice Society to prosecute. The edition sold widely – and
freely. This was the first of many Carlile victories against
the Society and the government.

Courteous as ever to Shelley, Carlile offered to withdraw
his edition of *Queen Mab* if 'the author wishes that the
publication be not proceeded with'. But Shelley never saw

the edition, and probably never even heard of it. Four
months after it appeared on the streets, he was drowned in
a storm in the Bay of Spezzia. The royalist press rejoiced.
John Bull, the nastiest of the nasty newspapers, put Shelley's
death down to the wrath of God:

Mr. Percy Bysshe Shelley, the author of that abominable and
blasphemous book, *Queen Mab*, was lately drowned in a storm
somewhere off the Mediterranean. His object in visiting that part
of the world, it was said, was to coalesce with some others of his
own opinions and to *write down Christianity*.
The visitation is therefore striking; and the termination of his
life (considering his creed) not more awful than surprising.[10]

It was Carlile and the *Republican* – not Hunt and the
liberals – who sprang to Shelley's defence. The same summer, Lord Castlereagh, promoted again to Lord Londonderry, had gone mad and cut his throat. On 23 August 1822
the *Republican* promptly printed a parody of the *John Bull*
obituary of Shelley:

The Marquis of Londonderry, the author of those detestable
measures which gave up the South of Italy to the most coarse and
leaden despotism in Europe, delivered up Genoa to a tyrant, in
the face of a British pledge of honour – and who indemnified the
employment of torture in Ireland to extort confession; lost his life
on Monday last in a fit of insanity, just as he was about to proceed
to the continent with the object of doing his best for the extinction
of dawning freedom in Spain and Greece. The visitation is therefore striking; and the termination of his life (considering his creed)
not more awful than surprising.

No wonder Carlile went to prison and was hated by the
authorities! The longer he stayed there, the more irreverent
grew the *Republican*. On 4 October 1822, for instance, it
heralded the state visit of George IV to Edinburgh with a
delightful little poem, modelled on an old Scottish royalist
ballad:

> Sawney, now the King's come.
> Sawney, now the King's come.

Kneel and kiss his royal bum.
Sawney, now the King's come.

No wonder, for that matter, that *Queen Mab* was so popular with the *Republican* readership. On 27 December 1822,
the paper could report: 'There are now no less than four
editions of this work on sale.' These included Clarke's,
against whom Carlile cautioned his readers. He went on: 'I
have also purchased the whole of the remaining copies of
the original edition printed by Mrs. Shelley in 1813. There
were but 180 copies and these will be sold at the same price
in sheets to those friends of Mr. Shelley, or others, who
may prize an original copy.'

The *Republican*, all the way to its demise in 1827, quoted
Shelley constantly – usually *Queen Mab*. Poems and letters
about Shelley were liberally printed, including, on 26 May
1824, a poem to Shelley of fourteen long stanzas by J. H.
Simson:

> . . . his warning voice
Is raised to wake the slumbering energies
Of countless multitudes.

On 11 February 1825, an article was published comparing
Shelley to Byron, and concluding: 'The aristocracy of England has not turned out a second man of Shelley's stamp.'
A correspondent to the paper from Tollington Park in
North London, Allen Davenport, was an enthusiastic admirer of Shelley. He caught the mood of Shelley which had
already invigorated thousands of working people:

He plants the standard of reason and philosophy in the citadel of
prejudice and superstition, and nobly challenges the multitude to
follow, conquer and destroy those ancient and implacable enemies
of the human mind. Such a poet must have appeared to many
persons more the poet of 1900 than one of the present age; and,
therefore, a cheap edition of his works was not to be contemplated; for who, when *Queen Mab* was written, contemplated the
unqualified freedom of the press?

The time is not far distant when public writers will find the necessity of paying due respect to the judgement of the class of people who have been denominated 'the swinish multitude'.

There needs no stronger proof of intellectual improvement amongst the common people than a cheap edition of *Queen Mab*. And I see no reason why the *Revolt Of Islam* should not follow *Queen Mab* into the hands of the mechanic and the labourer.[11]

Allen Davenport was right. There was in 1827 much more freedom of the press than anyone could have imagined in 1822 when Shelley died. For this, Carlile and his supporters were largely responsible. And his supporters were even more enthusiastic Shelleyans than Carlile himself.

These supporters were mainly young working men who collected around Carlile's London bookshop. When Carlile was imprisoned, they helped to publish the *Republican*. In the early spring of 1825 six of them were arrested and imprisoned at Newgate for the crime of 'serving in the shop of Richard Carlile'. Their reply was instant. They produced, from Newgate, the *Newgate Magazine*, which was even more rumbustiously offensive to the authorities than the *Republican*. Shelley was continually quoted.

Elijah Ridings, a reader in Manchester, wrote, in an early issue: 'There is yet no poet's works which contain golden strains of poetry and stronger attacks upon the absurd systems whose supporters have so long preyed on the industrious plebeians.'[12]

The editors replied the same month, long before the question attributed to Marx by Mehring: 'Byron in some respects gave way to the poison of religion. He was not willing, in this particular, to bear the full force of opposition. Shelley, on the contrary, gave his every feeling utterance clothed in the strength of manly eloquence: but alas! he was doomed to bear a corresponding neglect.'

In September 1825, the *Newgate Magazine* started a series of articles by 'C' – undoubtedly the old fighter Carlile himself, who was not only editing the *Republican* from Dorchester prison, but was also writing for his young friends' magazine in Newgate. The first article dealt with 'the character and writings of Shelley': 'He felt the tyranny by the few over the rights of the many with more than ordinary acuteness . . . Let us, friends of freedom, do that justice to him which he would have done to us had his existence been preserved.'

The series was taken up again in the spring of 1826. There was an article by 'C' in May (on *Queen Mab*); in June (on *The Revolt of Islam*); in July (on *The Cenci*); and in August a general summary. This was heralded as 'the last essay in the magazine before the prisoners were taken to the Compter'.

It matters not whether individual actions be good or bad. Are they sanctioned by those who rule over us? Are they permitted by our governors? This is the standard to which those who would seek immediate applause must resort. They must not foolishly give vent to their feelings without first ascertaining whether they will be agreeable to those who have the power to reward or punish.

Had Shelley consulted this standard – had he tuned his melodious language to the praise of the despoilers of humanity, then might the surrounding air have been filled with gratulations to his name, and his poetic merit blazoned across the world. But as true genius soars above the sphere of momentary applause, so did the unsullied mind of Shelley rest its claim upon the justice of the cause which it determined to advocate.

For this, Shelley has been assailed by the reviewers, and, by the cry of affected horror, his elegant productions have been kept in comparative obscurity.

There were signs that Shelley was doing more to Carlile and his circle than inspiring them. In one sense, he was changing their minds. Carlile's first comments on *Queen Mab* complained about Shelley's views on love and marriage. In the early editions of the *Republican*, the very few references to women are all patronizing. But in January 1825, the *Newgate Magazine* gave over two of its valuable pages to a remarkable article by 'a female materialist and republican'. It started with an unusual proposition:

No compleat reformation in the mind, morals or situation of *man* will ever take place till *woman* shall burst the fetters which have been imposed on her for ages – assert her right to be free and convince him that she is worthy to be treated like a rational thinking being . . .

Woman, in the present stage of society, is treated like a doll, considered incapable of reason and occupied through life with the most trifling concerns; but it is time for her at least to make an effort to be free . . .

Man has been enthralled, enslaved, deprived of his natural rights by the odious inventions of kingly tyranny and priestcraft; and the natural consequence of his degradation of mind has been that in all the relations of domestic life he has become as great a tyrant as the king or priest; recompensing himself for the loss of public freedom by being a private despot.

The article carries on relentlessly to a marvellous climax: 'But you, my countrywomen, possessed as I know you are of minds capable of the very highest improvement, shake off that lethargy which has so long benumbed your faculties – exert your reasoning power; read, reflect, inquire. Prove yourselves worthy of being not only conducted, but *conductors* of the great march towards truth and freedom . . .'

Who wrote this? Certainly not Carlile (who would not have been averse to pretending to be a woman to get his ideas in print). The style flows too freely. Perhaps it was the work of Jane Carlile, his wife, who stood in as editor of the *Republican* until she herself was arrested, and sent with her daughter to join Richard in prison in Dorchester. Imprisonment frustrated her more than it did her husband. Facilities were given to him to write and edit his magazine, but she, and her daughter, were provided with nothing. She was expected to sit in a corner and keep quite while the great emancipator got on with his work. Perhaps it was of Carlile himself that the 'female materialist and republican' wrote: 'men of the most liberal principles have studiously kept their wives in ignorance of their real sentiments . . . as if by some supernatural means it were possible for one sex to be free while the other is in bondage'.

Jane Carlile was devoted to Shelley. She insisted that a small bust of Shelley's head accompany her to prison. And her article, if hers it be, stirs from first to last with the poetry of *The Revolt of Islam*.

The posthumous debt which Shelley owes to the Carlile family is incalculable. They were not levellers, still less socialists. Carlile believed passionately in the sanctity of property, and in the 'motives to exertion' which the 'incentive of wealth' held out. But the Carliles discovered in Shelley a fellow freedom-fighter and enemy of censorship. They recruited him in their fight for the freedom of the press.

'Shelley,' wrote Carlile in 1826, 'has been kept in comparative obscurity.'[13] That was an understatement. Mary Shelley had published Shelley's relatively 'safe' posthumous poems – in 1824. But his collected works were not published until 1839; his prose works and essays not until 1840. While the upper classes and the literary establishment were kept in almost total ignorance of *Queen Mab*, the Carliles were pushing out more and more cheap editions of it to the working class.

There was one at the end of 1821, another in 1822, and then another. In the 1820s Carlile published four separate editions of *Queen Mab*, all with the notes translated, all cheap, all selling almost exclusively among the working class. In 1832, at the peak of the agitation around the Reform Bill, Henry Hetherington and James Watson, editors of the *Poor Man's Guardian*, the best-selling of the working class papers, published an edition of *Queen Mab*, at threepence, again with the notes all translated. This edition became the most popular of all. There is no record of how many it sold, but it went on selling all through the 1830s, 1840s, 1850s and even the 1860s. The *Poor Man's Guardian*, rather curiously, didn't have any articles on Shelley, but its voluminous advertisements for books and bookshops usually carried a reference to Shelley or to *Queen Mab*. Shelley's poem played a great part in the struggle of papers like the *Poor Man's Guardian* for the right to publish freely for the working classes – a struggle which was only won after Hetherington himself and Watson and countless *Poor Man's Guardian* sellers had gone to prison for offending against the Stamp Act.

The American scholar Newman Ivey White, in his research for his life of Shelley, read through every single British periodical and newspaper of the 1820s, 1830s and 1840s. He found that Shelley's reputation for the twenty years after his death was sustained in the main by the working class radical papers. From 1823 to 1840, he finds thirty-four references to Shelley in publications reflecting what he calls 'upper or middle class intellectual radicalism or extreme liberalism', and eighty-six in publications 'reflecting the working class radical interest in Shelley'.[14]

A good many of these were in the publications of Robert Owen, the philanthropist whose collectivist ideas earned him the title 'the father of English socialism'. Newman Ivey White remarks that if Owen *was* the father of British socialism, then Shelley could be regarded as its grandfather. Owen was devoted to Shelley's writings, and his publications, most notably the newspaper *New Moral World* of the late 1820s, bristle with Shelley quotations.

Anyone who published Shelley in any form – and particularly those who published *Queen Mab* – ran the risk of prosecution by the Society for the Prosecution of Vice. These 'guardians of morality' were supported by the government, and sought by prosecution or threat of it to suppress all radical material, especially that which opposed established religion or the sex and marriage laws. In 1841, Hetherington and his friends decided to challenge the Society to an open contest. They took out a 'test' prosecution against the rich society publisher Edward Moxon, who was making a lot of money from the first (1839) edition of Shelley's collected poems. The prosecution named *Queen Mab* as a 'blasphemous libel'. The charge sheet quoted great gobbets of atheism from the poem and stated the obvious fact that the poem was 'a scandalous, impious, profane and malicious libel of and concerning the Christian religion'.

Moxon hired his friend Thomas Talfourd, one of the most brilliant barristers of the time, to defend *Queen Mab* against this charge. Talfourd argued in court, with much flowery rhetoric, that Shelley's atheism was a flight of fancy. The court was unimpressed. Moxon was found guilty of blasphemous libel. It was then up to Hetherington to apply for sentence – which of course he didn't do.

Hetherington had proved to his own satisfaction that as far as the law of blasphemy was concerned, the courts were equally bigoted towards rich defendants as they were to the poor like himself. Practically, he had proved little else. He and Francis Place, who advised the *Queen Mab* prosecution, hoped that they might, by this example, shame the Vice Society into dropping their blasphemy prosecutions. But the Society was not to be shamed. The prosecutions went on. Charles Southwell, G. J. Holyoake, Thomas Paterson, Matilda Roalfe, William Baker and, in Scotland, Thomas Finlay and his son-in-law Henry Robinson – all these unsung champions of our press freedom were prosecuted and convicted of blasphemy during the next five years. And it was their courage and defiance of the law rather than the court games of Francis Place which finally put a stop to blasphemy prosecutions. But *Queen Mab*, at least, was never prosecuted again. Indeed, in the years that followed the Moxon prosecution – 1840–48, the years of the Chartist agitation for votes for the working class – *Queen Mab* and a lot of other Shelley poems were more widely read than ever before, and probably than ever since.

Eleanor Marx, I suspect, was voicing her own preferences when she suggested that Shelley was more 'worshipped' than Byron by the Chartists. The biographies and autobiographies of the Chartist leaders – even the more militant leaders like George Julian Harney – unanimously proclaim Byron as their favourite. But Shelley *was* read, learned and recited among the Chartists. The Rhymer Thomas Cooper included several Shelley poems in his programme for entertainment before huge Chartist audiences.

The Chartist *Circular* for 19 October 1839 had a short article entitled:'Percy B. Shelley. Among the few who had been called "Poets of the People" '. The article started, 'Assuredly the first and noblest name is that of Shelley. The treatment of the people by the upper classes roused in him violent emotions of indignation and compassion, and, inspired by these feelings, he wrote to teach his injured countrymen the great laws of union, and the strength of the passive resistance.'

The article started a series in the *Circular* on 'The Politics of Poets'. These included Byron, Milton and Burns (the latter more than once). The death of Wordsworth was greeted without great mourning. 'In announcing his death,' said a notice in the *Chartist Democratic Review* of May 1850, 'we must acknowledge that we are not impressed with any very heavy sense of sorrow, for we cannot include him in the list of those who like Burns, Byron and Shelley have secured the lasting worship of the people . . .'

A brilliant article in the *Northern Star*, the biggest-selling and best-known Chartist paper, by Thomas Frost, on 2 January 1847, showed that there were many socialists and freedom-fighters who had come to the same conclusion as had Marx in his disputed quotation on Byron and Shelley – before Marx could possibly have said it.

As Byron was the impersonation of the present transitionary state of the public mind, so was Shelley the representative and exponent of the future, not the futurity-idea inculcated by our clerical instructors, dim and shadowy as Ossian's Hall of Loda, but the moral summer of the world, the realization of the Arcadian fable and Hebraic myth. Shelley was the most highly gifted harbinger of the coming brightness, his whole aspirations were towards the future, as evinced in the *Queen Mab*, and the equally beautiful *Revolt of Islam*.

Byron's morbid imagination, the mother of those dark creatures of his fancy, the Laras and the Childe Harolds of his great poems, received many a scintillation of eternal light from his intercourse with Shelley, and its effect was visible in those cantos of *Childe Harold* which were written during their continental intimacy. The misanthropy which occasionally gleams forth in the writings of Byron – 'the stinging of a heart the world had stung' – was unknown to Percy Bysshe Shelley. He wrote not of the past like Scott, nor lingered over the present like Byron, but directed his whole thoughts and aspirations towards the future.

Byron, as he cast a melancholy glance at Spain and Italy, turned his eyes towards Greece . . . and he hoped. But Shelley gazed deeper into the gloom of futurity, and saw in the coming time the realization of his own bright visions of Utopia – not only Greece free from Moslem rule, and the unity and independence of Italy restored, but the unity and the fraternity of the whole human race . . .

Another expert witness to the appeal of Shelley to the working people was Frederick Engels. In his *Condition of the English Working Class* (1845) he wrote: 'Shelley, the genius, the prophet, Shelley and Byron, with his glowing sensuality and his bitter satire upon our existing society, find most of their readers in the proletariat; the bourgeoisie owns only castrated editions, family editions cut down in accordance with the hypocritical morality of today.'[15]

Ernest Jones, the Chartist leader, understood his Shelley better than most of the liberal Romantics who followed him. 'Shelley,' he wrote in *The Labourer* in 1847, 'had the happy power of never swerving from a practical aim in his most ideal productions.'[16] But by then, as the Chartist agitation subsided, the Shelley family, and a growing host of wealthy and respectable literary gentlemen, were combining to erase from Shelley all trace of that 'practical aim', and to establish Shelley-worship as an upper class fetish.

Lady Jane Shelley, who married Percy, Shelley's only surviving son, built a shrine to Shelley in Boscombe and mummified his effects. She commissioned statues and monuments to Shelley (including the Onslow Ford statue at University College, Oxford). She set in hand the writing of the Shelley Memorials, a ridiculous 'tribute' to the poet. Gradually, she prepared the ground for an orgy of cultured Shelley-worship, which reached its climax in the 1880s and 1890s.

The orgy really got under way when Shelley was adopted by W. M. Rossetti, whose 'Memoir' to Shelley, attached as a preface to a beautiful (if censored) edition of Shelley's poems in 1870, was full of extravagant language about 'the immortal poet'. It was uncritical and reverent. It allowed Shelley a 'belief in freedom', carefully skated over his atheism and did not even mention his femininism.

Over the next thirty years an increasingly hysterical literary establishment wailed and grovelled at the feet of the Great White Angel Shelley whom they had created. The 'standard biography' by Edward Dowden, published in 1886, snipped away at Shelley until he was just as his society readers liked him. Shelley's 'lyric poetry' was recited at countless literary soirées. It was as though the ghost of his own satire of cultured London – in *Peter Bell the Third* – had come to haunt his own reputation:

> And all these meet at levees;—
>   Dinners convivial and political;—
> Suppers of epic poets;—teas,
> Where small talk dies in agonies;—. . .[17]

Shelley – though never *Peter Bell the Third* – suddenly became popular in society circles. Great debates broke out after dinner over Shelley's private life. Scholars scraped around for titbits about the life of poor Harriet Shelley which would substantiate the prevailing view that it was *her* fault that Shelley left her, or, more scandalously, that she was loose-living and had had affairs with other men before Shelley left her. Others, a minority, took Harriet's side. The debate, and the hagiography, raged on.

As a model of all this, there is nothing to beat the essay on Shelley by the poet Francis Thompson, which was written in 1889, though not published until after his death in 1907. So popular was the essay that it was published in book form. It appealed instantly to a huge clientele among the literary well-to-do, and went into countless editions, many of which are still cluttering up second-hand bookshops today. A glimpse of Thompson's style will be enough to illustrate his purpose:

Coming to Shelley's poetry we peep over the wild mask of revolutionary metaphysics, and we see the winsome face of a

child . . . The universe is his box of toys. He dabbles his fingers
in the day-fall. He is gold-dusty with tumbling amidst the stars.
He makes bright mischief with the moon. The meteors nuzzle
their noses in his hand. He teases into growling the kennelled
thunder, and laughs at the shaking of his fiery chain. He dances
in and out of the gates of heaven: its floor is littered with his
broken fancies. He runs wild over the fields of ether . . . He gets
between the feet of the horses of the sun . . .[18]

This goes on for thirty pages. Even the hardest stomachs
have been heard to heave at the description of *Prometheus
Unbound* as: '. . . this amazing lyric world, where immortal
clarities sigh past in the perfumes of the blossoms, populate
the breathings of the breeze . . . where the very grass is all
a-rustle with lovely spirit-things . . .'[19]

And yet, Thompson mourns, Shelley was an *atheist*. 'We
reflect,' he writes, in what is a most unfair comment on Sir
Timothy and Lady Shelley, 'how gross must have been the
moral neglect in the training of a child who *could* be an
atheist from his boyhood.'[20]

But Thompson is sure that Shelley wasn't really an atheist.
He 'was struggling – blindly, weakly, stumbingly, but still
struggling – towards higher things.'[21]

The proof of that? Thompson has it: 'We do not believe
that a truly corrupted spirit can write consistently ethereal
poetry. We would believe in nothing if we believed that, for
it is the consecration of a lie . . . The devil can do many
things. But the devil can not write poetry.'[22] A poet couldn't
be an atheist, or he wouldn't be a poet: 'We cannot credit
that any Christian ever had his faith shaken through reading
Shelley . . .'[23]

No wonder the essay was popular. Here was one of the
literary giants of the age rescuing Shelley from the rim of
hell; dragging him back from the sinfulness and socialism
to which evil men and women had seduced him. Shelley,
numbed, castrated, angelic, could be put back on the shelves
of the most respectable libraries, taught in the most respectable school, even intoned in the most respectable churches.

Thompson's essay is not exceptional. It was typical of the

Shelley rescue operation carried out by the literary establishment of his time. The Shelley Society was formed in
1886. Its chairman was a Dr Furnivall, who joined because
his father had known Shelley. Other founder members
included the Reverend Stopford Brooke, whose opening
lecture to the society argued: 'The world will always be
drawn to Shelley for the religious gravity of his teaching';[24]
and the publisher Buxton Forman, who devoted a lot of his
time to persuading the society to forget about *Queen Mab*.

'To this day,' complained Forman in a lecture on 14 April
1886, 'Shelley is far more widely known as the author of
Queen Mab than as the author of *Prometheus Unbound*. As the
latter really strengthens the spirit, while the former does
not, we, who reverence Shelley for his spiritual enthusiasm,
desire to see all that changed. And the change is advancing.'[25]

Until then, as Forman well knew, for he collected Shel-
leyana and had in his library all the editions of *Queen Mab*,
Shelley had been read and appreciated among the working
class mainly for *Queen Mab*. Forman and his friends hoped
to win him back for respectable people who could understand about literature, by concentrating on his 'mysticism',
'lyricism' and 'spiritual enthusiasm'.

That campaign was successful, both in the immediate
battle and in the war. Queen Mab *was* relegated. The Oxford
edition of Shelley's poems – the standard work for the last
fifty years – has *Queen Mab* stuck at the back under the
heading which Buxton Forman had suggested: 'Juvenilia'.
And the efforts of the Shelley worshippers of that period –
from the extreme Francis Thompson to the more moderate
Buxton Forman – laid the basis for the disguising of Shelley
which has lasted for nearly 100 years.

They did not win without a fight, however. Not all the
founders of the Shelley Society were worshippers of the
Thompson school. Among those who were not was Henry
Salt, a delightful bananas-and-sandals socialist who had been
a teacher at Eton until he could stand it no longer. Salt
respected Shelley's opinions, and liked him the more for
them. His book on Shelley, *Poet and Pioneer*,[26] went into

many editions, and sold widely in the growing socialist organizations and trade unions.

A more vociferous contributor on behalf of the real Shelley was George Bernard Shaw. Shaw complained bitterly at Forman's lecture on *Queen Mab*, which was, he said, a 'perfectly original poem on a great subject'.[27] Even more ferocious was Edward Aveling, whose expulsion from the society was moved when it was known that he was living out of wedlock with Eleanor Marx. Only when it was pointed out that Shelley himself had eloped with the unmarried Mary Godwin was the motion for explusion withdrawn.

In general, the temper of debate in the Shelley Society was suitably calm and well-mannered. But, at a meeting on 13 April 1887, the differences between the two factions burst the bounds of politeness. A Mr A. G. Ross, B.A., spoke on *The Revolt of Islam*. Mr Ross was an objective academic Tory who believed that poetry should be restricted to those who knew about it. He had been enraged to discover that workers and even socialists were quoting a well-known English poet to their advantage. He gave full vent to the moderate expression which is the hallmark of academic objectivity: 'Now no one can contest the right of any one, even though he may be a mere sans culotte who runs about with a red rag, to quote Shelley when or where he pleases; but when the blatant and cruel socialism of the street endeavours to use the lofty and sublime socialism of the study for its own base purpose it is time that with no uncertain sound all real lovers of the latter should disavow any sympathy with the former . . .'[28]

Mr Ross went on to claim all literature for his class: 'It will be clearly understood that I strongly protest against any imaginative writer being cited as an authority in favour of any political or social action or inaction, and I will go so far as to say that I think the greatness of his writings affords a rough measure of his inability to manage the world's affairs, or to judge justly of another's management of them.'[29]

The Revolt of Islam, he decided (without any real discussion of the poem), had to be judged 'from the purely literary standpoint' and not by 'the vicious habit of judging poets by what they have taught'. Judged by that standpoint it was, inevitably, 'a failure'.[30] 'Let us then honour and reverence the man and his works for his and their godlike qualities, not the god for his manlike qualities.'[31]

Ross's lecture provoked a lively discussion. Henry Salt protested. So did Bernard Shaw – though he was quick to accept Ross's distinction between the 'socialism of the street' and 'the socialism of the study'.[32] 'Socialism,' he said, 'is not to be held responsible for many of the wild and wicked things that had been reputed to be done by street socialists.'[33]

Edward Aveling, on the other hand, 'maintained that the socialism of the study and the street was one and the same thing – and that constituted the beauty of modern socialism.'[34]

The debate continued, not so much in the Shelley Society, which did not last much longer, but outside. In 1892, the country gentlemen of Sussex celebrated the hundredth anniversary of Shelley's birth with a great feast, followed by a ceremonial opening of a new library at Horsham, Shelley's birthplace. Bernard Shaw was there. He commented gaily on the feelings of the guests:

On all sides there went up the cry, 'We want our great Shelley, our darling Shelley, our best, noblest, highest of poets. We will not have it said that he was a Leveller, an Atheist, a foe to marriage, an advocate of incest. He was a little unfortunate in his first marriage; and we pity him for it. He was a little eccentric in his vegetarianism; but we are not ashamed of that, we glory in the humanity of it [with morsels of beefsteak, fresh from the slaughter house, sticking between our teeth]. We ask the public to be generous – to read his really great works, such as the *Ode to a Skylark*, and not to gloat over those boyish indiscretions known as *Laon and Cythna, Prometheus, Rosalind and Helen, The Cenci*, the *Masque of Anarchy*, etc., etc. Take no notice of the Church papers; for our Shelley was a true Christian at heart.'[35]

Bernard Shaw chuckled to himself as he watched Edmund Gosse laboriously constructing this image of Shelley at the

Horsham library opening. He then fled to London for another meeting – at the Hall of Science, St Luke's parish in
East London.

That meeting, Shaw wrote, 'consisted for the most part
of working men'. 'It was summoned,' he went on, 'without
the intervention of any committee by Mr G. W. Foote, the
President of the National Secular Society, who, by his own
personal announcement and a few handbills, got a meeting
which beat Horsham hollow.'[36] After a few speeches, all
well received, Mr Foote 'recited Men of England, which
brought the meeting to an end amid thunders of applause.
What would have happened had anyone recited it at Horsham is more than I can guess. Possibly the police would
have been sent for.'[37]

Edward Aveling was a regular speaker at working class
meetings like the one at St Luke's. William Diack, in his
history of the Aberdeen Trades Council, recalls a 'crowded'
meeting that same summer of 1892 in the Oddfellows Hall,
Crooked Lane, in which Aveling 'thrilled his audience with
a dramatic rendering of some sonorous verses from Shelley's
Masque of Anarchy'.[38]

Salt, Shaw, Foote, Elanor Marx and Aveling had some
powerful allies. Edward Carpenter, the socialist poet whose
prose poems in the style of Walt Whitman sold thousands
of copies among working people, was an ardent Shelleyan.
Together with George Barnefield he wrote a rather complicated book called *The Psychology of the Poet Shelley* (George
Allen and Unwin, London 1925). In the early years of the
century these were joined by the women suffragists, led, as
we have seen, by Charlotte Despard.

It was an uphill battle. In the 1840s, as Engels noticed,
Shelley had been almost exclusively the property of the
working class. The Chartists had read him for what he was,
a tough agitator and revolutionary. The effect of the Shelley-
worship of the 1880s and 1890s was to weaken that image;
to present for mass consumption a new, wet, angelic Shelley
and to promote this new Shelley with all the influence and
wealth of respectable academics and publishers. A stream of

censored Shelley editions appeared on the market. In the lovely and popular series of selected poems of English poets published in the first quarter of the century by the Gresham Press, the introduction to the Shelley volume is by Alice Meynell, a close friend of Francis Thompson, and a fashionable poet and critic. 'This volume,' she wrote proudly, 'leaves out *all* Shelley's contentious poems.' The result is a horrible caricature – and there were scores like it.

The effect worked its way through to many influential writers and journalists on the Left, who, in an earlier age, might have read deeper and enjoyed Shelley, and passed on their enjoyment to others.

Henry Nevinson, for instance, chairman of the Men's Political Union for Female Suffrage, mused in his *Essays of Freedom* (1909) on the great English poets. He wrote at some length about Byron, Keats and Wordsworth – but when he came to Shelley he broke off, intimidated: 'And Shelley? – but his worshippers have made such a fool of Shelley that we dare not speak of him.'[39]

Robert Blatchford, editor of the *Clarion*, the largest-selling socialist paper of the time, loved books and was always urging his worker-readers to read and enjoy the best of English literature. But Blatchford had no time for Shelley – or rather for what he thought was Shelley.

'Is Shelley a great poet?' he asked in the *Clarion* of 16 February 1912. 'I say no . . . All that I ever want to read of Shelley I could put into one column of the Clarion.' Swinburne, Masefield, William Morris and even someone called Gould were, wrote Blatchford, better than Shelley. But Blatchford admitted he was reading Shelley only as a 'lyric poet'. He was reading only the Shelley who had been eulogized by Francis Thompson. Thompson's essay was, Blatchford declared, 'gorgeous nonsense'. But it had done the damage – even for Robert Blatchford. He tested Shelley by Francis Thompson's standard and he found Shelley boring.

When a volley of criticism greeted his first article on Shelley, Blatchford replied with another, almost as long, also on the front page. To one young worker who had written of his respect for Shelley, Blatchford replied: 'I hope he is not confusing art with politics. I was not, when I wrote of Shelley, thinking at all of his religious or political views. I don't go to Shakespeare, nor to Swinburne for sociology, nor for politics. I go to them for song, and for art. I ask from them the same kind of message that I get from the sunset and the moors, and the blackbird and the roses.'

But the sunset and the moors, the blackbird and the roses, do not use words. Poetry is made up of words. And words have meaning. Blatchford read Shelley without reading the words. He looked for a sort of soothing incantation, like the trilling of a blackbird, and he found that the expectation of Shelley built up by the Francis Thompsons was not fulfilled. Shelley was not especially good at trilling! And so Blatchford turned to savage him.

The readers of the *Clarion* did not agree. In spite of Blatchford, they continued to read Shelley. In 1925, thirteen years after Blatchford's outburst, the *Clarion* conducted a poll among its readers asking for nominations for the 'ten greatest British writers'.

The results, listed under the heading 'Shakespeare Dethroned', were as follows: 1) Dickens. 2) Shakespeare. 3) Hardy. 4) Walter Scott. 5) Thackeray. 6) Bernard Shaw. 7) William Morris. 8) Shelley. 9) Bunyan. 10) Chaucer. Shelley, then, was still among the top poets. Milton was eleventh, Keats twelfth, Wordsworth fourteenth, Tennyson fifteenth and Byron was not even in the first thirty! Blatchford, incidentally, had crept into the running himself. He was twenty-seventh.

By this time, the *Clarion* was losing popularity on the Left. The Russian Revolution had led to the formation of the British Communist Party, which attracted to itself a new band of confident and assertive Marxists. Many of these started to write for *Plebs*, a monthly 'paper of the people' which was started in 1919. In April 1921, Ernst Johns, a Communist Party member who often contributed on literary subjects, wrote an article about Rudyard Kipling. At the start of this article, Ernest Johns wrote:

Britain has long ago passed this stage and the erstwhile revolutionary English capitalist has settled down to respectability and orthodoxy; though not until their early struggles had inspired a poet of revolt in the person of Shelley.

This throwaway reference at the start of the article brought down on Ernst Johns' head a terrific hail of outrage. It came from a young Communist at Oxford University called Ralph Fox. Fox, later to become one of the outstanding Communist intellectuals of the 1920s and 1930s, wrote back furiously to denounce Johns for 'materialist misconception' and 'airy dogmatism'.

But it is when we come to Shelley—he inspired of revolutionary capitalism!—that I must make my loudest protest. For here is neither sense nor history . . .

In this proletarian movement, for it was proletarian in England, Shelley was not backward; rather was he in the full front of the battle. Mary Shelley tells us: 'He looked on all human beings as inheriting an equal right to possess the dearest privileges of our nature—the necessities of life when fairly earned by labour and intellectual instruction.' And we can be sure that Shelley's interpretation of the words 'necessities' and 'intellectual instruction' would still make the average Briton's hair rise.

After quoting two verses from *Song to the Men of England*, Ralph Fox urged any reader of *Plebs* who was still in doubt about what Shelley thought of the capitalists of his day to read *Peter Bell the Third*. And if anyone *still* wanted to understand the nature of class society at the time that Shelley was writing, Ralph Fox recommended Mark Rutherford's *Revolution in Tanner's Lane*, which, he said, should be written on vellum in letters of gold and placed on the altar of the English revolution'.

Fox ended his long letter with a rousing attack on the 'misuse' of materialism which divided history into stages and lumped all the writers and poets of each age into those stages. This attitude, he said, inspired 'the well-deserved ridicule of our movement'.

Ernest Johns, however, stuck to his airy dogma. In another long letter, printed in the June issue of *Plebs*, he asked:

Does Fox seriously class Shelley as a 'proletarian poet'? Is it not a more reasonable proposition that his atheism and republicanism are significant of the ideals of the advanced section of the revolutionary capitalist class which had still to wrest complete political dominance from the hands of the landed proprietors?

No, replied Ralph Fox. In the August 1921 issue of *Plebs* he had another wonderful letter, entitled *In Defence of Shelley*. After ridiculing the notion that the capitalist class in England from 1789 to 1832 was revolutionary, he came directly to the point:

Are we then to class Shelley as a liberal, a sort of humanitarian Byron, or is he as Beer indexes him in *The History of English Socialism* 'the poet of labour and communism?' There is, I think, only one test to distinguish the liberal from the socialist revolutionary. The first wants only political equality, the second demands in addition economic equality. In this, Shelley was beyond all equivocation a socialist, for the very basis of his philosophy was economic communism. That is why he was a human outcast when Byron was a popular and rather naughty hero.

Ralph Fox ended his long letter, which was spiced with quotations from *Queen Mab*, by dealing with some of the 'witnesses' produced by Ernest Johns for the view that Shelley was basically a bourgeois writer. 'Of course, old men like Saintsbury, W. M. Rossetti etc. have an interest in sneering at and glossing over the essence of Shelley, but that a Communist should help them, as Johns does, is a painful surprise to me.'

Ernest Johns made a weak stab at a reply, returning once more to the letter pages of *Plebs* in September 1921. His chief argument in this letter was that Shelley was a friend of Byron and Hunt, who were both obviously liberals. It followed that Shelley was a liberal! Ralph Fox did not bother to reply. The correspondence was closed.

But the argument went on among Communists. At first, Ralph Fox's view prevailed and Shelley was widely recommended as a revolutionary poet. The review page of the *Sunday Worker*, for instance, printed as article on 17 January 1928 by Lewis Wynne entitled 'Shelley—a Great Poet and a Great Rebel'. Shelley was described as 'a rebel in politics, philosophy and religion—a poet of revolution'. After outlining the state of England in Shelley's time, Lewis Wynne went on: 'Such was the poisonous social system which drove Shelley from England. Against it, he opposed the whole force of his genius. In the *Revolt of Islam*, *Prometheus Unbound*, *The Masque of Anarchy* and in many of his shorter poems and satires, Shelley showed himself a real propagandist as well as a noble creative spirit.'

But Shelley did not last long in the esteem of the Communist Party hierarchy. The openness and freedom among socialists to read, enjoy and criticize all kinds of literature, whoever the author and whatever their formal political persuasion, rapidly vanished. In its place came a crude party line which told people what they should and should not read. The All Russian Association of Proletarian Writers was set up in 1928 to 'eliminate liberal tendencies' in culture. In 1932, it was abolished in place of the even stricter Soviet Writers Union. You had to be a member of the union if you wanted to write anything at all. The censorship and aridity of the S.W.U. were faithfully accepted by the Communist Parties of the West – and most faithfully of all by the British Communist Party.

Shelley was a casualty of this new line. His name vanished from the pantheon of British writers approved by the Moscow-based Foreign Languages Publishing House. 'English literature,' decreed the 1936 edition of *International Literature*, 'will be represented by editions of the works of Dickens, Walter Scott, Tennyson, Byron and Oscar Wilde.' It was not until after the 'destalinization' of 1956 – the Khruschev speech which exposed some of what had happened under Stalin – that the Foreign Languages Publishing House brought out an edition – and a very good edition, too – of Shelley's works.

In a book called *Illusions and Reality*,[40] the most brilliant of all the young Communist intellectuals of the day, Christopher Caudwell, wrote on 'the sources of poetry'. His aim was to establish the party line, that all previous poetry had been written in the interests of another class, and was therefore useless for the new proletarian revolution which had come in Russia and was to come elsewhere.

Christopher Caudwell had read and enjoyed Shelley. But

this was not a time for enjoyment. Caudwell's conclusions are those of a party warrior: 'Shelley speaks for the bourgeoisie . . . The bourgeois trammelled by the restraints of the era of mercantilism is Prometheus, bringer of fire, fit symbol of the machine-wielding capitalist . . .'[41]

Well, here is Shelley 'speaking for the bourgeoisie' in *Queen Mab*:

> Commerce has set the mark of selfishness,
> The signet of its all-enslaving power
> Upon a shining ore, and called it gold:
> Before whose image bow the vulgar great,
> The vainly rich, the miserable proud, . . .[42]

Or in 'A Philosophical View of Reform':

. . . They have supplied us with two aristocracies. The one, consisting of great land proprietors, and merchants . . . The other is an aristocracy of attornies and excisemen and directors and government pensioners, usurers, stock jobbers, country bankers, with their dependents and descendants. These are a set of pelting wretches . . . Both in the habits and lives of this new aristocracy . . . there is nothing to qualify our disapprobation. They eat and drink and sleep, and in the intervals of those things performed with most ridiculous ceremony and accompaniments, they cringe and lie. They poison the literature of the age in which they live . . . Their hopes and fears are of the narrowest description. Their domestic affections are feeble, and they have no others. They think of any commerce with their species but as a means, never as an end, and as a means to the basest forms of personal advantage.[43]

Shelley *detested* the bourgeoisie.

The idea that Prometheus represents the new capitalist chained by 'the era of mercantilism' is even more grotesque. Prometheus, as he, his supporters and his enemies stress again and again, represents science and progress, not for one class but for all humanity. The whole point of *Prometheus Unbound* is that he is freed not by the efforts of people with knowledge and education (who alone are powerless properly to free their knowledge and education) but by the actions of the masses. Caudwell blunders on into the thicket:

Although Shelley is an atheist, he is not a materialist. . . . This idealism is a reflection of the revolutionary bourgeois belief that, once the existing social relations that hamper a human being are shattered, the 'natural man will be realised' – his feelings, his emotions, his aspirations, will all be immediately bodied forth as material realities. Shelley does not see that these shattered social relations can only give place to the social relations of the class strong enough to shatter them, and that in any case these feelings, aspirations and emotions are the product of the social relations in which he exists and that to realise them a social act is necessary, which in turn has its effect upon a man's feelings, aspirations and emotions.[44]

But Shelley *did* see all these things. He *did* see that a social act was necessary to shatter the social relations whereby the rich and powerful enslaved the poor majority. That is the theme of *Prometheus Unbound*, *The Mask of Anarchy* and *The Revolt of Islam*. He also saw that the 'social relations' which follow any such revolution must, if the revolution is to be worthwhile, be followed by the full development of human potential. That was the purpose of revolution. Barren talk of the social relations of a class strong enough to shatter the old order could never be an inspiration to people to rise in revolution.

And here is the dreadful paradox which confronted Caudwell and thousands of Communist intellectuals like him. He believed that the Communist Party was the only instrument of revolution and change. Yet the Russian government (and therefore the world Communist Parties) were engaged in a relentless assault on everything revolutionary. The central drive of Stalin's purges in the 1930s was not directed against the governments of the West or their agents. It was directed against the memory and meaning of the Russian Revolution. All contact with that revolution had to be annihilated; its leaders and theorists had to be publicly broken. Above all, the ideas of the revolution, chief among which was the liberation of human potential, had to be destroyed.

It followed that all culture which mattered was, by defi-
nition, culture which started after the revolution – 'proletarian culture', culture here and now, as laid down by
Stalin's cultural policemen. All apparently revolutionary literature in the past, especially poetry, had to be written off
as 'idealism', or part of a 'bourgeois revolution'. So Christopher Caudwell, a brave and brilliant young Communist,
tugged his own instincts and those of his readers away from
the thrill and inspiration of their revolutionary literary her-
itage. He patronized Byron and Keats, ridiculed Wordsworth, and expelled Shelley to the 'idealist' wilderness.

Sadly, Christopher Caudwell's close colleague and mentor,
Ralph Fox, did not criticise this 'misuse of materialism' in
considering Shelley, as he had so effectively demolished it in *Plebs*
in 1921. Perhaps Ralph Fox too had had his enthusiasm and
better instincts blunted by the crudeness of the Party line. At any
rate, not long after the publication of *Illusion and Reality*,
Christopher Caudwell and Ralph Fox both died heroes' deaths
fighting for Republican Spain.

The new, Communist cultural orthodoxy, so powerfully
attacked at the time and later by George Orwell, persevered
throughout the explosion of reading which took place on the
Left at the end of the 1930s. The Left Book Club was set up
largely under the influence of the Communist Party. In twelve
years it published 257 books, and the circulation of the 'book of
the month' quickly soared to 40,000. It says something about the
philistinism of the club's organizers that only one of those books
was about literature. It was called *Literature and Society* and was
by David Daiches, whose view of Shelley was even cruder than
Caudwell's.

'Shelley,' he wrote, 'lacks sophistication. He has the outlook on life of a sensitive and intelligent child. He never
faced the real problems of earthly existence, though on the
other hand he never consciously retired into a dream world.
If he did spend his time in an unreal world he did not realize
it: he thought it was the real world and judged accordingly.
That is why Shelley, for all his great lyrical faculty, is a poet
whom we find, sooner or later, to be unsatisfying.'[45]

Like Blatchford, Daiches was reading the Shelley presented to him by his idolaters of the late nineteenth century. Once the straw Shelley was set up, it was easy to knock him down. But how could any intelligent socialist or radical describe the author of *Queen Mab*, *The Mask of Anarchy*, *Peter Bell the Third*, *Swellfoot the Tyrant*, 'Song to the Men of England' and 'England in 1819' as 'never facing the problems of earthly existence'?

All this was damaging enough for Shelley's reputation. Yet, at exactly the same time, another, still fiercer attack was being made on Shelley from an even more influential quarter.

By 1936 F. R. Leavis had established himself as one of Britain's top literary critics. From his base at Downing College, Cambridge, he was editing his own literary journal, *Scrutiny*. He had the reputation of being a bit of a maverick. He had fought for English literature against the hierarchy of Cambridge University (and Oxford), which took the view that most readable English literature is in Anglo-Saxon, and that a young man's (and certainly a young woman's) reading should stop at *Beowulf*.

In his *Revaluation*, published in 1936, Leavis attacked many of the sacred figures of English literature, including even Milton. His fiercest essay in the book is directed against Shelley. Shelley, wrote Leavis, is 'almost unreadable'. 'It is impossible,' he continues, 'to go on reading him at any length with pleasure.'[46]

To establish this assertion, Leavis develops some harsh textual criticism of some of Shelley's most famous poems. From sections of the 'Ode to the West Wind' he shows that Shelley's metaphors are often sloppy. He takes the line: 'Loose clouds like earth's decaying leaves are shed', and asks, 'In what respect are the "loose clouds" like "decaying leaves"? The correspondence is certainly not in shape, colour or way of moving.'[47] The passage in the poem about the coming storm is subjected to the same sort of criticism.

The same technique is rigorously applied to one of Shelley's weaker poems, 'When the Lamp is Shattered'. Shelley's poetic description of Mont Blanc is unfavourably compared to that of Wordsworth; and a passage from Shelley's *The*

Cenci is shown to have been plagiarized from Shakespeare's
Measure for Measure. Needless to say, the Shakespeare passage reads better.

But Leavis was far too serious a critic to rest his case
against Shelley on four fleeting gobbets. He used these,
rather, as examples of his general theory about Shelley.

'There is,' he wrote, 'nothing grasped in his [Shelley's]
poetry.'[48] In another place he referred to 'The earnest struggle to grasp something real',[49] and 'Shelley's weak grasp
upon the actual'.[50] Or again: 'There is no object offered
. . . no realized presence . . .'[51] Or: 'He is peculiarly weak
in his hold of objects'.[52] Or: 'Quivering intensity . . . is
offered instead of any object'.[53]

As a result of this incapacity to grasp real objects, Leavis
argued, Shelley's poetry had 'little to do with thinking'. It
could be enjoyed only by immature or lazy minds. It had
'nothing to do with discipline'.[54]

Nothing irritates Leavis more than this 'lack of discipline'.
He quotes – and grumbles about – a particularly beautiful
passage from Shelley's 'Defence of Poetry': 'for the mind in
creation is as a fading coal, which some invisible influence,
like an inconstant wind, awakens to transitory brightness;
this power arises from within, like the colour of a flower
which fades and changes as it is developed, and the conscious
portions of our natures are unprophetic either of its approach
or its departure.'[55]

This moves Leavis to fury. Inspiration, he insists, is not
something that can be written about in this undisciplined
way. It must be 'tested, clarified, defined and developed in
composition'.[56] Inspiration must, in other words, have a
tag on it. The reasons why some people can express themselves more spontaneously or more clearly than others must
be reduced to some discipline. Otherwise, how can the critic
deal with them?

But inspiration does not work like that. As long as a critic
tries to put a tag on inspiration, he is lost. That is not of
course to say that the results of inspiration cannot be assessed
or criticized. Nor is it to say that inspiration has nothing to
do with thought or discipline. But any assessment of such

thought or discipline must depend on the cause of the inspiration. What causes people to write inspired poetry? Without the answer to this question, any measurement or criticism of poetry is futile.

Some poetry is inspired by a sight, a feeling or a passion. Other poetry – including most of Shelley's – is inspired by ideas which bind up sights and feelings and passions, and incorporate them in a political philosophy. That is what Shelley was talking about when he wrote in the Preface to *The Revolt of Islam* about 'the passions which rise and spread, and sink and change, amongst assembled multitudes of men'.[57] These passions and the ideas which they presented to Shelley were the inspiration of his poetry. Any assessment of that poetry and its inspiration, then, must include an assessment of his ideas, and the way in which his poetry conveys them.

Yet, from the beginning of his essay, Leavis refuses to discuss Shelley's ideas. He ducks behind his expertise: 'When one dissents from persons who, sympathising with Shelley's revolutionary doctrines and with his idealist ardours and fervours – with his "beliefs", exalt him as a poet, it is strictly the poet one is criticizing.'[58] These 'beliefs' (the inverted commas are revealing: perhaps Leavis thought that no one really believed anything) are, he went on, irrelevant to poetry.

'Shelley, of course had ideas and ideals; he wrote philosophical essays, and it need not be irrelevant to refer, in discussing his poetry, to Plato, to Godwin, and other thinkers. But' – and here is his theme again – 'there is nothing grasped in the poetry, no object offered for contemplation, no realized presence to persuade us or move us by what it is.'[59]

Leavis reiterated this insistence on the literary critic's duty not to allow his judgement to be affected by politics or political ideas in a later book, *The Common Pursuit*. 'Philosophy and literary criticism,' he scolded, 'are very different things.'[60] Or again: 'The poet's essential belief is what can most readily be extracted as such from his works by a philosopher.'[61]

A critic's job was criticism; a philosopher's job was ideas and ideals. There was a strict demarcation line which, when discussing Shelley, Leavis insisted on observing. As a result, he came to discuss a poet who was not Shelley at all, but the miserable image of Shelley who had been created by the Francis Thompson school. Leavis falls into the same trap as Robert Blatchford and David Daiches: 'It is at any rate universally agreed that . . . Shelley's genius was "essentially lyrical". '[62]

The test, then, is of Shelley as a lyricist, a warbler, of a Shelley divorced from his ideas and his opinions, and from the effect they had on his imagination, intuition and inspiration.

And of course, as a warbler, Shelley *is* at fault. There is a sloppiness and excess in his language and in his metaphors which the discipline of a Keats or a Wordsworth would have ironed out. Similarly, if 'objects' are only the things of nature – winds or clouds or skylarks or rivers or glaciers – then it is true that Shelley's descriptions of them can be inaccurate or even faintly ridiculous.

If Shelley is judged by the standard laid down by his idolaters of the late nineteenth century, then a scrupulous wordsmith like F. R. Leavis can find him wanting, or even 'unreadable'. But it is the wrong test. Again and again, the images which Shelley paints are representative of his ideas. It is the ideas which are there to be grasped; the ideas are the objects to be realized. They emerge from page after page of Shelley's descriptions of the society in which he lived – of the human beings, their passions and their natural surroundings, all wrapped up together.

Out of *Queen Mab* comes the description of a ravaged and divided society; out of *The Revolt of Islam* the potential of the masses to change that society; out of *Peter Bell* the dungeon which awaits poets and writers who forswear the ideals in which they believe; out of 'Ode to the West Wind' the despair of someone who believes the world must be changed but can find no one to help him change it; out of *Prometheus Unbound* the possibility – and the dangers – of revolution. Demogorgon, writes Leavis, is 'vague'. Yes, he is vague, just as the working class movement at the time was vague, unformed, scarcely recognizable, yet strong enough to bind its collective identity into a single, vague creature.

There is plenty to be grasped in Shelley, plenty of clear, descriptive writing. Some of it is written for mass consumption, like *The Mask of Anarchy*, or the shorter political poems of 1819. Leavis, rather curiously, pays grudging respect to these poems. 'Had he used and developed his genius in the spirit of the *The Mask of Anarchy*, he would have been a much greater, and a much more readable, poet.'[63]

But, he goes on, '*The Mask of Anarchy* is little more than a marginal throw-off'.[64] It is not. It is one of Shelley's most important poems, and its political theme is the same as that of his other great poems, including the ones described by Leavis as 'essentially lyrical'. Without this theme, all these poems lose their shape. With it, they become clear and sharp. To hive off the theme into some other area of expertise – into philosophy or politics – is an act of literary and intellectual buffoonery.

F. R. Leavis was not a buffoon. He knew perfectly well that poetry cannot be divorced from the social conditions in which it is written. In his *New Bearings on English Poetry: A Study of the Contemporary Situation*, published in 1932, Leavis ridiculed the preoccupation of Victorian poets with a 'dream world'. He described the 'essential qualification of the poet' as 'the need to communicate something of his own'. Poetry, he argued, with some passion, is part and parcel of the age in which it is written, and, if it does not reflect that, it is not good poetry:

Poetry tends in every age to confine itself by ideas of the essentially poetical which, when the conditions which give rise to them have changed, bar the poet from his most valuable material, the material that is most significant to sensitive and adequate minds of his own day; or else sensitive and adequate minds are barred out of poetry. Poetry matters because of the kind of poet who is more alive than other people, more alive in his own age. He is, as it were, at the most conscious point of the race in his time . . . He is a poet because his interest in his experience is not separate from his interest in words . . . Poetry can communicate the actual quality of experience with a subtlety and precision unapproachable by any other means. But if the poetry and the intelligence of the age lose touch with each other, poetry will cease to matter much. . . .[65]

These principles were applied very strictly by Leavis to the poets he admired. T. S. Eliot was always one of Leavis's favourites. In his *Retrospect*, published in 1950, he wrote of Eliot's *Four Quartets*: 'One doesn't need to be able to share Mr. Eliot's personal Anglo-Catholicism or even to be able to sympathize with it or anything akin to it, in order to feel indebted to Four Quartets, and to see that his poetry has the most important relevance to the interests of anyone fully alive in our time.'

The test is 'relevance of interest to anyone fully alive'. There is nothing here about what may or may not be 'grasped'. There is no textual nit-picking. There is no scoffing at 'vagueness'. On the contrary, 'the *only technique* that matters is that which compels words to express an intensely personal way of feeling'.

When laying down the ground rules for his own criticism in *New Bearings*, and when following those rules in dealing with T. S. Eliot and other poets of whom he approved, Leavis insisted that poetry must be relevant to the time and that it must reflect the definite ideas and interests of the poet. Yet when dealing with Shelley, he slipped back into the tradition of G. A. Ross, who had told the Shelley Society fifty years earlier that imaginative writers should not be associated with any political or social action.

How to explain this contradiction? Why does Leavis apply different standards of criticism to different poets? There can be only one answer. Leavis's objection to Shelley, like his affection for Eliot, was political: he preferred the dry conservatism of Eliot to the revolutionism of Shelley. Just as no poet, no novelist, no writer, is politically 'objective', so no literary critic is 'objective' either.

Where did Leavis stand? In his heyday, in the 1930s and 1940s, he kept his political views to himself. In an essay in

Scrutiny in 1949, he wrote admiringly of Beatrice Webb and her brand of Fabian socialism. Fabian politics had obvious attractions for Leavis. It proposed not 'wild ideas' but tangible reform. It held out a realizable 'object' to be 'grasped'. It offered change without upheaval. It also reserved politics for professionals and experts. The people who needed reforms need do nothing about it. Beatrice Webb and her friends would see to it that reforms were carried out. They were experts in politics just as F. R. Leavis was an expert in literary criticism.

Leavis liked people who proposed specific reforms much better than people who sought to stir up the multitude to take things for themselves. And, like countless others with the same limited aspirations, Leavis was very quick to forget all about reform when it seemed to threaten the 'rights' of the cultured few.

In a revealing essay in the last number (May–August 1974) of a failed literary journal called the *Human World*, the ageing Leavis spoke of a by-election meeting at which he had signed the nomination papers and contributed to the fund of the Liberal candidate. He was appalled to hear the Liberal leader, Mr Jeremy Thorpe, supporting comprehensive schools. 'I suspect,' he wrote, 'that the liberal leader knows well enough that education matters and that the triumph of democratic egalitarianism is disastrous for humanity. . . .'

This was *always* Leavis's view. He resented the Cambridge academic establishment not out of any radical fervour, but because they would not let him join it. More education, for Leavis, meant worse education. Education, he believed, should be strictly limited to a few intelligent people. Education for all was 'disastrous for humanity'.

Shelley, on the other hand, believed above all else in 'democratic egalitarianism'. He argued that people were not ineducable, nor unwilling to learn. More education meant that everyone would learn more and be better for it. While Leavis saw the mass of people as a rubbish heap, Shelley saw them as a reservoir of unfulfilled ambitions.

This difference between the two men's ideas explains the

ferocity of Leavis's attack. His objection to Shelley was not, as he pretended, purely literary. It was political. And because his criticism refuses, in the name of literary objectivity, to engage Shelley in the real argument which Leavis had with him, it is criticism by subterfuge.

Leavis's *Revaluation* caused terrible havoc to Shelley's reputation among the young men and women at university at the time. Leavis was so influential – especially, perhaps surprisingly, among the more radical teachers and students of English literature – that many read Leavis on Shelley before they read Shelley, and dismissed Shelley without even reading him. A typical experience was that of Geoffrey Matthews, who went to Oxford to read English in 1939.

'We all revered Leavis so much that when I read Leavis on Shelley, I didn't want to read Shelley very much,' Geoffrey Matthews told me. 'I tried without much enthusiasm to read *Prometheus Unbound*, and then went to my tutor and said, "Look, I can't understand this." And he said: "No, neither can I. Let's leave it alone, and read some Keats." '

Geoffrey Matthews didn't take up Shelley again until after the war. 'I then became hooked,' he told me. He now teaches English at Reading University, and is one of the very few teachers in Britain who understands, loves and passes on the real Shelley. But he was the exception. Ever since *Revaluation* was published, the academic world has shunned Shelley, or confined him to a narrow seam.

Leavis's assault on Shelley in the universities combined with and fortified the assault from the Communist Party and its Left Book Club periphery. The results for the reading of Shelley both in the universities and among working people were catastrophic.

Even in the great social upheavals which followed the Second World War, there was little sign of a Shelley revival. Leavis grew more fashionable in English literature departments. Shortly before his death in 1978 he was awarded the highest honour in the land and was made a Companion of Honour – along with Jack Jones, the transport union leader, who had also spent his life 'grasping' at 'realizable objects' only to see them all vanish – all, that is, except his own honours. The Labour Party, whose early years had been marked by a keen interest in the self-education of its supporters, grew fat on votes – and entirely careless of education or literature. And so Shelley was snuffed out in the 1950s and 1960s almost as effectively as he had been when he was alive.

Does that matter? Surely, some might argue, so much has changed since Shelley's day that his ideas *are* irrelevant. His lyrical splendour may still be enjoyed. But of what use are his diatribes against a society where king, aristocracy and Church ruled without any democratic check whatever? Haven't all Shelley's aims been realized? Haven't we, for fifty years and more, elected our governments by universal suffrage? Are we not living in a parliamentary democracy?

Here we go back to Shelley's doubts about universal suffrage. For a brief moment he wondered if granting the vote to everyone would be a big enough extension of democracy to break the most undemocratic feature of his society: inequality of property. Would votes for the masses give them control over the property which they produce? Would the election of Labour governments provide those governments with the economic power necessary to carry out the reforms which they held out to the people who elected them?

Fifty years after adult suffrage in Britain the answer to these questions is still No. By clinging to the control of every area of power and influence except Parliament – the judiciary, the police and armed forces, the civil service, newspapers and television, bigger and bigger corporations – the rich have managed to defend and extend their power and their privilege. Again and again they have forced the Labour governments away from Labour promises and Labour supporters. They have even persuaded those governments that policies in the interests of big corporations are 'in the national interest'. The result has been an extension of irresponsible power in our society.

In these circumstances, the Parliamentary reformers have less and less to offer the bemused and harassed masses. For a brief instant in the 1950s and 1960s they seemed to hold out a 'practical' and possible programme for more equality and more wealth for all. All this has been dashed to pieces. Suddenly, the 'practical reformers' who were arguing in the sixties about the distribution of the fruits of economic prosperity are grappling with an economic crisis which none of them predicted and which none of their policies can contain. Now no one asks how best to distribute increasing wealth. Now the problem is how to keep people in work, and out of prisons or mental hospitals. The reformers are forced to lower their sights so drastically that their targets are indistinguishable from those of the reactionaries.

The impotence of elected office quickly works its way through to the working people who cast the votes. Their confidence is shattered. They lose faith in their own judgement and their own ability, and turn back to the dark myths of God and king. They become proud, not of their achievements, but of their colour and their nation. They start to search for a 'strong man'. Suddenly we are reminded that aspirations can fall as fast as they can rise. Tyranny in England may not be as savage as it was in Shelley's time, but the consequences of a relapse into tyranny – in the century of the concentration camp and the atom bomb – would be far more horrible.

Shelley's time, like ours, was a time of reaction after a period of reform. He sought to lift people's aspirations out of the gloom, to fix them once again on the vision of a new society, where people were not divided by wealth or class and were therefore able to behave decently to one another. In the 'Address to the Irish People', which he wrote in 1812, when he was nineteen, he challenged his readers to lift up their eyes from the wretchedness around them.

This vision inspires *Prometheus Unbound*, written seven years later, in his prime. After the freeing of Prometheus and the overthrow of Jupiter, the Spirit of the Hour reports on the changes which have taken place on earth:

> I wandering went
> Among the haunts and dwellings of mankind,

And first was disappointed not to see
Such mighty change as I had felt within
Expressed in outward things; but soon I looked,
And behold, thrones were kingless, and men walked
One with the other even as spirits do,
None fawned, none trampled.[66]

People have stopped lying to one another to prop up their ephemeral power:

None wrought his lips in truth-entangling lines
Which smiled the lie his tongue disdained to speak; . . .
None talked that common, false, cold, hollow talk
Which makes the heart deny the *yes* it breathes, . . .[67]

Women are:

From custom's evil taint exempt and pure;
Speaking the wisdom once they could not think,
Looking emotions once they feared to feel, . . .[68]

All the trappings of undemocratic power are redundant:

Thrones, altars, judgement-seats, and prisons; wherein,
And beside which, by wretched men were borne
Sceptres, tiaras, swords, and chains, and tomes
Of reasoned wrong, glozed on by ignorance,
Were like those monstrous and barbaric shapes,
The ghosts of a no-more-remembered fame,
Which, from their unworn obelisks, look forth
In triumph o'er the palaces and tombs
Of those who were their conquerors, mouldering
round . . .[69]

What is left?

The loathsome mask has fallen, the man remains
Sceptreless, free, uncircumscribed, but man
Equal, unclassed, tribeless, and nationless,
Exempt from awe, worship, degree, the king
Over himself; . . .[70]

Many writers, including many revolutionary writers, have dismissed this part of Shelley's writing and his thought as 'idealist'. 'Idealist' is a nasty word in the received vocabulary of modern Marxists. Ever since Frederick Engels wrote *Socialism, Utopian and Scientific* (1892), distinguishing between the 'idealist' philosophers who longed for a better society and the 'scientific' socialists who worked for one, some Marxists have concluded that all talk of a new society, all attempts to awaken people's imaginations with the vision of a new society, is idealist, and therefore suspect. Marxism, we are told, is a science. Surely, socialism follows capitalism as certainly as the mingling of hydrogen and oxygen produces water. Doesn't this dreaming of a new society simply distract from the urgent task of mixing the chemicals? Shelley's new world, according to this theory, is not only idle rant, but also a distraction from the real socialist objective.

Yet Marx and Engels – and indeed all socialists worth the name – were inspired above all else by their vision of a new social order. The *Communist Manifesto* ends with the ringing phrase 'You Have a World to Win'.

It was part of the propaganda of a divided society that 'sceptres, tiaras, thrones' were inevitable products of human nature. The only effective argument against that was that human nature, freed from the constrictions of class division, would change, and would thrive in a different sort of society. The vision of the new society is an indispensable part of the case for changing the old society. Those who are not inspired by it are usually those who do not really want change at all.

What annoyed Marx and Engels about the utopians was not their belief in a new, classless social order, but their belief that the new society was something which could not be won out of the old. The utopians' vision was completely cut off from the reality around them. It was proclaimed as a dreamer tells about his dream. As Marx put it in an early letter about Romantic poetry (though not about Shelley): 'Everything real becomes hazy and loses all bounds. The poems in the first of the three volumes that I sent Jenny are therefore characterised by attacks on the present, feeling without moderation and form, nothing natural, everything built on moonshine. What is and what ought to be are depicted as wholly opposed . . .'[71]

Was Shelley such a poet?

In one sense, yes he was. There is very little guide in any of his writing as to how his new society was to come about. More importantly, his analysis of political events often slipped into the very generalizations about human nature which so infuriated him when they were used to justify wealth and aristocracy. He analysed what he thought was the failure of the French Revolution not in economic terms, but in terms of the 'bestial nature' of the masses before (and therefore after) the revolution.

In his analysis, Shelley was constrained by the economic circumstances of his time. The French Revolution, though it proclaimed equality, could not have introduced it. Production could only grow through the promotion of a few entrepreneurs, what Shelley called 'a new aristocracy', who could afford leisure and education. When Shelley advocated an egalitarian society founded on plenty and increased production, he was ahead of his time. In that sense, he was idealistic. In that sense, and in that sense alone, what 'ought to have been and what was' were 'depicted' by him as 'opposed'.

And in that sense Shelley is no longer idealistic. For now there *is* the capacity to produce enough for everyone. The businessmen and entrepreneurs of today, far from increasing production, are applying the brakes to it. Now we *can* have a society where no one fawns and no one tramples, where more and more is produced, where all the important decisions – including the economic ones – are taken by elected representatives. Shelley's visions have lost their idealism and their utopianism. They have taken on real life and meaning. They are more realistic now than they were in Shelley's day, and therefore more inspiring.

But in another sense, a more important sense, Shelley's writing is not utopian or idealistic at all. His political comment was rooted in his belief that a new social order could be fashioned with tools made in the old society; that the people – the real, working people of the time – could themselves create that social change. Just as his excitement about science stemmed from what could be done with the existing forces of nature – the lightning, the earth, the waves – so his excitement about human change stemmed from his belief about what human beings could do with their existing powers. He was the precise opposite of the utopian dreamer, the 'ineffectual angel' invented by his critics and his worshippers. He was – and is – first and foremost an agitator.

Agitation comes at us from every corner of his poetry: from Cythna's speech to the sailors; from Iona's urging of the Pigs; from Asia's indignation before Demogorgon. It comes from the odes to the West Wind and to the Skylark. It streams through all his shorter political poems and his love poems. Everywhere there is an echoing, irrepressible call to people to get up off their knees and realize their potential.

Just as his vision of a new society is more relevant today than it was then, so his agitation is more powerful. No one listened to his call when he was alive. The people whom he called were unorganized. The working class was in the making. Now it is made. The purpose and direction of his agitation are clearer than they have ever been.

Yet the relevance of Shelley's vision and his agitation are in themselves not enough to demand people's attention today. If all we had left of Shelley was his prose, he would be of little interest to anyone outside a university. He would deserve – though he still does not get – a few paragraphs in a history of socialism or even a whole chapter in a detailed study of radical thought, in the section entitled 'From Godwin to Marx'.

Shelley's writing lives not just because of his vision, nor because of his agitation, but because both were expressed in poetry – some of the most magnificent poetry ever written in the English language.

Just as the Shelley worshippers of the late nineteenth century pretended that Shelley's ideas were irrelevant to his poetry, so some Shelley worshippers of this century have pretended that his poetry was irrelevant to his politics.

In the essay quoted earlier in this chapter about the centenary of Shelley's birth, George Bernard Shaw wrote that the working men who came to the memorial meeting in East London 'took Shelley quite seriously, and were much more conscious of his opinions and of his spirit than of his dexterity as a versifier'. Sylvia Norman, in her lovely book on the reputation of Shelley after his death (called *The Flight of the Skylark*), described the people who came to that meeting as 'A community that claimed Shelley as a fellow socialist and ignored his verse'.[72]

Fabians like Shaw and Sylvia Norman could be as snobbish as the lords and ladies of literature, whose patronage of Shelley they ridiculed. According to them, the masses could not understand poetry. The interest of the common man or woman in Shelley was, therefore, restricted only to his politics.

Yet for Shelley, and for his unsung followers, politics and poetry were inextricably entwined. In his 'Defence of Poetry', Shelley wrote: 'The most unfailing herald, companion, and follower of the awakening of a great people to work a beneficial change in opinion or institution, is Poetry. At such periods there is an accumulation of the power of communicating and receiving intense and impassioned conceptions respecting man and nature.'[73] In the preface to *Prometheus Unbound*, he wrote: 'The great writers of our own age are, we have reason to suppose, the companions and forerunners of some unimagined change in our social condition or the opinions which cement it.'[74] Most, if not all, of his poetry, was written with that 'unimagined change in our social conditions' in sight. It was written to loosen the 'cement' which bound people's opinions to the existing system of society.

Critics and professors who seek to claim Shelley for a small circle of people who 'understand literature' are fond of quoting Shelley's attacks on didactic poetry. In the same

preface to the *Prometheus*, he wrote: 'Didactic poetry is my
abhorrence.'[75] A thousand murmurs of 'hear hear' can be
heard. The attack on 'didactic poetry' sounds like a contradiction of Shelley's view that poetry is 'the most unfailing
herald . . . of a great people to work a beneficial change in
opinion'. But there is no such contradiction. The two statements complement one another. Shelley's poetry is agitational; it is not didactic.

The distinction can be discovered by anyone who tries to
spread radical ideas among working people. On the one
hand, there is a respect for openly expressed opinion, however extreme; on the other, a contempt for ideas which seem
to come from someone else. The agitator whose ideas sound
or read as though they have not been independently thought
out becomes an outcast or an irritant or both.

How do people tell the difference between independently
held ideas and dogma recited by rote? The first test is the
ability of the agitator to listen and to learn from people who
do not agree. So often, socialists and radicals disgorge gobbets of dogma which someone else has fed them. They seek
to shield their parcel of received ideas from challenge or
discussion, and so appear to their audiences as fanatics, intolerant of anyone who does not agree with them.

Shelley was not like that at all. He held and expressed his
ideas very fiercely. His friend Peacock disagreed with almost
all of these ideas. But Peacock paid Shelley this marvellous
compliment:

I must add, that in the expression of these differences, there was
not a shadow of anger. They were discussed with freedom and
calmness; with the good temper and good feeling which never
forsook him in conversations with his friends. There was an
evident anxiety for acquiescence but a quiet and gentle toleration
of dissent . . .

Indeed, one of the great charms of intercourse with him was the
perfect good humour and openness to conviction with which he
responded to opinions opposed to his own.

Peacock went on to contrast Shelley to others of his
acquaintances:

I have known eminent men, who were no doubt very instructive as lecturers to people who like being lectured; which I never did; but with whom conversation was impossible. To oppose their dogmas, even to question them, was to throw their temper off its balance.[76]

That is one difference between didacticism and agitation. It was the good humour, openness and tolerance of Shelley's conviction which made it so persuasive. He believed in collective responsibility and collective endeavour, out of which individual freedom would flourish – and he expressed his belief, therefore, in an individual way. His ideas, he conceded, could only be improved by democratic argument and challenge, and he expressed himself accordingly.

The second criterion for judging between frankly held opinion and dogma is the language used.

Shelley loved and treasured language, not for its own sake but for its power to communicate ideas. 'Words,' he wrote to Godwin, 'are merely signs of ideas.'[77] More lyrically, the Earth in the *Prometheus* proclaims:

> Language is a perpetual Orphic song,
> Which rules with Daedal harmony a throng
> Of thoughts and forms, which else senseless and shapeless
> were.[78]

'He believed,' wrote Newman Ivy White in a brilliant passage, 'that custom always degraded language and modes of expression just as it debased institutions and conduct. Words, like creeds, naturally wore smooth and meaningless, and lost their original brightness. It was the function of poets to revitalize language as well as thoughts.'[79] If people's ideas were to be changed, then the language to which they were accustomed had to be changed too. Predictability was the death of propaganda.

Poetry, for Shelley, was language at its most powerful. Poetry arranged words and sentences in rhyme and rhythm so as to fix them in the memory, together with the ideas which they heralded. Shelley wanted his ideas to go, in his famous phrase,

> Ringing through each heart and brain
> Heard again, – again, – again . . .[80]

And therefore he shunned predictable language. He hated rhetoric. He looked for the surprising, the unsuspected words and images which would thrill people and stir them to action. He invented the 'vision of poesy', the 'ghastly masquerade' of Murder, Fraud and Anarchy, to capture the full horror of the Castlereagh tyranny and of Peterloo; the visit of a devil to satirize the apostasy of Wordsworth; a herd of rampaging bulls, a volcano, the West Wind at full blast, to symbolize the might of the masses in motion.

Shelley was a master of words, of rhyme and rhythm. And he used his mastery to paint his pictures and his metaphors – from landscape, from the world of animals, from the deepest recesses of the imagination – to conjure up the ideas which he was expressing. He was not just an agitator. He was perhaps the most eloquent agitator of all time.

Our world, like his world, needs agitators. People's aspirations need to be lifted and guided into action. Yet what passes for agitation today is stunted by a hideous language.

The trade unions which have grown up to defend the working people from the ravages of the rich have constructed for communication with themselves and with the outside world a constipated gobbledegook of 'heretofores' and 'negotiated settlements' which isolate the trade union leaders not so much from the employers as from their own rank and file. The language of the Labour Party – long since divorced from any need to convince the masses – slides all the time into Parliamentary politeness or ridiculous conference rhetoric.

None of this is surprising or new. What is remarkable is that the revolutionaries and radicals who have turned their back on the conventional means of change – the people, that is, who depend above all else on the success of their communication with the masses – have adopted a language which is even more grotesque than that of their adversaries.

It is as though the discovery of the class divisions in society and the revolutionary means of ending them is a passport into a ghetto of the enlightened. There, the revolutionaries can converse with one another in their own language. The bulk of the literature, journalism and speech which has emerged from this ghetto in the past twenty years is, in the words which Marx and Engels used to describe the socialist literature of Germany in 1848, 'foul and enervating'.[81]

It is a dreadful jumble of imperatives and assertions. It is almost entirely humourless. It depends upon didactic, the 'putting of the line'. It serves only to irritate the masses to whom it is directed. As they turn away, embarrassed rather than outraged, they are castigated by the revolutionaries as 'backward'. Yet more often than not, the new revolutionary language is not ahead of but behind that of the masses. The humblest and most desperate people often describe their plight and the need to end it far more powerfully than the 'correct' revolutionaries.

This dead sectarian language springs from isolation and fear of a hostile world. It is the language of people who prefer to stay out of the world as disgruntled enemies of it rather than to change it. And its most astonishing effect is to make the revolution dull. Sometimes, indeed, revolutionaries even exult in their own dullness, as though commitment to a lifetime of boredom is mere proof of 'seriousness' (a very important word for modern revolutionaries).

Shelley was not dull. His poems reverberate with energy and excitement. He decked the grand ideas which inspired him in a language which enriches them and sharpens communication with the people who can put them into effect. That is why he was loved and treasured by the Chartist workers, the socialist propagandists of the 1890s, the suffragists and feminists of the first twenty years of this century. And that is why socialists, radicals and feminists of every hue should read Shelley today – read him, learn him by heart and teach him to their children.

If Shelley's great revolutionary poetry – all those glaciers and winds and volcanoes – can get to work on the imaginations of the hundreds of thousands of people who have had enough of our rotten society and of the racialism and corruption off which it feeds; if that poetry can inspire them to write and talk with a new energy, a new confidence and a new splendour, then there is no telling what will happen.

Certainly the police will have to be sent for.

Select Bibliography

BOAS, Louise, *Harriet Shelley: Five Long Years*: Oxford University Press, London 1962.

CAMERON, K. N., *The Young Shelley: Genesis of a Radical*: Victor Gollancz Ltd., London 1951.

——, *Shelley: The Golden Years*: Harvard University Press, Cambridge, Mass. 1975.

A Discourse on the Manners of the Ancient Greeks, Relative to the Subject of Love, ed. Roger Ingpen: privately printed in London, 1931.

DOWDEN, Edward, *The Life of Percy Bysshe Shelley*: Routledge and Kegan Paul, London 1969.

The Esdaile Notebook, ed. K. N. Cameron: Faber and Faber, London 1964.

GLOVER, A. S. B. (ed.), *Shelley*: Nonesuch Press, London 1951.

GRAHAM, William, *Lost Links with Byron, Shelley and Keats*: Leonard Smithers and Co., London 1898.

GRYLLS, R. Glynn, *Mary Shelley: A Biography*: Oxford University Press, London 1938.

HOLMES, Richard, *Shelley: The Pursuit*: Weidenfeld and Nicolson Ltd., London 1974.

HUTCHINSON, Thomas (ed.), *Shelley: Poetical Works*, 2nd edition: Oxford University Press, London 1970.

INGPEN, Roger (ed.), *The Letters of Percy Bysshe Shelley*: Sir Isaac Pitman and Sons Ltd., London, and Charles Scribner's Sons, New York, 1909.

INGPEN, Roger, and PECK, Walter (eds), *The Works of Percy Bysshe Shelley*, 10 vols: Ernest Benn Ltd, London, and Charles Scribner's Sons, New York, 1926–30.

JONES, Frederick L. (ed.), *Mary Shelley's Journal*: University of Oklahoma Press, Norman, U.S.A. 1947.

——, *The Letters of Mary W. Shelley*: University of Oklahoma Press, Norman, U.S.A. 1944.

——, *The Letters of Percy Bysshe Shelley*: Clarendon Press, Oxford 1964.

KING-HELE, Desmond, *Shelley: His Thought and Work*: Macmillan, London 1960.

LEAVIS, F. R., *The Common Pursuit*: Chatto and Windus, London 1952.

——, *New Bearings in English Literature: A Study of the Contemporary Situation*: Chatto and Windus, London 1932.

——, *Revaluation*: Pelican paperback, London 1972.

MEDWIN, Thomas, *The Life of Percy Bysshe Shelley*, ed. H. B. Forman: London 1913.

NORMAN, Sylvia, *The Flight of the Skylark*: Max Reinhardt, London 1954.

Notebook of the Shelley Society: Reeves and Turner, London 1888.

PEACOCK, Thomas Love, *Memoirs of Shelley and Other Essays and Reviews*, ed. Howard Mills: Rupert Hart-Davis, London 1970.

PECK, Walter, *Shelley: His Life and Work*: Ernest Benn, London 1927.

A Philosophical View of Reform, with an introduction and appreciation by T. W. Rolleston: Oxford University Press, London 1920.

ROGERS, Neville (ed.), *The Complete Poetical Works of Percy Bysshe Shelley*: Clarendon Press, Oxford 1975.

SALT, Henry, *Shelley: Poet and Pioneer*: Allen and Unwin, London 1924.

Shelley and His Circle 1773–1822: vols I and II, ed. K. N. Cameron: Harvard University Press, Cambridge, Mass. 1961; vols III and IV, ed. K. N. Cameron: Harvard U.P., 1970; vols V and VI, ed. D. H. Reiman: Harvard U.P., 1973.

THOMPSON, Francis, *Shelley*: Burns and Oates, London 1909.

TRELAWNEY, Edward, *Records of Shelley, Byron and the Author*, New Universal Library edition: George Routledge and Son Ltd., London, and E. P. Dutton and Co., New York, 1878.

WHITE, Newman Ivey, *Shelley*: Secker and Warburg, London 1947.

WOODINGS, Robert Bertram (ed.), *Shelley, Modern Judgements*: Macmillan, London 1968.

Notes

Unless otherwise stated, the following three works have been used for quotations from Shelley's writings:

POEMS: *Shelley: Poetical Works,* edited by Thomas Hutchinson, second edition, Oxford University Press, London 1970, referred to as *Poetical Works.*

PROSE: The Works of Percy Bysse Shelley, edited by Roger Ingpen and Walter Peck, ten volumes, Ernest Benn Ltd, London 1926-30, referred to as *Works.*

LETTERS: *The Letters of Percy Bysse Shelley,* edited by F L Jones, two volumes, Clarendon Press, Oxford 1964, referred to as *Letters.*

INTRODUCTION

1 Oxford University Press, London 1931.

2 *Shelley, A Selection,* p. 19.

3 *Shelley,* 1973, p. 18.

4 Letter to Sir Richard Rees, Bt, 28 July 1949, Sonia Orwell and Ian Angus (eds), *The Collected Essays, Journalism and Letters of George Orwell,* vol. IV *In Front of Your Nose, 1945–50,* (Secker and Warburg, London 1968), pp. 504–5.

5 Paul Arthur Schilpp (ed.), *The Philosophy of Bertrand Russell,* 'My Mental Development' (Evanston, Illinois and Cambridge University Press, New York 1946), p. 8.

6 Victor Gollancz Ltd., London 1963, and Penguin, London 1970.

7 Weidenfeld and Nicolson Ltd, London 1974.

8 *Shelley: His Thought and Work* (Macmillan, London 1960) and *Doctor of Revolution, The Life and Genius of Erasmus Darwin* (Faber and Faber, London 1977).

9 The Press of Case Western Reserve University, Cleveland, Ohio 1972.

CHAPTER ONE: *The Ghastly Masquerade: England 1810–22*

1 stanzas II–VII, *Poetical Works,* p. 338.

2 *The Complete Works of William Hazlitt,* ed. P. P. Howe, after the edition of A. R. Walker and Arnold Glover, vol. 17 (J. M. Dent and Son, London 1933), p. 299.

3 *The Spirit of the Age,* first published 1825, World's Classics edition (Oxford University Press, London 1904), pp. 241–2.

4 *Memoirs of the United Irishmen* (Dublin 1857).

5 Quoted in the *Dictionary of National Biography, From the Earliest Times to 1900,* vol. XVIII, ed. Sir Leslie Stephen and Sir Sidney Lee (as originally published in 1897–8, Oxford University Press, London, reprint 1973), p. 1244, quoting Cornwallis's *Correspondence,* iii, p. 506.

6 Figures from the Annual Register for 1812.

7 Figures from the Census of Population for 1811.

8 G. M. Trevelyan, *History of England* (Longman, London 1926), p. 583.

278

9 ibid., p. 582.
10 Figures from the Annual Register, May 1811, and 1812.
11 Figures from the Annual Register, 19 July 1821.
12 Trevelyan, op. cit., p. 582.
13 Figures from the Annual Register for 1819.
14 ibid., 1818.
15 ibid., 7 May 1812.
16 ibid., 24 May 1811.
17 ibid., 1811, Appendix on Criminal Libel Cases.
18 Criminal Cases Supplement to Annual Register for 1812.
19 *The Three Trials of William Hone for publishing Three Parodies*; viz.— *The Late John Wilkes's Catechism, The Political Litany and The Sinecurist's Creed* (Freethought Publishing Company, London 1818), p. 134.
20 Annual Register, 13 April 1812.
21 ibid., 1 May 1812.
22 ibid., 1812.
23 ibid., 27 August 1812.
24 ibid., 8 April 1812.
25 *The Making of the English Working Class* (Penguin, London 1970), p. 663.
26 Letter from Fox in 1798 to the Duke of Grafton, quoted in *Autobiography and Political Correspondence of Augustus Henry, Third Duke of Grafton K.G.*, ed. Sir William R. Anson (John Murray, London 1898), p. 404.
27 Quoted in the Annual Register for 1810.
28 ibid., 1810.
29 ibid., 2 March 1817.
30 ibid., 5 July 1816.
31 Quoted in the Annual Register for 1812.
32 Quoted in the Annual Register for 1817.
33 Figures from the *Gorgon*, 12 September 1818.
34 Figures from the *Gorgon*, 15 August 1818.

CHAPTER TWO: *Republican*

1 stanza XV, *Poetical Works*, p. 608.
2 Newman Ivey White, *Shelley*, vol. I (Secker and Warburg, London 1947), p. 12, quoting Maud Rolleston, *Talks With Lady Shelley* (London 1925).
3 'The Voyage: A Fragment', Neville Rogers (ed.), *The Complete Poetical Works of Percy Bysshe Shelley*, vol. I 1802–1813 (Clarendon Press, Oxford 1975), p. 131.
4 canto III, *Poetical Works*, p. 770.
5 canto III, ibid., p. 771.
6 canto III, ibid., p. 772.
7 ibid., p. 574.
8 20 June 1811, *Letters*, vol. I, no. 86, p. 110.
9 stanzas XIV and XV, *Poetical Works*, p. 879.
10 act II, scene II, ibid., p. 406.
11 12 July 1820, *Letters*, vol. II, no. 576, p. 213.
12 act II, scene II, *Poetical Works*, p. 409.
13 27 December 1812, *Letters*, vol. I, no. 219, p. 346.
14 *Poetical Works*, p. 526.
15 *Works*, vol. V, p. 260.
16 ibid., vol. VII, p. 42.
17 ibid., vol. VII, p. 25.
18 ibid., vol. VI, pp. 73–4.
19 *Poetical Works*, p. 103.
20 canto IV, ibid., p. 777.
21 canto IV, ibid., p. 777.
22 Letter to Elizabeth Hitchener, 15 December 1811, *Letters*, vol. I, no. 153, p. 208.
23 stanza II, *Poetical Works*, p. 871.
24 *Works*, vol. V, pp. 238–9.
25 ibid., vol. V, p. 261.
26 'An Address to the Irish People', ibid., vol. V, p. 215.
27 act V, scene II, *Poetical Works*, p. 323.
28 canto IV, ibid., p. 777.
29 ibid., p. 550.

279

CHAPTER THREE: *Atheist*

1 A. S. B. Glover (ed.), *Shelley* (Nonesuch Press, London 1951), pp. 252–3.

2 Thomas Medwin, *The Life of Percy Bysshe Shelley*, ed. H. B. Forman, a revision of the two volume edition published by Newby, London 1847 (London 1913), p. 88.

3 6 February 1811, *Letters*, vol. I, no. 45, p. 45.

4 *Poetical Works*, pp. 822–3.

5 ibid., p. 824.

6 *Works*, vol. VI, p. 40.

7 ibid., vol. VI, pp. 47–8.

8 ibid., vol. V, pp. 289–90.

9 ibid., vol. VI, p. 213.

10 canto IV, *Poetical Works*, pp. 777–8.

11 canto VIII, stanza VIII, ibid., p. 117.

12 *Works*, vol. V, p. 217.

13 ibid., vol. V, p. 218.

14 canto X, stanza XXXII, *Poetical Works*, p. 137.

15 canto X, stanza XXXIII, ibid., p. 137.

16 canto X, stanza XXXV, ibid., p. 138.

17 'A Ballad', quoted in William J. McTaggart, *England in 1819: Church, State and Poverty* (The Keats–Shelley Memorial Association, London 1970), p. 9.

18 ibid., pp. 9–10.

19 3 November 1819, *Letters*, vol. II, no. 527, p. 136.

20 23 December 1819, ibid., vol. II, no. 543, p. 166.

21 *Works*, vol. VII, p. 94.

22 *Teresa: The Story of Byron's Last Mistress* (George Harrap and Co. Ltd., London 1948; published in America in 1945 under the title, *Teresa, or Her Demon Lover*, Charles Scribner's Sons, New York).

23 *Shelley: His Life and Work* (Ernest Benn, London 1927), p. 246.

24 ibid., p. 246.

25 *Poetical Works*, p. 458.

26 ibid., Note (2), p. 478.

27 ibid., Note (2), p. 478.

28 ibid., p. 471.

29 *Shelley: The Pursuit* (Weidenfeld and Nicolson, London 1974), p. 678.

30 *Letters*, vol. II, no. 699, p. 699.

31 Edward Trelawney, *Records of Shelley, Byron and the Author*, New Universal edition (George Routledge and Son Ltd, London, and E. P. Dutton and Co., New York, 1878), p. 50.

32 ibid., pp. 256–7.

33 stanza LII, *Poetical Works*, p. 443.

34 stanza LV, ibid., p. 444.

35 *Prometheus Unbound*, act IV, Speech by the Earth, ibid., p.264.

CHAPTER FOUR: *Leveller*

1 *Works*, vol. VI, p. 79.

2 'On Leaving London for Wales', penultimate verse, *The Esdaile Notebook*, ed. K. N. Cameron (Faber and Faber, London 1964), p. 55.

3 'England in 1819', *Poetical Works*, p. 575.

4 Letter to Elizabeth Hitchener, 7 January 1812, *Letters*, vol. I, no. 158, p. 223.

5 *Poetical Works*, p. 175.

6 'A Ballad', quoted in William J. McTaggart, *England in 1819: Church, State and Poverty* (The Keats–Shelley Memorial Association, London 1970), p. 9.

7 *Works*, vol. V, p. 266.

8 'A Tale of Society as it is: From Facts, 1811', Neville Rogers (ed.), *The Complete Poetical Works of Percy Bysshe Shelley*, vol. I 1802–1813 (Clarendon Press, Oxford 1975), p. 101.

9 Letter to Elizabeth Hitchener, 7 January 1812, *Letters*, vol. I, no. 158, pp. 223–4.

10 canto V, *Poetical Works*, p. 780.

11 Quoted in Olive D. Rudkin, *Thomas Spence and His Connections* (Allen and Unwin, London 1927), p. 37.

12 canto III, *Poetical Works*, pp. 771–2.

13 'Song to the Men of England', stanza II, ibid., p. 572.

14 act II, scene II, ibid., p. 406.

15 scene I, ibid., p. 492.

16 scene I, ibid., p. 492.

17 scene I, ibid., p. 492.

18 ibid., p. 804.

19 ibid., pp. 804–5.

20 15 December 1811, *Letters*, vol. I, no. 153, p. 207.

21 *Poetical Works*, p. 805.

22 stanzas LIII–LV, ibid., p. 342.

23 ibid., p. 805.

24 'A Philosophical View of Reform', *Works*, vol. VII, p. 43.

25 canto V, stanza XLIX, 3, *Poetical Works*, p. 91.

26 Note to line 27, p. 8 of 'A Philosophical View of Reform', *Works*, vol. VII, p. 334.

27 *Works*, vol. VII, pp. 14–15.

28 ibid., vol. VII, p. 15.

29 ibid., vol. VII, p. 27.

30 ibid., vol. VII, p. 30.

31 *A Philosophical View of Reform*, with an introduction and appreciation by T. W. Rolleston (Oxford University Press, London 1920), p. 75.

32 *Works*, vol. VII, p. 30.

33 ibid., vol. VII, p. 30.

34 ibid., vol. VII, pp. 24, 25.

35 ibid., vol. VII, p. 41.

36 ibid., vol. VII, p.41.

37 ibid., vol. VII, p. 34.

38 ibid., vol. VII, p. 35.

39 ibid., vol. VII, p.34.

40 ibid., vol. VII, p. 37.

41 ibid., vol. VII, p. 36.

42 ibid., vol. VII, p. 37.

43 ibid., vol. VII, p. 36.

44 'What Men Gain Fairly', *Poetical Works*, p. 574.

45 *Puritanism and Liberty: The Army Debates 1647–9*, selected by A. S. P. Woodhouse (Dent, London 1938), p. 38.

46 *Works*, vol. VII, p. 10.

47 stanza XVII, *Poetical Works*, p. 609.

CHAPTER 5: *Feminist*

1 canto II, stanza XLIII, *Poetical Works*. p. 63.

2 Quoted in George Catlin's introduction to the Everyman edition of Mary Wollstonecraft's *Vindication of the Rights of Woman* (J.M. Dent and Son, London, and E.P. Dutton and Co., New York, 1929), p. XXV.

3 Marquis de Condorcet, *Sur l'admission des Femmes au droit de Cité*, 1790, quoted (and translated) in Claire Tomalin, *Life and Death of Mary Wollstonecraft* (Penguin, London 1977), p. 135.

4 *An Enquiry Concerning Political Justice and Its Influence on General Virtue and Happiness* (G.G.J. and J. Robinson, London 1793).

5 Facsimile reproduction with an introduction by Eleanor Louise Nicholas (Scholars' Facsimiles and Reprints, Gainsville, Florida 1960), (a) p. 43, (b) p. 24, (c) p. 142, (d) p. 143, quoting Burke, (e) p. 144, (f) p. 148, (g) p. 149.

6 ibid., p. 152.

7 Everyman edition, ed. G.E.C. Catlin and also containing J. S. Mill, *The Subjection of Women* (J. M. Dent and Son, London 1929), p. 20.

8 ibid., p. 21.

9 ibid., p. 154

10 ibid., p. 38.

11 ibid., p. 161.

12 ibid., p. 28.

13 ibid., p. 154.

14 ibid., p. 189.

15 Tomalin, op. cit., p. 251.

16 ibid., p. 260.

17 'The Voyage: A Fragment, Au-

281

gust 1812', *The Esdaile Notebook*, ed. K. N. Cameron (Faber and Faber, London 1964), p. 102.

18 *Poetical Works*, pp. 171–2.

19 17 August 1812, *Letters*, vol. I, no. 201, p. 323.

20 *Poetical Works*, p. 806.

21 ibid., p. 806.

22 ibid., p. 807.

23 ibid., pp. 807–8.

24 ibid., p. 808

25 ibid., p. 808.

26 ibid., p. 808.

27 ibid., p. 415.

28 ibid., p. 415.

29 *A Discourse on the Manners of the Ancient Greeks, Relative to the Subject of Love,* ed. Roger Ingpen (privately printed in London, 1931), p. 14.

30 'A Defence of Poetry', *Works*, vol. VII, pp. 123–4.

31 17 August 1812, *Letters*, vol. I, no. 201, p. 323.

32 *Poetical Works*, p. 18.

33 ibid., p. 18.

34 ibid., p. 18.

35 ibid., pp. 18–19.

36 ibid., p. 19.

37 ibid., p. 20.

38 ibid., p. 30.

39 ibid., p. 20.

40 ibid., pp. 14–15.

41 Manuscript in the Pierpont Morgan Library, New York.

42 *Works*, vol. VII, p. 228.

43 *Poetical Works*, p. 175.

44 11 December 1817, *Letters*, vol. I, no. 432, p. 577.

45 canto II, stanza XXXVI, *Poetical Works*, p. 61.

46 canto II, stanza XXXVII, ibid., pp. 61–2.

47 canto II, stanza XXXVIII, ibid., p. 62.

48 canto II, stanza XXXIX, ibid., p. 62.

49 canto II, stanza XXXIX, ibid., p. 62.

50 canto II, stanza XLII, ibid., p. 63.

51 canto II, stanza XLIII, ibid., p. 63.

52 canto IV, stanza XVIII, ibid., p. 76.

53 canto IV, stanza XX, ibid., p. 76.

54 canto IV, stanza XXI, ibid., p. 76.

55 canto IV, stanza XXII, ibid., p. 77.

56 canto V, stanza LI, 4, ibid., p. 92.

57 canto V, stanza LI, 4, ibid., p. 92.

58 canto V, stanza LI, 6, ibid., pp. 92–3.

59 canto VI, stanzas XXXIV–XXXVI, ibid., p. 102.

60 canto VII, stanza I, ibid., p. 107;

61 canto VII, stanza VI, ibid., p. 108.

62 canto VIII, stanzas XIV–XV, ibid., p. 119.

63 canto VIII, stanza XIII, ibid., p. 118.

64 canto IX, stanza X, ibid., p. 124.

65 canto IX, stanza XVI, ibid., p. 126.

66 From *Loose Hints Upon Education*, 1781, quoted in H.L. Mencken (ed.), *New Dictionary of Quotations* (A. A. Knopf, New York 1942), p. 1318.

67 Thomas Love Peacock, *Memoirs of Shelley and Other Essays and Reviews*, ed. Howard Mills (Rupert Hart-Davis, London 1970), p. 57.

68 Quoted in Louise Boas, *Harriet Shelley: Five Long Years* (Oxford University Press, London 1962), pp. 78, 79.

69 *Poetical Works*, pp. 762–3.

70 'To Harriet', ibid., p. 876.

71 ibid., p. 877.

72 op. cit., p. 37.

73 op. cit., p. 125.

74 op. cit., p. 55.

75 ?14 July 1814, *Letters*, vol. I, no. 258, pp. 389–90.

76 14 September 1814, ibid., vol. I, no. 260, p. 394.

77 ibid., vol. I, no. 260, pp. 394–5.

78 26 September 1814, ibid., vol. I, no. 262, p. 397.

79 Boas, op. cit., p. 168.

80 op. cit., p. 54

81 Frederick L. Jones (ed.), *Mary Shelley's Journal* (University of Oklahoma Press, Norman, U.S.A. 1947), pp. 23–6 *passim*.

82 ibid., pp. 39–41 *passim*.

83 'Frankenstein, or the Modern Prometheus', Peter Fairclough (ed.), *Three Gothic Novels* (Penguin English Library, London 1968), p. 260.

84 ibid., p. 264.

85 ibid., p. 386.

86 stanza I, *Poetical Works*, p. 37.

87 stanza VIII, ibid., p. 39.

88 stanza XI, ibid., p. 39.

89 stanza XIV, ibid., p. 40.

90 Jones, op. cit., p. 122.

91 'The Choice', quoted in R. Glynn Grylls, *Mary Shelley: A Biography* (Oxford University Press, London 1938), p. 298.

92 *Poetical Works*, p. 582.

93 Note on *Swellfoot the Tyrant*, ibid., p. 410.

94 4 August, Jones, op. cit., p. 159.

95 'The Aziola', *Poetical Works*, p. 642.

96 Jones, op. cit., p. 180.

97 ibid., pp. 183, 184.

98 ibid., pp. 193, 198.

99 30 September 1817, Frederick L. Jones (ed.), *The Letters of Mary W. Shelley*, vol. I (University of Oklahoma Press, Norman, U.S.A. 1944), no. 36, p. 36.

100 M. M. Stocking and D. M. Stocking (eds), *The Journals of Claire Clairmont* (Harvard University Press, Cambridge, Massachusetts 1969), p. 100.

101 ibid., p. 178.

103 ibid., p. 154.

104 William Graham, *Lost Links with Byron, Shelley and Keats* (Leonard Smithers and Co., London 1898), p. 25.

105 ibid., p. 83.

106 stanza III, *Poetical Works*, pp. 539–40.

107 Neville Rogers (ed.), *The Complete Poetical Works of Percy Bysshe Shelley*, vol. II 1814–1817 (Clarendon Press, Oxford 1975), pp. 317–18.

108 *Shelley: The Pursuit* (Weidenfeld and Nicolson, London 1974), pp. 481–4.

109 8 October 1818, *Letters*, vol. II, no. 482, p. 41.

110 See the original letter in Keats' House, Hampstead, London.

111 *Letters*, vol. II, no. 591, pp. 241–2.

112 ibid., vol. II, no. 595, pp. 249–50.

113 ibid., vol. II, no. 672, p. 367.

114 *Poetical Works*, p. 419.

115 Jones, *Mary Shelley's Journal*, p. 134.

116 Stocking, op. cit., p. 153.

117 *Poetical Works*, p. 415.

118 *Letters*, vol. I, no. 132, p. 168.

119 'To Harriet', *Poetical Works*, p. 522.

120 ibid., p. 419.

121 18 June 1822, *Letters*, vol. II, no. 715, p. 434.

122 *Letter to Maria Gisborne*, 1820, *Poetical Works*, p. 370.

123 ibid., p. 583.

124 ibid., p.627.

125 *Letters*, vol. II, no. 489, p. 66.

126 Quoted in Edward Dowden, *The Life of Percy Bysshe Shelley* (Routledge and Kegan Paul, London 1969), p. 515.

127 Quoted in Graham, op. cit., p. 83.

128 Longman, etc., London 1825.

129 Quoted in Richard K. F. Pankhurst, *William Thompson 1775–1833* (Watts and Co., London 1954), p. 72.

130 Quoted in F. A. Huyak, *John Stuart Mill and Harriet Taylor* (Routledge and Kegan Paul, London 1951), p. 42.

131 Longman, etc., London 1873, p. 186.

132 Michael St John Packe, *The Life of John Stuart Mill* (Secker and

Warburg, London 1954), p. 313.
133 ibid., p. 313.
134 Bertrand and Patricia Russell (eds), *Amberley Papers*. vol. II, 'Kate's Journal', 28 September 1870 (Hogarth Press, London 1937), p. 375.
135 T. C. and E. C. Jack, London, p. 6.
136 canto VIII, stanza XXVII; see Richard Pankhurst, *Sylvia Pankhurst: Artist and Crusader* (Paddington Press, London 1979), p. 40.
137 S. C. Crownwright-Schreiner (ed.), *The Letters of Olive Schreiner: 1876–1920* (T. Fisher Unwin, London 1914), p. 33.
138 ibid., pp. 254–5.
139 Reprinted in *The Death of the Moth and Other Essays* (The Hogarth Press, London 1942), p. 83.

CHAPTER 6 *Reform or Revolution?*

1 canto III, *Poetical Works*, p. 773.
2 canto IV, ibid., p. 775.
3 canto IV, ibid., p. 776.
4 canto III, ibid., p. 773.
5 Note (4), ibid., p. 479.
6 canto IV, ibid., p. 775.
7 7 May 1812, *Letters*, vol. I, no. 187, p. 297.
8 Note to letter no. 222 (26 January 1813), ibid., vol. I, p. 351.
9 15 February 1813, ibid., vol. I, no. 224, p. 353.
10 'Address to the People on the Death of Princess Charlotte', *Works*, vol. VI, p. 80.
11 *The Making of the English Working Class* (Penguin, London 1970), p. 733.
12 *Works*, vol. V, p. 225.
13 ibid., vol. V, pp. 225–6.
14 ibid., vol. V, pp. 229–30.
15 20 November 1816, *Letters*, vol. I, no. 370, p. 513.
16 *Poetical Works*, p. 34.
17 August 1819, *Letters*, vol. II, no. 511, p. 115.
18 3 November 1819, ibid., vol. II, no. 527, p. 136.
19 *Works*, vol. VI, p. 68.
20 30 July 1820, *Letters*, vol. II, no. 580, p. 223.
21 *The Life of Percy Bysshe Shelley* (Routledge and Kegan Paul, London 1969), p. 437.
22 Note to 'Poems Written in 1819', *Poetical Works*, p. 588.
23 canto V, ibid., pp. 780–1.
24 canto I, stanza XXXI, ibid., p. 47.
25 ibid., p. 460.
26 6 November 1819, *Letters*, vol. II, no. 528, p. 149.
27 *Poetical Works*, p. 575.
28 ibid., p. 575.
29 'Song to the Men of England', stanza I, ibid., p. 572.
30 stanza V, ibid., p. 572.
31 stanza VI, ibid., p. 573.
32 canto V, stanza XXXII, ibid., p. 86.
33 *Letters*, vol. II, no. 585, p. 234.
34 *Works*, vol. VI, pp. 163–4.
35 'Ode to Liberty', stanza XIII, *Poetical Works*, p. 608.
36 canto II, stanza XIV, ibid., p. 56.
37 Robert Bertram Woodings (ed.), *Shelley, Modern Judgements* (Macmillan, London 1968).
38 act II, scene II, *Poetical Works* p. 408.
39 act II, scene II, ibid., p. 409.
40 *Shelley: The Pursuit* (Weidenfeld and Nicolson, London 1974), p. 532.
41 stanza II–VII, *Poetical Works*, p. 338.
42 stanza VIII–IX, ibid., pp. 338–9.
43 stanza XVI, ibid., p. 339.
44 stanza XXI, ibid., p. 339.
45 stanza XXII, ibid., p. 339.
46 stanza XXV, ibid., p. 340.
47 stanza XXXI, ibid., p. 340.
48 stanza XXXII, ibid., p. 340.

49 stanza XXXIII, ibid., p. 340.
50 stanza XLI, ibid., p. 341.
51 stanza XLII, ibid., p. 341.
52 stanza XLVI, ibid., p. 341.
53 stanza LXIV, ibid., p. 343.
54 stanza LXIV, ibid., p. 343.
55 stanza LXV, ibid., p. 343.
56 stanza LXVIII, ibid., p. 343.
57 stanzas XLVII–XLVIII, ibid., p. 341.
58 stanza LXXIX, ibid., p. 344.
59 stanza LXXXIV–LXXXV, ibid., p. 344.
60 stanza LXXXVIII, ibid., p. 344.
61 stanza LXXX, ibid., p. 344.
62 op. cit., p. 753
63 stanza LXXXI and LXXXII, Poetical Works, p. 344.
64 stanza LVII, ibid., p. 342.
65 stanza LXXXIX–XCI, ibid., p. 344.
66 stanza XXXVII–XXXVIII, ibid., p. 341.
67 Works, vol. VII, p. 34.
68 ibid., vol. VII, pp. 43–4
69 ibid., vol. VII, pp. 44.
70 canto II, stanza XLIII, Poetical Works, p. 63.
71 Works, vol. VII, p. 46.
72 ibid., vol. VII, p. 47.
73 ibid., vol. VII, pp. 47–8.
74 ibid., vol. VII, p. 48.
75 ibid., vol. VII, pp. 49–50.
76 ibid., vol. VII, p. 50.
77 ibid., vol. VII, p. 52.
78 ibid., vol. VII, p. 53.
79 See Donald H. Reiman, Shelley and His Circle 1773–1822, vol. VI (Harvard University Press, Cambridge, Massachusetts 1973), p. 1062.
80 Works, vol. VII, p. 54.
81 ibid., vol. VII, p. 54.
82 ibid., vol. VII, p. 54.
83 26 May 1820, Letters, vol. II, no. 568, p. 201.
84 Works, vol. VII, p. 6.
85 ibid., vol. VII, p. 31.
86 act I, Poetical Works, p. 222.
87 act II, scene I, ibid., p. 229.
88 'Fragments on Reform', Works, vol. VI, p. 295.
89 'A Philosophical View of Reform', ibid., vol. VII, p. 50.
90 Works, vol. VII, p. 23.
91 act II, scene IV, Poetical Works, p. 236.
92 act II, scene IV, ibid., p. 236.
93 act II, scene IV, ibid., p. 236.
94 act II, scene IV, ibid., p. 236.
95 act II, scene IV, ibid., p. 236.
96 act II, scene IV, ibid., p. 236.
97 act II, scene IV, ibid., p. 236.
98 act II, scene IV, ibid., p. 238.
99 act II, scene IV, ibid., p. 238.
100 act II, scene IV, ibid., p. 238.
101 act II, scene IV, ibid., p. 238.
102 act II, scene IV, ibid., pp. 238–9.
103 act II, scene IV, ibid., p. 239.
104 op. cit., p. 505.
105 act III, scene I, Poetical Works, p. 244.
106 2 March 1811, Letters, vol. I, no. 49, p. 54.
107 ibid., vol. I, no. 141, p. 185.
108 ibid., vol. I, no. 155, p. 213.
109 Works, vol. V, p. 256.
110 ibid., vol. V, pp. 256–7.
111 4 March 1812, Letters, vol. I, no. 170, p. 260, note 8.
112 8 March 1812, ibid., vol. I, no. 173, p. 267.
113 14 March 1812, ibid., vol. I, see under letter no. 173, p. 270.
114 ibid., vol. I, no. 176, p. 276.
115 ibid., vol. I, no. 175, p. 275.
116 18 March 1812, ibid., vol. I, no. 176, p. 277.
117 Poetical Works, pp. 33–4.
118 'Letter to Maria Gisborne', Leghorn, 1 July 1820, ibid., p. 368.
119 Letters, vol. I, no. 153, p. 208.
120 16 January 1812, ibid., vol. I, no. 160, p. 231.
121 Note on Peter Bell the Third, Poetical Works, p. 363.
122 part VI, stanzas XXXII and XXXIII, ibid., p. 359.
123 part VI, stanzas XXXVI–XXXVIII, ibid., p. 360.

124 part VII, stanzas XI, XIII, and XVIII, ibid., pp. 361–2.

125 16 August 1820, *Letters*, vol. II, see under no. 579, p. 222.

126 *Poetical Works*, pp. 193–4.

127 Letter to Mary Shelley, 7 August 1821, *Letters*, vol. II, no. 650, p. 317.

128 Quoted in Dowden, op. cit., p. 515.

129 *Letters*, vol. I, no. 66, p. 77.

130 11 December 1821, ibid., vol. II, no. 672, p. 368.

131 18 June 1822, ibid., vol. II, no. 715, p. 436.

132 ibid., vol. II, no. 511, p. 114.

133 'Letter to Maria Gisborne', *Poetical Works*, p. 368.

134 *Letters*, vol. II, no. 530, p. 151.

135 ibid., vol. II, no. 557, p. 181.

136 ibid., vol. II, no. 563, p. 191.

137 ibid., vol. II, no. 568, p. 201.

138 23 December 1819, ibid., vol. II, no. 543, p. 166.

139 Arthur H. Bevan, *James and Horace Smith* (London 1899), p. 176.

140 *Letters*, vol. II, no. 542, p. 165.

141 Letter to Thomas Love Peacock, 23–24 January 1819, ibid., vol. II, no. 491, p. 71.

142 17 January 1870, ibid., vol. II, no. 545, p. 169.

143 stanza I, *Poetical Works*, pp. 603–4.

144 12 July 1820, *Letters*, vol. II, no. 576, p. 213.

145 7 January 1812, ibid., vol. I, no. 158, p. 221.

146 stanza XXXIX, *Poetical Works*, p. 440.

147 'Ode to the West Wind', ibid., p. 577.

148 'Ode to the West Wind', ibid., p. 577.

149 Newman Ivey White, *Shelley*, vol. II (Secker and Warburg, London 1947), p. 193.

150 stanza IV, *Poetical Works*, pp. 578–9.

151 stanza IV, ibid., p. 579.

152 stanza V, ibid., p. 579.

CHAPTER SEVEN: The Trumpet of a Prophecy: 1822–1980

1 Quoted in Newman Ivey White, *Shelley*, vol. II (Secker and Warburg, London 1947), p. 416.

2 Franz Mehring, *Karl Marx, The Story of His Life* (Allen and Unwin, London 1939), p. 504.

3 Clarendon Press, Oxford 1976, pp. 396–7.

4 H. S. Salt, *Company I Have Kept* (Allen and Unwin, London 1930), pp. 50–1.

5 *Letters*, vol. II, no. 632, p. 298.

6 ibid., vol. II, no. 633, p. 300.

7 ibid., vol. II, no. 634, p. 302.

8 ibid., vol. II, no. 636, pp. 304–5.

9 ibid., vol. II, no. 421, pp. 566–7.

10 *John Bull*, 30 June 1822.

11 *Republican*, 15 December 1826.

12 *Newgate Magazine*, June 1825.

13 ibid., August 1826.

14 White, op. cit., vol. II, p. 398.

15 Panther, London 1969, p. 265.

16 vol. I, p. 284.

17 part III, stanza XII, *Poetical Works*, p. 352.

18 Francis Thompson, *Shelley* (Burns and Oates, London 1908), pp. 45, 46.

19 ibid., p. 59.

20 ibid., p. 68.

21 ibid., p. 69.

22 ibid., p. 69.

23 ibid., pp. 72–3.

24 *Notebook of the Shelley Society*, vol. I (Reeves and Turner, London 1888), p. 4.

25 ibid., p. 29.

26 First published by William Reeves, London 1896; reprinted Watts and Co., London 1913, Allen and Unwin, London 1924.

27 *Notebook of the Shelley Society*, vol. I, p. 31.

28 ibid., p. 190.

29 ibid., pp. 190–1.

30 ibid., p. 192.
31 ibid., p. 192.
32 ibid., p. 193.
33 ibid., p. 194.
34 ibid., p. 194.
35 'Shaming the Devil about Shelley', *The Albemarle Review*, September 1892, reprinted in Bernard Shaw, *Pen Portraits and Reviews* (Constable and Company, London 1932), p. 241.
36 ibid., pp. 243–4.
37 ibid., p. 243.
38 William Diack, *History of the Trades Council and the Trade Union Movement in Aberdeen* (Aberdeen University Press, Aberdeen 1939), p. 105.
39 Duckworth, London, p. 304.
40 Lawrence and Wishart, London 1937.
41 *Illusion and Reality: A Study of the Sources of Poetry* (Lawrence and Wishart, London 1937), p. 91.
42 canto V, *Poetical Works*, p. 779–80.
43 *Works*, vol. VII, pp. 28–9.
44 op. cit., p. 92.
45 Victor Gollancz Ltd, London 1938, p. 199.
46 Pelican, London 1972, p. 198.
47 ibid., p. 192.
48 ibid., p. 197.
49 ibid., p. 216.
50 ibid., p. 194.
51 ibid., p. 197.
52 ibid., p. 208.
53 ibid., p. 198.
54 ibid., p. 197.
55 *Works*, vol. VII, p. 135.
56 op. cit., p. 192.
57 *Poetical Works*, p. 34.
58 op. cit., p. 192.
59 op. cit., p. 197.

60 Chatto and Windus, London 1952.
61 ibid.
62 *Revaluation*, p. 194.
63 ibid., p. 215.
64 ibid., p. 215.
65 Chatto and Windus, London, pp. 13–14.
66 act III, scene IV, *Poetical Works*, p. 252.
67 ibid., p. 252.
68 ibid., p. 252.
69 ibid., p. 253.
70 ibid., p. 253.
71 Karl Marx and Frederick Engels, *Werke*, vol. I (Berlin 1956–8), p. 4, quoted in S. S. Prawer, *Karl Marx and World Literature* (Clarendon Press, Oxford 1976), p. 19.
72 Max Reinhardt, London 1954, p. 274.
73 *Works*, vol. VII, p. 140.
74 *Poetical Works*, p. 206.
75 ibid., p. 207.
76 Thomas Love Peacock, *Memoirs of Shelley and Other Essays and Reviews*, ed. Howard Mill (Rupert Hart-Davis, London 1970), p. 63.
77 Roger Ingpen (ed.), *The Letters of Percy Bysshe Shelley*, vol. I (Sir Isaac Pitman and Sons Ltd., London, and Charles Scribner's Sons, New York, 1909), no. 150, p. 347.
78 act IV, *Poetical Works*, p. 264.
79 op. cit., vol. II, p. 437.
80 *The Mask of Anarchy*, stanza XC, *Poetical Works*, p. 344.
81 *The Manifesto and the Communist Party* (1848), quoted in *Marx and Engels: Selected Works*, vol. I (Moscow 1969), p. 132.

INDEX